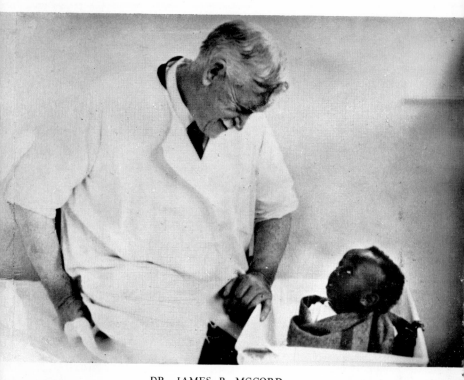

DR. JAMES B. MCCORD

MY PATIENTS
WERE ZULUS

by James B. McCord, M.D.

with John Scott Douglas

RINEHART & CO., INC.
NEW YORK   TORONTO

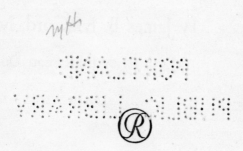

CONTENTS

CHAPTER ONE

A BABY IS BORN,
ZULU STYLE

IT WAS MIDNIGHT WHEN THE HEADLIGHTS DANCED across a reflecting surface and the thinning, junglelike tangle of low "bush" beyond. Brakes failed to stop the car; it swung half around and slued into a mud wallow. The native guide beside me grunted but slumbered on, until the silence, broken only by a frog chorus, awakened him. He had walked twenty-five miles to ask my help, and I hadn't the heart to disturb him even when we'd become mired along the way.

"The road ends here," he murmured drowsily, taking my bag as he stepped from the car.

The moon had set, but by watching my guide's silhouette and following the swishing sounds of grass against his legs, I stayed on a trail leading up a hill and dropping sharply to open veld on the other side. Half a mile of rough travel brought us to a kraal or yard, surrounded by a fence of spiny branches designed to keep out wild hogs. Rising above this formidable fence was a thatched hut, dome shaped like an old-fashioned beehive.

3

A figure moved dimly across the kraal and through the gateway.

"Mabanyi comes," my guide explained. It was Mabanyi, head of this small kraal, who had sent the runner twenty-five miles to find me.

"Your wife still lives?" I asked in Zulu as he approached.

"Yes," he said. "I will take you to her."

He was a magnificent man with iron-gray hair, naked except for an *umutsha*—a belt supporting an oxhide apron behind and a fringe of monkey tails in front. As we crossed the bare ground to the hut, he told me about the birth of his first child, a son born the year before.

"After he was born, Setaba wrapped him in a blanket, cleaned up the hut, and walked to the garden to select tender ears of corn to grind to a paste for his first meal."

"Then your wife is now having her second child?" I asked.

"A second son, the first of twins, was born twelve hours ago," answered Mabanyi. "But this time my wife prepared no corn and the remaining twin stays inside, though a midwife and women from neighboring kraals have beaten her to make her give it up. The midwife wished to call a witch doctor, for she says my wife is bewitched."

It was good news that the witch doctor had not yet taken charge. Probably he would have cut the woman with his "scalpel"—a broken piece of bottle, a rusty knife or perhaps a short spear known as an *assegai*—removing the baby piecemeal.

The Zulus look upon twins as monstrosities and though the practice of killing them has died out, a second child usually dies of neglect. Knowing that many Zulu women died or were lifetime cripples after being mutilated by witch doctors, Mabanyi ignored the native mid-wife's advice and sent for Elizabeth Njapa, whose husband had a near-by kraal.

Zulu women will not help in a difficult birth until past childbearing years because of a belief that their future children will then be stillborn. But Elizabeth, having received nursing and midwifery training in my hospital, ignored this superstition, and assisted in any confinement cases near her kraal, calling on me for help when a delivery threatened complications. It was she who inspired Mabanyi to send a runner to Durban to find me.

Light glowed from the entrance of one thatched hut, and Mabanyi paused before it. No male Zulu except a witch doctor enters a hut during childbirth, so he asked me to enter alone. For a large man like myself it was necessary to stoop double to pass through the three-foot entrance into a room without chimney or windows. Six nearly nude, sweating crones knelt in a half circle before a woman on a grass mat. The stench of their unwashed bodies would have driven a strange white doctor from the hut, but after years of South African practice, I was accustomed to it.

Elizabeth was bathing the woman on the mat. "They were beating Setaba to make her give up her second child," she explained, pointing to the sticks and barrel staves in the hands of the old women.

Since Zulu women shrink from pain, and seem able to inhibit labor by force of will, native midwives prevent relaxation by furnishing sticks to all women present. The mother bears down again with the effort to hold her breath to avoid any outcry, which, in a Zulu woman, would be regarded as disgraceful.

Now, more older women from neighboring kraals began arriving. To allow myself more room, I sent them to boil more water than I'd need, and the others took places in a circle around me, watching with wide and curious eyes. To give me better light, Elizabeth raised the only light in the hut, an earthenware lamp, with a rag wick for the kerosene, as I leaned beside the woman on the mat. Moisture beaded her upper lip and forehead, and her dark, tortured eyes regarded me listlessly.

"I think the second baby lies sidewise in her body," Elizabeth said. "One arm reaches out from the womb. In the hospital, you said normal delivery never follows in arm-presentation cases."

The nurse was right. The muscular contractions that usually expel a child had twisted its head backward toward the spine; in this wedge shape the baby could not pass through the birth canal. Something must be done immediately to relieve the mother.

First I scrubbed my hands and arms with antiseptic soap, and then I held the chloroform mask under Setaba's flaring nostrils until her straining body had relaxed. I handed the mask to the nurse, in case it should later be needed, and warned her to watch our patient's weak pulse.

This was a case where instruments would be useless, where a surgeon must have "eyes in his fingers," as we say. In such instances, I was extremely fortunate. The index and middle fingers of my right hand had been lost in an accident on my grandfather's farm. That accident, which had seemed so tragic in my boyhood, had in reality proved a blessing. For the narrowness of my hand and the strength that had developed in the remaining two fingers had frequently saved the lives of my patients in difficult surgical or maternity cases.

Now, after an exhausting hour of digital manipulation, I was able to move the child into position for a breech delivery, one of the normal positions for birth. But the baby, unfortunately, was stillborn . . . had, in fact, been dead for hours.

Stiff from working so long in a cramped, kneeling position, I stepped from the hut, and informed Mabanyi that the second twin was dead but that his wife would grow strong and well.

He smiled broadly. "I have one new son. What more could a man want? When the women have gone," he added, "you can sleep in my house."

The idea had little appeal. For although each of Mabanyi's wives had her own hut, and he had another, I knew from experience that he'd feel it his duty as a host to sleep where I slept; and the visiting Zulu matrons, for social reasons, would do likewise. But the only alternative was to sleep in my car, and a medical colleague doing that had recently died from the bites of malarial mosquitoes, so I chose the lesser of two evils.

We waited until the women had cleaned up the hut, and then entered. But there were so many visiting women that the "female side" of the hut was heavily overbalanced, and there was space on the "male side" for but one man. I told Mabanyi to lie there, and chose for myself the space before the entrance, wrapping myself in four blankets that a woman brought me.

As I dozed off, a wife climbed over me to go outside, for Zulus' sanitary arrangements are the nearest bush. Then a daughter was prompted by the same thought, and presently several other daughters and visiting women found me a convenient steppingstone for their nocturnal prowling.

Again I dozed, this time to be startled awake by a squawking and beating of wings. Mabanyi was thrusting an indignant rooster toward my face.

"What am I supposed to do with it?" I asked, drowsily.

"It's a thanksgiving present for your work."

I appealed to the nurse. "Am I supposed to hold this rooster all night?" The fowl was scratching, trying to peck my mustache, and beating me with its wings. "What do others do when given a chicken, Elizabeth?"

"Sometimes they say they are hungry and ask to have it cooked."

"A fine idea!" I said with enthusiasm.

While the rooster was stewing, I slept—until two wives dragged Setaba across my body, insisting she had to go outside. Heavy-eyed, I waited for them to haul her back. Then the bird was served, but my attempts to chew the stringy meat were unavailing.

"Elizabeth," I said in English, "this bird is either made of leather or uncooked. What shall I do with it?"

"Who knows what the doctor will do with his own?"

"What do others do at a time like this?"

"Sometimes they ask the family to eat with them."

"Good! Tell them I've satisfied my appetite, and now leave the heroic old bird to them."

After the last bone was picked, the hut quieted down, and I slept undisturbed (except by fleas) until awakened by the cold of dawn. I groped for my top blankets, and found they now covered one of the visitors.

Stiff and shivering, and having nothing else to do while waiting for Mabanyi's neighbors to come and help me free my car, I recalled various Zulu maternity cases, involving problems my professors at medical school could never have foreseen. Even if Setaba's second twin was stillborn, I reflected, it had come out whole. Not as much could be said of many babies delivered by witch doctors.

Odds oppose a Zulu woman and her child when labor

is prolonged. I recalled a case only a short time before when a native midwife faced with a foot-presentation case called a witch doctor to help. Wearing only an *umutsha* of monkey tails, a fur cap, and a necklace of antelope horns in which he kept his medicines and charms, and equipped with a very sharp spear, he had taken one look at the infant's feet in the mother's womb and then amputated the right one. The father objected to removal of the other, and while the men argued, the baby was born normally. One of my colleagues was called to the kraal at that point, and he bound up the stump, saving the child's life. But it had angered us both that a boy's foot had been needlessly sacrificed.

Knowing almost nothing of human anatomy, native witch doctors and midwives often brutally butcher a mother following the birth of her child, under the impression that they are removing the afterbirth. In one case of this type, where I was fortunately called in time, a midwife had been attempting to remove a prolapsed womb.

One of my most persistent surgical problems during years of practice in Natal was vesicovaginal fistula resulting from ignorant cutting by black "surgeons." And my most stubborn case of this kind was Nolaka's.

Nolaka was slashed so deeply by her witch doctor when her child was slow in coming that vesicovaginal fistula resulted, making it impossible for her to retain urine or bowel contents. Loathesome and malodorous, she was avoided by her husband and his other wives until her embittered disposition earned her the Zulu name of Nolaka, meaning "with anger."

A couple stopped at her kraal one night, the husband explaining that his wife had been badly cut by their witch doctor at the birth of their child.

"She could never bear another child," he said. "But I

heard that at the Hospital UDokotela McCord they could help a woman. My wife was operated on there, and now she can bear other children."

The next day in spite of Nolaka's protests that she had suffered all she could stand, her husband started carrying her the fifty miles to the nearest railroad.

Nolaka reached the hospital in pitiable condition. Nurses opened all windows, but the smell of foul discharges was almost overpowering when I entered the examination room. The little woman's face was wizened from long suffering. To make her more comfortable, my wife carried her like a child to the bathroom. Though she used abusive language and beat Margaret's chest until my wife had lowered her into the tub, Nolaka found the warm water so soothing that she said nothing when she was borne away the following day. Her fondness for bathing led me to call her *Umtokoloshe*, after the Zulu water spirit, and the new name so pleased her that it almost brought a smile to her face.

Before attempting to repair the fistula, her urine had to be rendered as aseptic as possible with frequent doses of acid phosphate for many weeks.

Then Nolaka was wheeled into the operating room, and my wife Margaret, serving as matron of the hospital at the time, gave ether. Nolaka clung to my wife's apron as she drifted off, the apron from then on giving her a feeling of strength and comfort.

I had performed the same operation so many times that I had developed a variation of the accepted technique, an innovation which increased the chances of mending the broken walls. But sometimes the operation had to be repeated several times, and there were rare cases which never healed.

Nolaka was one of the stubborn cases. Within a few

weeks, I realized that her first operation was less successful than I had hoped for. This was a misfortune in every
way. Her bitter tongue and ingratitude were causing the
nurses great distress, and patients needing weeks more
convalescence were obliged to suffer from her violent
tongue.

One night when Margaret gave Nolaka castor oil to
relieve constipation, the little black woman screwed up
her face, and turned her head to the wall to spit it out.
Margaret's frayed patience snapped; she held her patient's
nose. Nolaka swallowed in surprise. But she was so angry
she refused to say good night.

A short time later, however, she sent for Margaret,
and instead of the outburst my wife expected, Nolaka
smiled meekly. "Please, Nkoskanzi, may I hold your
apron?" And she clung to it until she fell asleep.

Margaret assumed our problem patient had realized
that no one in the hospital had ever addressed a harsh
word to her or treated her unkindly, but she did not expect the about-face to last. In the morning, however, the
startled nurse almost dropped Nolaka's breakfast tray
when, instead of the usual vituperation, the small patient
addressed the nurse with a cheery good morning. If a
Zulu turns over a new leaf, the page is likely to remain
turned; Nolaka was as bright from then on as she had been
sullen before.

A few mornings later when I informed her she must
have another operation, her only question was, "May I
hold Nkoskanzi's apron?" Assured that she could, she
smiled contentedly.

My first operation had brought some improvement
in Nolaka's condition, though it had not drawn the tissues
together in a completely normal manner. The second operation likewise failed in this result, and so did the third

and fourth attempts to repair the breach by surgery. By then I would have conceded defeat had it not been for the cheerful fortitude with which Nolaka faced her operations and endured a condition that was undoubtedly causing her great distress. Unwilling to fail anyone with such courage, I performed a fifth, a sixth and a seventh operation. The seventh attempt at last sealed up the vaginal outlet, converting bladder and vagina into one sac—not the ideal solution, but at least affording her fair control over her discharges so that she would no longer be offensive in the kraal.

Then I sent for Nolaka's husband, and he came to the hospital, a tall and aged Zulu whose skin stretched taut across his bony frame. With puckered brow he listened while I explained that his wife would no longer be a trial to others.

"But never again," I concluded, "can she have children."

He frowned darkly at that. "What do I want her for then? If I had a cow which gave no milk, I would kill it. I cannot kill Nolaka but I do not want her."

Nolaka's father likewise refused to take her back, for if he did, tribal law would then require him to return as many cattle as he'd received for her, and he knew no other man would wish to buy a sterile woman.

So I returned Nolaka to her husband. Often afterward, however, I wondered how an unwelcome wife had been received.

Three years later, when a missionary friend was making a back-country trip, I asked her to inquire about Nolaka, describing the large kraal on a high, lonely hillside as my patient had pictured it. When my friend reached a kraal which answered the description, she asked some native children whether Nolaka lived there. The children shook their heads, and my friend would have passed on if a native woman had not come up to hear the question repeated.

"You want Nolaka? There is no one here by that name. The woman known as Nolaka is now called Nomusa."

The missionary was startled by the answer because *nomusa* meant "with kindness." But deciding that it might be the same woman, she asked to see her. Nomusa came from the field where she'd been working, eager to hear news about her friends in the hospital.

"When I returned home, no one liked me," she explained, smiling. "A woman who can bear no children cannot be respected."

"But now they like you," my friend pointed out. "They call you Nomusa."

The shriveled little woman smiled. "Yes; they like me now."

And she explained the change. Her only friend at first was a hulking imbecile girl who tormented the children and would turn fiercely on any woman attempting to punish her. Nomusa realized the big girl was starved for affection, and won her devotion by helping her plant the finest garden in the kraal. Slipping off when the girl was working, she took charge of the children while their mothers labored, teaching them songs and games learned at the hospital. Rarely does a childless wife command respect, but Nomusa proved an exception because she had increased the resources of her small community.

On the outskirts of Durban, surrounded by an impenetrable snarl of vines, brush and trees, stands a little tea garden. Monkeys are numerous in the trees, swinging from the branches, chasing one another up the trunks, chattering and scolding when another monkey, making a perilous leap across space with the aid of a swinging vine, rocks the branch upon which they are perched. Friends who frequented this tea garden spoke of a strange occurrence when a mother monkey appears with a newborn baby.

The mother, my friends declared, is quickly hemmed in by other female monkeys. One snatches the babe, examining it minutely before passing it along to the next. Eventually it is returned to the mother unless one of the monkeys discovers an imperfection or deformation, to which she calls attention by a loud chattering. The mother monkey, in that case, utters a shrill sobbing cry, but she never succeeds in reaching the little monkey before it is dropped to its death.

Now, I ask no one to place credence in a story received secondhand, and I relate it simply because it draws a curious parallel to a custom among the Zulus. They eliminate defective children in somewhat the same way to make sure that only the fit shall survive. Even today unchristianized Zulus allow imperfect babies—often babies with easily correctible defects—to die of neglect.

I had a brush with this custom one afternoon when I was on a back-country medical jaunt. After climbing a steep trail, I paused to rest beside a kraal and was admiring the golden hills, broken by a tracery of green where they were cut by densely wooded streams, when a young man stepped from the hut. His handsome face was troubled as he courteously inquired whether I would examine his baby.

The contrast between the bright sunlight and the darkness of his hut prevented me from seeing, at first, that the earthen floor had been *sindaed* with cowdung until it had a high gloss, the sign of a scrupulous Zulu housekeeper.

And then I saw the housekeeper herself, a buxom woman with a round and childlike face, who wore the knee-length hide petticoat which replaces a girl's bead apron at marriage. Her expression turned sullen when my glance fell on a baby not over two days old that lay at the side of the hut, neglected and weakly crying.

The father picked it up, gently turning it over to show me an imperforate anus. Without a rectal opening, it could not live much longer. Luckily my pocket kit of instruments included an artery forceps, so I placed it and a scalpel in a pot over the fire, removed a bottle of iodine from my pocket as well, and prepared to operate.

The mother continued cooking, showing no interest even when I removed the sterilized instruments from the pot. It was the work of but a few minutes to correct the defect, and suture the edge of the opening into the rectum. The father beamed when I told him that he now had a fine baby girl, as perfect as one born normal. Taking the child in his arms and cooing softly to it, he held it toward the mother to nurse.

The mother shuddered, her childlike face contorted with revulsion as she drew back. "*Monstrosity!*" she cried sharply.

"It's a beautiful child," I said, explaining in Zulu that the original imperfection would never mar the child.

But the mother kept repeating, "Monstrosity! monstrosity!"

Silent and miserable, the father cradled the baby in his arms, tenderly stroking its back. Then, hopefully, he thrust it again toward his wife, but she shook her head, refusing to nurse it.

As I left, tears rolled down the father's cheeks and he still held the crying baby in his arms, while the mother went stoically about her cooking.

When I passed the kraal a week later, the father came out to speak, his eyes glistening as he described how the baby grew weaker and weaker until death came from starvation. The mother never once touched her baby after discovering that it had no rectal opening.

Later I performed an identical operation on a baby born to a Christianized Zulu mother who had abandoned primitive beliefs. When I placed the baby in her arms, her face brightened with happiness and she bared her breast to nurse it. Neither she nor her husband showed any prejudice against a baby born not quite perfect.

Zulu women love children and pride themselves on the number they have, but they have definite ideas about the years when a woman should conceive. So general is the prejudice against childbearing when nearing menopause that I was astonished one day when a woman well past middle age entered my dispensary with five children ranging from a baby in arms to a seven-year-old.

"Whose babies are these?" I asked.

"Mine," she said.

"You mean they're children by one of your husband's younger wives?"

"No," she said, her black face set stubbornly; "they are mine—my own children!"

"That's impossible. You're too old to have children!"

The children had digestive troubles, and while examining them, I questioned the woman until she reluctantly told me her story.

She was sold for a good price in cattle, but failed to conceive, a failure which could not be laid to her husband, since his other wives had borne many children. As she neared menopause, he returned her to her father's kraal.

"You must give back my cattle," he said. "Your daughter is barren."

Unwilling to repossess a sterile daughter, for whom no other man would pay cattle, the father suggested another plan: "Take my youngest daughter; she is healthy and will give you many children."

"If she does not," the husband said, "I will return your oldest daughter and you must replace my cattle."

The sister moved into her brother-in-law's kraal (a custom the Zulus regard as in no way immoral) and within eight years gave birth to five children. The father felt that the fifth child discharged his debt, and called his younger daughter home. Her prestige was enhanced in the eyes of Zulu men by the fivefold proof of her fertility.

"So these children," the woman ended triumphantly, "are mine, for they were given my husband to pay a debt. But I cannot allow them to become sick or to die, for my younger sister is now married, and would no longer give me children by my husband."

CHAPTER TWO

MY DREAMS
HAD A BLACK LINING

NOW, I WAS NOT AFRICAN BORN, NOR WAS THERE ANY romantic notion of becoming a Zulu surgeon in my youthful dreams.

My boyhood was a prosaic one; my school years were spent in various villages where my father, a Congregational minister, had his parishes, and my summers devoted to work on my grandfather's large farm in Illinois. I might have followed my grandfather into farming if Paul Du Chaillu's books of African travel and the adventures of David Livingstone hadn't opened vistas to another world. The glimpses they gave of Africa seemed more vivid to my brother Joel and me than the creeks and emerald meadows we passed with unseeing eyes on our walks. In the fading light of summer afternoons, driving the cows through the wooded pasture at milking time, we planned exciting adventures when adulthood would, in some miraculous way, take us to the Dark Continent. Many a night in our darkened upstairs bedroom we elaborated on these plans in conspiratorial whispers.

Advancing years, though failing to dim this longing, brought a dawning sense of realism. Farming was the only means we knew of financing African exploration, for we could see, as a clergyman's sons, that the ministry offered only meager earthly rewards. As we lay in the hayloft of grandfather's barn one day, trying to estimate the number of years that must pass before a farm could pay for our travels, Joel straightened and, with a look of consternation, cried:

"Gee, Jim—we'll be old men before we can see Africa!"

Reluctantly we laid away our dreams in moth balls. My brother sensibly left his there and turned his thoughts toward the making of money, eventually to become a banker. But I still hoped some day to dust off the naphtha, and in time chance helped me shape my life somewhat along the pattern of our dreams.

My parents, though deeply religious, held advanced views for their day, and when I had exhausted the educational opportunities of the nearest school, they sent me at fifteen to the preparatory school of Oberlin College in Ohio. A classical college and theological school, it was still looked upon in 1886 as a radical experiment because of its pioneering in eliminating racial barriers to higher education and in becoming the first American co-educational college.

I arrived at Oberlin feeling like a tall and awkward rustic. My elder brother, who had a fluent tongue and a quick wit, had always been the leader, and now, without his guiding hand, I felt painfully self-conscious among students who seemed not only more confident but more sophisticated than I. However, my shyness had its limits, for when an older and larger boy in the town of Oberlin taunted me, I tried to thrash him. Beaten I was, of course, but at least it established the fact that my lack of confidence ran only in certain channels.

In time I gained a little confidence, and with it a few friends who included me in discussions which could be started at Oberlin at the drop of the slightest hint of controversy. The callow, often specious logic of other small-town boys glaringly revealed their inexperience, but shyness still made me better listener than talker. Nor could I force myself to veer discussion to Africa, the subject on which reading had best informed me.

The Student Volunteer Missionary Movement then sweeping through American colleges found fertile ground at Oberlin, where students from homes of liberal viewpoint already possessed a crusading spirit. Before the emotional high-water mark of the movement was reached, many students had enrolled.

Except for a religious background, it's hard to explain today why I was among them. I had scant zeal for "converting the heathen." And though my reading had acquainted me with the backwardness of African natives, I saw Christianity as a means of advancing them to a better way of life rather than as an end in itself. Back of all this, perhaps, lay the desire to live on the mysterious continent which had for so long gripped my imagination. Missionary work might make that possible.

Among the youthful zealots attending weekly meetings of the missionary volunteer band were two missionaries' daughters of my own age, from the Oberlin high school. Tall girls, with the high coloring of perfect health, Margaret Mellen and Clara Davis looked so much alike that at first I mistook them for sisters. Unlike the other girls, they wore their hats in meetings, and when I learned of the prank which made this necessary, they rose in my estimation. Margaret had, in a mischievous moment, dared

Clara to enter a barbershop and have her hair cut. Without a moment's hesitation, Clara marched into the shop and sat in an empty chair. Margaret, with sinking heart but unwilling to desert her friend, took another chair. And the disapproving barber, intending to teach them a lesson, sheared both girls like sheep.

A friend enlightened me on their backgrounds. Clara's father was a former missionary to Japan, with an imposing A.B. and C.F.M. appended to his name. Years later, although I had no suspicion of it then, her brother Jerome Davis was to become a world figure in education and sociology. However my interest, which had heretofore played no favorites, turned toward Margaret upon learning that her parents, the Reverend and Mrs. William Mellen, were retired missionaries who had worked among the Zulus of Natal. The girl herself had been born in Zululand.

Shyness prevented me from speaking to her at missionary meetings, but I haunted Oberlin's main street after classes, hoping for a glimpse of Margaret. And later, discovering that she attended my church, I sat where I could watch her unobserved.

For months I secretly admired the girl without finding any way to meet her. At a church social, late in December, I spied the blue hair ribbon Margaret wore in chestnut hair now grown long enough to arrange in a pompadour. I made a resolve so daring that it suddenly became hard to breathe: before the evening had passed, I would meet Margaret Mellen!

But the time slipped away, with that desired end no nearer realization. And at the hour when Oberlin girls must leave, it was my misfortune to be talking to a college girl; etiquette decreed that I escort her home. Never was a girl escorted home with greater haste, a good night said

with more unflattering abruptness! For I remembered
that high-school girls, unlike those in college, were not
bound by 7:30 rules.

Disheveled from sprinting back to the church, I
looked around the gathering and saw a friend talking to
Margaret. He strode over, inquiring with concern
whether I'd been in an accident.

"You must introduce me to Miss Mellen!" I gasped.

Amusement lighted his face. "So that's it!"

After the introduction, my old difficulty in finding
words struck me speechless. The girl waited expectantly
while I stared at her in mounting confusion. Finally she
said understandingly, "Shall we sit down, Mr. McCord?"

Her smile and manner were as natural as an old
friend's. She was more mature than I, more experienced
in meeting people and situations, so unaware of her vivacious charm that it didn't intrude to make me feel her a
stranger.

"I wanted to speak to you about Africa."

Her eyes were eager. "Are *you* interested in Africa?"

Her sympathetic attitude struck the shackles from
my tongue; I told her my dream of becoming an African
missionary. And she described Unsunduzi Mission where
her father had been stationed for many years and where
she was born.

"I left there at six," she admitted, "but I remember
many events at Unsunduzi more clearly than those of last
school year. Besides," she added with twinkling eyes, "I
plan to go back—I'm a Zulu princess."

My face must have expressed disbelief.

"It's true." And she laughed. "Father was the most
influential man in our district when the native chief died,
and the Zulus asked him to become their leader. Father's
other duties left him no time to watch the tribe's inter-

ests, so he declined. But when the Zulus were insistent, he said:

"'Will you obey me as your chief? Will you work when there is work to be done? And will you all come to meetings when I set the time?' The natives agreed. 'Then,' said Father, 'a meeting will be held each Sunday morning at the church. I will expect you to be there.' "

"And your father remained their chief?" I asked in astonishment.

She nodded. "The British legally approved the appointment because there was no question about Father's desire to help the Zulus. So you see," she concluded hastily, as a high-school boy approached, "I'm a real Zulu princess, and so is my older sister, Laura."

The boy, John Ellis, had come to ask if she were ready to leave. I couldn't catch her answer, but I imagined that she was explaining she must first dismiss this tall and awkward college boy, who had so many questions to ask about Africa. Flushing hotly when at length she rose, I asked if I might see her home.

"Of course," Margaret said. "I told John that I was going with you, Mr. McCord."

Africa was brought very close by that conversation with a sympathetic girl, and it was hours before I could sleep. But even after that brief acquaintance with her, I saw that my dreams of Africa must be redesigned to include Margaret Mellen. . . .

Long talks with the Mellens strengthened my desire to go to Africa. Margaret was too young to consider marriage, but, without anything said, we made plans with the confident assumption that we'd go together to South Africa to work among the Zulus. She even duplicated my courses at Oberlin to qualify for missionary work.

Several years after my enrollment in Oberlin, however, doubts shook the foundations of this plan. My defects as a missionary were appalling. Still self-conscious speaking before groups, I envied students who improvised long prayers without preparation, prayers that at times seemed more eloquent than meaningful. Even repeating psalms with Margaret in church was painful. Honesty compelled me to admit to myself that these limitations would cause a native congregation as great misery as myself if I ever became a preacher.

Undoubtedly I should have disclosed these doubts to Margaret. But my missionary plans were so enmeshed with our plan to build our future in Africa that it was not until shortly before my graduation that I could bring myself to do it. Our backgrounds were so different that I was afraid Margaret wouldn't understand. At home in the country I met only our neighbors and congregation, and conversation then fell into well-grooved channels. Mission life and environments as widely separated as Africa and the United States during her formative years had accustomed Margaret to making friends, and words flowed with her thoughts.

When I explained my trouble, she asked, with an anxious note in her voice, "Don't you believe in helping native peoples, Mr. McCord?"

"More than ever, now that your father has shown me the Zulus' need for it."

"Can't you help them with head and hands rather than vocally?" she asked. "You enjoy your science courses, don't you? Couldn't you go to Africa as a medical missionary?

I had underestimated this young girl's gift for understanding. With those two questions, she parted the dark clouds that had hung over me so long! And then in the same calm voice, she described the need for medical missionaries.

"Miss Mellen," I interrupted, summoning all my courage, "will you marry me and go to Africa when I have my medical degree?"

"You know I will, Mr. . . ." She hesitated, color creeping into her cheeks as she realized that with our changed status as an engaged couple, last names were no longer appropriate. "*Jim*," she added, smiling.

After I was graduated from Oberlin in 1891, I went home to work for a summer on my grandfather's farm. Both my grandfather and my father were relieved that I'd given up the idea of preaching; they now entertained high hopes that medical school might knock all nonsensical ideas about Africa from my head as well.

From the first week in the Chicago Medical College of Northwestern University, I felt solid ground under my feet. The hours of classroom work and study, the lectures, dissection and observation in the operating theatre, seemed all too short. Three years sped by like one.

My internship was to be served in the Mercy Hospital in Chicago, but before it began I was granted a two-week vacation in mid-August to marry Margaret at Oberlin and to go to my home in Iowa, the only honeymoon an intern's pay would allow.

Nearing the end of my internship, I wrote the American Board of Commissioners for Foreign Missions of the Congregational Church, believing a missionary appointment to be a mere formality. The Board's answer, in consequence, was a crushing disappointment. The Zulu Mission, which included the Adams Mission, the Esidumbini Mission and the Inanda Mission, had a doctor and lacked funds to pay another. Money only partially explained why I failed to receive an appointment. Many missionaries then believed that faith and prayer was sufficient to insure native health—a statement that may today cause a skeptical lift of brows. Medical missionaries were expected in that day to be first preachers, then medical men, if time remained for that. And roundabout word had reached the Zulu Mission of my alarming shortcomings as a preacher.

Before Margaret and I could gather the fragments of our dreams and decide what to do, a letter came from Dr. Robert Cavett of Lake City, Iowa. Ill health made it difficult for him to care for his large practice, and when he asked the Chicago Medical School to recommend a graduate, they had suggested that I'd make a suitable partner.

"If I accept," I said unhappily to Margaret, "we'll never reach Africa."

"Yes, we will," she said with conviction. "Your Scotch-Irish stubbornness won't allow you to forget that easily, Jim. Can't we consider it a detour, with Africa as its end?"

So we entrained for Lake City. But instead of the elderly doctor we expected, we found Dr. Cavett still in his early thirties. Nor was there anything in the appearance of the young doctor who met us at the station to suggest the poor health that had prompted him to take a partner. He was a man of medium height, solidly built, with a broad and ruddy face made almost handsome by his warm smile. The only thing to hint at a hidden factor in Dr. Cavett were the gray streaks in his jet-black hair, surprising me a little when he lifted his hat in a cordial and carelessly formal gesture to Margaret. Prematurely white hair is so common, however, that it gave rise to no misgivings at the time.

After Dr. Cavett had helped my wife into the carriage and had started his span of chestnut mares along the tree-bordered street, the looks of pleasure on the faces of passers-by when the doctor smiled and tipped his hat showed that he was regarded with affection and respect by the townspeople.

The following morning my new partner stopped his buggy before the cottage Margaret and I had rented, and I climbed in. But prior to leaving town to make our calls, Dr. Cavett drew up in front of the drugstore, explaining that he must have something for his cough. When we left Lake City behind, the fall wind sweeping across the prairie was raw, stinging our faces, forcing us to raise collars and pull up the lap robe. The horses plodded through the mud, heads down, their tails limp with dejection. Frequently Dr. Cavett reached under the robe for a bottle in his pocket. Undisturbed by my refusal to have a drink, he would tip back the bottle several times before corking it.

At each bare little shack we visited, Dr. Cavett's pronouncement was the same, "You're a very, very sick person."

Our sixth call was paid to a family of settlers living in a one-room board shack, a shack with so many cracks that the wind whistled through it almost unimpeded. Eight children in misfit clothing and named in Swedish numerals, according to the order of their birth, stood huddled around a glowing stove. The father of this family, coming in with a partial pail of foamy milk, removed a cap with ear flaps and followed the doctor to a rough board bed in one corner.

Though the woman lying there could not have been thirty-five, the lines that exhaustion had left in her face made her appear, at first, to be a grandmother. Dr. Cavett made a careful examination, frowning gravely as he repeated his formula, "You're a very, very sick woman, Mrs. Swanson."

Deep satisfaction, like a gleam of sunlight, lighted her face, and when she glanced, with a triumphant expression, at her husband, he shifted uneasily. Children left the stove to walk to the bedside, looking down on their mother with rounded and anxious eyes.

"A very, very sick woman!" Dr. Cavett repeated emphatically, opening his bag to tap some pills into a paper. "But, fortunately, you called me in time. You'll pull through all right if you take this medicine and remain quietly in bed. Don't let me hear of you getting up before I call on Friday."

After we were in the buggy, driving away, I asked, "Wasn't that a sedative you gave her?"

"Yes, Jim."

"But she had no temperature. Her chest was clear, her pulse normal. She just seemed tired out."

"That's correct, Jim. Too many babies; too much work."

"But you told her she was very ill."

"So I did, so I did. Pleased her, too."

"Yes, but . . . was it honest?"

"Jim, they taught you medicine in school. Now I'll teach you about humans. Freida Swanson is tired and discouraged, sure that no one appreciates her hard work. For five days she'll have her husband and her kids fussing over her. She'll feel *wanted*. On Friday I'll tell her she's made a wonderful improvement, and can get up. And it will be the truth—she needs both rest and the feeling that she's needed!"

Dr. Cavett's approach to medicine as a human rather than a medical problem was upsetting to a young doctor freshly hatched from medical school. But when our patients, often those with serious illnesses, rose with monotonous regularity from their beds, I began to see a strongly recommending element in my partner's approach —it worked!

His approach worked because somehow or other he had learned what all good doctors must sooner or later learn—that nature herself is a great healer. Drugs or surgery, properly used, are an aid to nature, but nature herself must ultimately do the work.

But even with his knowledge that the human constitution is a fairly rugged thing, Dr. Cavett never spared himself to lend a helping hand. The fiercest blizzards, the deepest snow, the most slippery roads never once prevented him from visiting patients in need of medical assistance.

After a time he gave up any pretense of a cold when drinking the quart of whiskey a day that was his normal allowance. However, I didn't know that he was also addicted to morphine until one day when I surprised him with his sleeve rolled up, and his arm revealed numerous punctures. He tried to hide the hypodermic needle, but was not quick enough.

"It's the only way I keep from having delirium tremens, Jim," he explained, only slightly abashed.

"But if you'd stop drinking—" I began, shocked by this fresh development.

"This is my normal state," he interrupted. "Whiskey and morphine!"

The discovery that he was seeing patients while both drugged and partially intoxicated deeply disturbed me, and I decided to watch him closely. But I found no evidence that my partner ever confused the Mr. Hyde role of his private life with the Dr. Jekyll role of his practice. He could, to an amazing degree, exert physical control over his drugged body. Sometimes, after a long and arduous round of calls, nightfall would find Dr. Cavett in a dead stupor, while there were still patients to visit. He'd mumble unintelligibly as I helped him from the buggy and supported him to the door of our next patient. At the sound of footfalls within, he'd wrench himself up with visible effort, and when the door opened, his eyes would be clear, his hand steady, his step firm and brisk as he entered the house. Nor did I ever detect him making the slightest error in the kind or amount of drugs he measured out. However, a few moments after he had called a cheerful good-bye from the carriage and I had urged the chestnut mares on, he would slump against me, completely unconscious once more.

His bodily demand for liquor and drugs had reached an alarming point before he would agree to enter a Chicago hospital specializing in narcotic cases.

After his treatments, he returned to Lake City, completely cured but with the disposition of a wounded ogre. Thereafter he was subject to black depressions, and his sullen silences bordered on actual hostility. One morning, however, I entered our office to find him singing lustily. His greeting was gay, his smile warm. It was an indication that he'd resumed the use of drugs and liquor, and though we both knew the end of that trail, it seemed too late for Dr. Cavett to turn back.

One day when he did not appear, I went to his room. He lay on his bed, his hair tousled, his eyes wide with panic. Suddenly he shrank back and began screaming. "Don't let them get me, Jim!" It was delirium tremens, and Dr. Cavett saw policemen rather than snakes. For three days I stayed with him, sleeping on the bed beside him nights so that I would be there to calm him when he had hallucinations. The fourth day, appearing quite rational, he asked for the newspaper. After a while, he laid it aside and discussed the Fitzsimmons-Corbett fight he'd just read about. Then, his interest lagging, he rolled over as though exhausted, and slipped away. . . .

I inherited Dr. Cavett's practice, and shortly after the birth of my daughter, Jessie, I bought a home near my office, in the center of town. There my second daughter, Mary, was born. Margaret and I were rebellious to find our roots sinking deeper and deeper into the Iowa soil, but we saw no way of realizing our dream of creating a different kind of life in Africa.

After Margaret's older sister, Laura, resigned her instructor's position at Mills College to return to missionary work, her letters from Natal urged us not to lose hope. In one letter she mentioned that the wife of Dr. Bridgeman, of the Zulu Mission, was in poor health, and that he might retire. I wrote the American Mission Board, but received only a brief explanation that Dr. Bridgeman had not yet decided to retire, and, until he did, no successor would be named.

That fall, however, I was asked to take his place. In six weeks unpaid bills were collected, possessions sold, and we bought complete African outfits. From Boston, on a cattle boat England-bound, we sailed on October 11, 1899, the day the Boer War broke out in South Africa. And two weeks later we booked passage on a ship carrying troops to Natal. At dusk, a few days after rounding the Cape of Good Hope, we saw the white line of breaking surf curving away from below the serried ranks of green hills, out along the base of a high ridge that pierced the Indian Ocean. Topping the outer point of this ridge was a light, blue-white against the darkening sky.

"That's the Durban lighthouse," someone shouted.

I hurried below to find Margaret and our two daughters. When we reached the deck, her hand sought mine.

"We've taken a long time reaching Africa," she said. "It seems like coming home, Jim."

British soldiers with jaunty caps tilted over their ears

crowded the rail to look. Engines ceased throbbing, and the anchor clanked overside abreast of a landlocked harbor. To the south was the bluff on which the lighthouse stood. Across two miles of shimmering water lay the opposite shoreline, lined with warehouses. Northeast of the circular harbor were buildings and homes, their modern appearance a little startling, here in the heart of a subtropical wilderness. And soaring above them was an eminence that Margaret called Berea Ridge. Finer, larger mansions than those below dotted its steep slopes, but in the fading light little could be seen except the white blurs of walls below the darker expanses of tile roofs.

Neither of us could have dreamed then of the part the Berea was one day to play in our lives, of the plans we were to attempt on that hill, of the bitter opposition they were to arouse, of the part those plans were to play in the life and health and growth of the Zulu people. For the Berea was one day to become the scene of our life work, of our often frustrated efforts, of a project whose worth we never doubted but which was to seem at times, nevertheless, to have been conceived in one of our unluckier moments.

Yet, having no gift of foresight, we were more interested in a soldier's question, asked of a passing ship's officer, than in Berea Ridge. "When are we going to dock, sir?"

"Never cross the sandbar with this ship," answered the officer cheerily. "The old lady's too big. But a tug will be out bright and early."

With dead engines, the ship rolled in ever-widening arcs in the heavy ground swells. Passengers deserted the deck, Margaret among them. For the first time since leaving America, I felt queasy, and fled to my cabin where, if the worst must happen, I could be seasick in privacy.

Shortly after dawn, a tugboat hove to on our lee side. A dozen of us were helped into a big, rickety basket, the cargo winch whisked us from the deck, and we hung suspended over the wildly dancing tug. Then, with a rush, we descended in the basket, striking deck with an emphatic thud. Staggering out, we lay on the deck to think of happier times. Before other travelers and soldiers had joined our miserable company, we had acquired the greenish hue of freshly caught lobsters.

This churning ceased after the tug had pounded, grating and swaying, across the sandbar into quiet water. A few minutes later, when we crossed the gangplank to the dock, I was carrying Mary, a chunky and altogether unhappy ten-month-old baby, and leading Jessie by the hand. Margaret somehow contrived to make it on her own. Laura Mellen drew my wife into her arms, but Margaret, still shaky and with the motion of the sea stirring within her, was not what you'd call demonstrative.

CHAPTER THREE

IN AFRICA,
PATIENCE IS A VIRTUE

LAURA MELLEN, MORE SLIM AND BROWN THAN WHEN we'd last seen her at Oberlin, radiated vitality and good health to a degree that was depressing after the punishment we'd taken on the tug. I had but a moment, however, to observe her contrast with that of my seasick family.

A fierce-looking band of natives had descended upon me looking like something from a nightmare in their cotton suits and strings of beads, and with enormous oxhorns fastened to their heads. Bracelets clinked on the slim ebony arms waving in my face; whitewashed legs swished nearly to my shoulders as the men jumped and kicked.

"Don't be alarmed, Jim," Laura said, laughing. "They're not angry. They're just rickshaw boys, demonstrating how agile they are!" And she directed the two highest kickers to pack off our baggage to the hotel where we were having lunch.

Margaret had given me an idea of Durban's size, telling me that it was half as populous as Columbus, Ohio, without preparing me for its beauty. As the rickshaw boys trotted along, Laura pointed out blue jacaranda and other flowering trees. The homes, mostly one-story stucco dwellings, were smothered in bougainvillia or golden glory, gardens were paintings in riotous colors. Although streets and buildings stretching three miles back to Berea Ridge were inviting, it was the hilltop, with its beautiful homes, which we most wished to see. Unfortunately, there was only time to remove travel stains and eat before catching a southbound train.

Tales of Stanley and Du Chaillu made it hard to shake loose impressions of an equatorial Africa, but our train passed through country that Laura compared with Central California. True, heavy rainfall accounted for dense forest along the rivers, but aside from these strips of forest, the open veld, with only sparse clumps of green dotting the golden hills, would have seemed familiar to a San Franciscan. Jessie and Mary flattened small noses against the train windows as we passed native kraals, their beehive-shaped huts surrounded by a wall of stakes.

Only a shed in a forest clearing marked the Umbogintwini River stop where we disembarked that afternoon. After the train had disappeared into a shadowy cavern of trees, we followed Laura along wagon tracks leading through the bush. Jessie, skipping along childlike beside Margaret, suddenly squealed, "Prairie schooner!" and darted past us toward a small covered wagon. Yokes were laid out for six oxen, but there was no sign of oxen or driver.

"The driver must have 'outspanned' the oxen to graze," Laura suggested. "In Africa, patience is a virtue."

Minutes later a native with a sparse and grizzled beard ran up, his tattered trousers flapping around his bony knees.

"Where is the leader-boy, Richard?" Laura asked.

With a vague gesture, the aged Zulu explained that the boy was with the oxen. Laura sent Richard off to find him. But when the sun had declined and the driver had not returned, I set off along the road with one small daughter. I saw none of the poisonous snakes Laura warned me might drop unsuspectingly, but Natal monkeys scolded from the treetops. Finally I found our boy roasting an unplucked bird, while other black urchins watched hungrily. Short of African virtue, I hustled him off to bring the oxen.

The purpose of a leader-boy was to guide the two foremost oxen by a rope after they were "inspanned," or hitched to their yokes. Richard's "driving" consisted of cracking his whip.

My respect for American pioneers deepened with every lurching, jolting, swaying mile the covered wagon traveled. We climbed hillocks, plowed through creeks and riverbottom sands, and only on open veld were our aching joints and muscles given any relief. The worst part of the ride was when Richard dropped off to speak to a friend, and an ox recognized the bawling of its calf in the kraal we were approaching. The drowsy leader-boy came to with a start, prudently dropping his rope when the oxen began running. The top-heavy wagon rolled side to side like a small boat in a beam sea as the oxen raced toward the kraal stockade. With visions of us all being impaled on the sharp stakes, I tried to help Laura, Margaret and the children over the high backboard, but we tumbled in a heap at each attempt.

Shouting, Richard and his friend headed the runaways away from the kraal. We missed the stockade, scattered frightened cattle, including the calf responsible for the trouble, and came to a stop when entangled reins and yokes made it impossible for the oxen to run farther.

It was dark before the harness was straightened and repaired. Boughs scraped the canvas top and the wagon pitched and swayed in deep ruts. Not a star showed through the forest roof. Suddenly the wagon tilted, and the oxen ran at the crack of Richard's whip.

"Amanzimtoti River," he shouted.

Imagining that the sleepwalking leader-boy had led us down into a river, I held Mary tighter and prepared for a ducking. Water splashed through floorboard cracks, but in a moment the oxen climbed a bank and halted.

I stepped stiffly out, staring with interest at a sprawling building of brick and thatch, its walls partially covered with vines. In general appearance, it somewhat resembled pictures I'd seen of picturesque early Spanish ranch houses. Candles burned in the windows, and a native girl, neatly dressed in a short and simple frock, welcomed us at the door.

Everyone else at Adams Mission had retired, but this girl had remained up to keep our dinner warm. She led us into the dining room, where candles showed us that the old walls, and the thatched roof above, had been well maintained. We took places at the end of a long table, and when the girl had served us, Laura began to tell us about Ireland Home.

This dwelling had long been the home of a couple serving Adams station, but following the death of Reverend Ireland, his wife had opened a school for native girls. The school was a great success. Young girls objecting to marrying a decrepit ancient, with perhaps six wives and the ten head of cattle to pay for another, could escape a distasteful marriage by coming to Ireland Home. The British had impressed on the natives that white men's houses must not be invaded, so fathers tried to recapture their daughters on the grounds, but this proved difficult after the girls set up a "father-raid-warning" system. Fathers could pay a fee to a native magistrate, who then served papers requiring a girl to return home, but as the daughter might run away again the same night, legal methods fell into disfavor.

Most heathen maids attended school to enforce their choice of a mate, but as a by-product of their wilfulness, they became Christians, acquired habits of cleanliness, and learned of better medical practices than those of witch doctors. Other missions opened girls' schools, however, so Adams Mission closed theirs upon the retirement of Mrs. Ireland, devoting their limited funds to an industrial school for boys.

"The Zulus have no words for our tools," Laura explained. "They speak of 'learning to shoot with plane and saw'."

Daybreak found Margaret and me exploring the luxuriant and well-tended garden surrounding Ireland Home. Then, after a time, we passed through a gate into the main yard of the mission, laid out on a bare slope and dotted with missionaries' homes. Through the bare windows of a small building to the right of the gate, we looked into the industrial shop where the shooting was done with plane and saw. Opposite it was the chapel, a plain and barnlike building with an iron roof, large enough to accommodate perhaps a hundred people, its wooden benches standing in rows on the dirt floor.

Farther up the hill, we came upon a house with cracked and pitted walls. Fresh paint failed to conceal its age. While we were speculating on its builder, a woman of pleasantly maternal appearance opened the door. Clearly she didn't expect to see us, for she said, "Oh!" and for several moments, although she made no movement, I half expected her to close the door. Then she smiled, a smile that was withdrawn, with no hint of friendliness.

Margaret, embarrassed by the woman's coolness, said, "We didn't mean to stare, but this house . . . it seems so old . . ."

"So it is," said the woman. "It's the oldest house in Natal. . . . You must be the McCords; we've been expecting you. I'm Mrs. Bunker, and this," she added, turning to a man who had come to the door, "is Dr. Bunker. Won't you come in?"

Her manner invited refusal, and I saw that Margaret, usually at home in any situation, was plainly flustered by this reception. "Oh, no thank you, Mrs. Bunker. It's so early."

Dr. Bunker stroked his beard, a little nervously, as if he felt they might have been too brusque. "This is the house Dr. Adams built, shortly after the War of 1812. He lived here until he died."

"The Adams house!" Margaret exclaimed, turning to me. "Why, Mother and Father came to live in this very house ten years before Lincoln became president. They just missed knowing Dr. Adams; he died the day of their arrival."

This announcement seemed to thaw the Bunkers somewhat, and now they insisted that we come in. We tried to refuse, but when Mrs. Bunker also urged us, we could hardly decline. I had the feeling, as the Bunkers showed us the house, that they were normally friendly people, and that there must be some reason for their original restraint, though I could not think what it was.

Face liftings with mud and coats of whitewash prevented the house from showing its seventy-five years. The Bunkers' hobby was Adamsiana, and they had preserved

letters in Dr. Newton Adams's copperplate handwriting.
Though the letters gave evidence of a dogmatic character, that may have explained the bristling among his con-
temporaries, the Bunkers found much to justify it.

Dr. Adams, they explained, was the first missionary
and doctor in Natal when only a handful of white adven-
turers and traders lived there on the sufferance of a powerful and unconquered Zulu nation. He needed mental
and spiritual toughness to hold his own against soldiers
of fortune who respected only brawn and bullets. Severely
limited in funds, Dr. Adams had appeared mornings in
work clothes to supervise the native servants felling trees
and breaking virgin soil behind his span of oxen; at noon
he dressed in white to tend his patients; Sundays found
him preaching, in ministerial coat, in the church built
with his own hands and those of his converts. Hence his
native name, "The Man With Three Coats."

When Natal blazed into rebellion against the
whites, and those escaping massacre fled to populous centers, Dr. Adams remained at his station, refusing to return home even when the American Mission Board withdrew its support to enforce the order. His response was to
break more ground for a larger garden. He treated the
war wounds of natives and whites alike; on Sundays, he
preached to all who came. By the time peace came, he
had won the respect of both sides.

In later years, Dr. Adams's fame as a surgeon spread
far beyond Natal, though in his day he was obliged to
operate without anesthesia. Besides preaching and doing
medical work, he played a dominant role in the political,
social and industrial movements in Natal, dying at only
forty-seven, burned out by the prodigal expenditure of his
energy.

Adams Mission didn't have another medical mission-

ary until Dr. Bridgeman, my predecessor, was appointed
forty years later, in 1893.

"I like to think," said Dr. Bunker, "that it was because no other doctor could be found to match Newton
Adams's stride."

We thanked the Bunkers, and he followed us outside to help us orient ourselves.

"Along the slope," he explained, "are two missionaries' homes, the larger belonging to Mr. Kilbon, chairman of this mission. Near it is the schoolhouse. The station lies between two valleys, and across the right-hand
one is the boys' dormitory, Jubilee Hall. Higher on the
slope, you'll see a cluster of smaller dwellings beyond the
valley to your left. Native theological students and their
families live there."

"What is that house on the crest?" Margaret asked.

"That's Hilltop, where you'll live. Over the brow of
the hill is a bridge spanning a stream. Cross it, and you'll
find the dispensary and hospital Dr. Bridgeman built six
years ago when he came here."

Nothing would restrain Margaret longer. We started
up the hill, intending to pass the missionaries' houses,
trailing smoke at this hour from breakfast fires. But before we could pass the door of Mr. Kilbon's house, the
door opened, and a man of medium height, black bearded
and with an ear trumpet, waved to us.

"You're the McCords, I know. I'm Mr. Kilbon.
Come in, come in. You're just in time for breakfast."

He wouldn't hear of a refusal, seizing Margaret's arm
and ushering her into the house, where Mrs. Kilbon came
to greet us, her smile, her manner as cordial as her husband's. It was in sharp contrast to the Bunkers' reception,
and when I asked, at breakfast, whether the Bunkers were
always so reserved, Mr. Kilbon laughed.

"You'll find most of the missionaries a little stand-offish, I expect, Dr. McCord. For a while, anyway. Quite a few of them feel that a doctor is not necessary in our work. And you have another obstacle—you're American."

Margaret and I must have looked startled, for Mrs. Kilbon smiled, and added, "Mr. Kilbon means that you'll have to live down the reputation of one of your country-men, the Elder Weavers."

"He was a wild and woolly character, as I believe you call it, with extreme ideas of holiness," Mr. Kilbon went on. "Missionary work was in a turmoil here for years after he left, the result of his influence on the natives. Ever hear of him?"

I leaned toward the ear trumpet and explained that I'd heard only a little about the unrestrained elder.

"Better tell you about him, then," said Mr. Kilbon, "because he's sown a thorny path for you medical mission-aries."

The Elder Weavers, he told me, was an Iowan of the John-the-Baptist type, a forceful personality and a preacher who could capture a congregation by his impas-sioned speech and earnestness. He was even able to draw large numbers of Zulus and hold them as if hypnotized, when he first came to Natal as a missionary, though he preached entirely in English. In time, he employed an in-terpreter to translate as he spoke.

No one had any quarrel with the Elder Weavers when he preached straight gospel, which he usually did, but he had a few unorthodox ideas which more and more frequently crept into his sermons and in the end were to do an immense amount of mischief.

One of his idiosyncrasies was a belief in confession in open meeting. The Zulus, who in many cases had much to confess, would listen with enthusiasm to others confessing their sins and would, when their turn came, relate with gusto their own wrongdoings. This was not, however, sufficient for the Elder Weavers, for he had gained a strong following among the missionaries, and he insisted that they also publicly acknowledge their sins. They had little enough to confess in most cases, and one old missionary, who had led an exemplary life, had to think back to his childhood to recall anything sinful enough to seem worth relating. The effect of the missionaries' confessions was not a good one so far as the natives were concerned. They listened, openmouthed, and decided that if these good people had pecadilloes, perhaps sin was a normal human failing.

The Elder Weavers's most unfortunate idiosyncrasy, however, was his belief that he could heal the sick. True, there were some remarkable recoveries in cases where psychic treatment was all that was necessary. But his idea that taking medicine was a sin was a severe handicap to patients who needed it. If such patients failed to respond to their own and his prayers, the elder was certain they were either still living in sin or lacked faith.

Elder Weavers left South Africa after years there as a missionary, and when he retuned, in his later life, he was a medium-sized old man with graying hair, a bushy beard and a piercing eye, but without all of his former zeal. His influence on the natives was nevertheless still strong. He rose each morning with the sun to climb a high hill, and there, under a tree, he spread an antelope skin to protect his trousers, and prayed. For years after he departed a second time from Natal, many Zulu disciples carried antelope skins to use when they desired to pray.

Although I had no suspicion of it when Mr. Kilbon was telling me the story, I was to feel the effect of the

Elder Weavers's teachings for many years. On occasions when I had made long trips by boat or on foot to remote missions, I found missionaries still under his influence. A sick missionary, badly in need of medicine, would not touch it, believing that faith alone would effect a cure. The other missionaries would confess that I'd been called merely to write a death certificate in the event the sick person died. Natives who also believed that faith and prayer would cure physical ills, would likewise refuse medicine that would have hastened their recovery.

I smiled and assured Mr. Kilbon that our fellow missionaries need have no fear that all Americans were like the Elder Weavers, and certainly my resemblance to him, particularly as a preacher, was slight.

After leaving the Kilbons, Margaret and I climbed the hill to the comfortable wattle house at the crest, which was screened on three sides. But we'd forgotten to ask Mr. Kilbon for the key to Hilltop, and the door to our new home was locked.

We descended toward the stream, crossed the footbridge which spanned it, and climbed perhaps a quarter mile to the dispensary, which was open. It was a plain brick building, with a small porch and a sheet-iron roof, a building with four small rooms, the largest only a little over twice my own length. But that seemed sufficient at the time, with rooms for assembly, operating and examining, consulting, and a cubbyhole room for drugs.

Only a few steps beyond the dispensary was the mission hospital built by Dr. Bridgeman, with a small thatched-roof hut behind to serve as a kitchen. The hospital itself, a building of three rooms, with a veranda running around three sides, was of the construction known as wattle and daub. Laura had already explained the term. Posts are driven into the ground, and vines woven be-

tween them are plastered with mud. When the dried mud
is whitewashed, it resembles stucco.

My medical school professors would have shaken
their heads at this hospital, with its dirt floor and thatched
roof, at the kitchen hut which I must use as a sterilizer
room; but I had envisioned conditions so much more
primitive in South Africa that I was well pleased.

When we climbed to Hilltop again, we stopped to
admire the view from its porch. To the west, we had a
sweeping view of golden hills, valleys, twisting river channels, thickly banked with trees; and in the distance, waves
of green mountains reaching far into the heart of Africa.
To the east there were rippling green hills, with the Indian Ocean beyond, metallic blue in the morning light,
and at certain times, we knew, we could watch ships beating northward toward the spice ports, the Red Sea and
China.

"Jim," Margaret asked anxiously, "is it what you expected?"

"I hope there's no serpent," I laughed.

"Not in this Eden!" she declared.

But there was; and we learned about it at the morning tea where me met our fellow missionaries—Mr. Kilbon, chairman of the mission; Reverend Bunker, who
bustled about, to talk eagerly for a while and then lapse
into meditative silence as though composing a sermon;
Miss Hattie Clark, a spinster of indefinable age and as-
cetic manner; Mr. Cowles, head of the boys' school, a
man as humorless as an undertaker; and Mr. Pixley, a
bearded gentleman with a smile which never faded
whether he was speaking of Mrs. Bridgeman's bad health
or the pranks of the girls at near-by Inanda, the girls'
school where he taught. It was Mr. Pixley who told us,
with his unchanging smile, of an inflexible rule that no

one could serve at the mission until he could speak Zulu.
This was a blow, for I had expected to start practice that
day, with an interpreter's assistance.

I shouted this intention into Mr. Kilbon's ear trumpet, while at the same time trying to face the chairman.
He nodded his black beard.

"Trouble is, Dr. McCord," he said kindly, "we can't
always provide an interpreter, nor can I spare anyone at
present to teach you Zulu."

Laura, overhearing him, must have noticed my crest-
fallen look.

"Wonderful, Jim!" she cried, coming to my rescue.
"You and Margaret and the girls can come to my station.
I'll be your teacher."

Laura originally worked at Esidumbini (a mission
station established by her father) with two maiden missionaries. But when one retired and the other married,
she became sole spiritual guardian of scores of Christianized Zulus living on the 5,000-acre mission reserve. Her
work also encompassed heathen settlements scattered
over 100 miles of veld and bush. She covered this territory on foot because rinderpest had killed most of Natal's
cattle a few years before; walking was easier than finding
ox or horse.

But foot travel was too difficult for two small girls
and Margaret, then pregnant. So Laura went ahead to arrange transportation. Even with her flair for accomplishment, it was two weeks before she could find a horse and
buggy.

Our trip by covered wagon and train to Tongaat was
more comfortable than the only hotel there. Our room
perched over a saloon, where boisterous British soldiers
and hotel guests sang and argued. It was a relief to hear a
knock at three in the morning.

I carried the sleeping children outside. A horse with skin hanging loosely on a bony frame was hitched to a wagon belonging in a museum. The native owner of this ancient equipage was obviously too decrepit to walk, yet the buggy would hold only the two children and one adult.

"I thought Margaret and I could take turns riding," Laura explained apologetically. "I could find no other transportation."

My low estimate of the horse was over-optimistic; he could not even keep pace with Margaret. When daylight broke over the green hills, however, waiting for the plodding animal on a pinnacle was not unpleasant. Mountains rippled away to every compass point, the green of hillsides here and there broken by native kraals or sloping gardens. To the eastward the distant ocean spread like purple velvet until it merged with the horizon. The endlessly pitching hills were less appealing under a flaying midday sun. Each climb became greater strain on legs and back, and the view seemed less worth the effort.

The dipping road prevented me from realizing we were on a high plateau until we reached its edge as the light began to fail. A thousand feet below lay a lost world, an immense fertile valley of kraals and gardens, cupped in the hills. The meager road carved from the white sandstone cliffs snaked dizzily downward, the plateau plunging in a sheer precipice on one side.

Laura's assurance that "no horse has run off the cliff for a long time" failed to satisfy Margaret or me. We lifted Mary and Jessie from the wagon. The rear end of the vehicle skidded dangerously as the driver rode his brakes all the way to the bottom. The flatness of the valley from above was illusory, for there were still foothills to cross before we mounted a final hill ringed with flame. The natives, Laura enlightened me, burned the grass so the rains would enrich the hills with fresh pasturage for their cattle.

After leaving the blazing grass and an orange grove behind, we came to a bungalow of sun-dried bricks with an inviting veranda. A tall, solemn Zulu, as thin as a willow wand, stood beside a platoon of schoolchildren who appeared to have waited hours for us to complete our twenty-five-mile journey. He raised his hand and the children burst forth with "Shine On, Oh Star of Hope," and then, blissfully unaware of any incongruity, led his pupils in, "Welcome Home to the Prodigal."

Men in white pants and shirts, and women in drab, shapeless dresses, walked up to speak as the song ended. Grinning broadly, they kept repeating, "*Umkwenyana . . . Umkwenyana . . .*"

"They're calling you 'Brother-in-Law,'" Laura laughed. "Have you forgotten you married into the royal family?"

A Zulu of prepossessing stature addressed me, his dark eyes gleaming with mischief.

"He welcomes the husband of Princess Margaret," Laura translated, with a smile. "He knows you'll wish to follow Zulu custom. A man marrying into the royal family kills a beast and feasts his people."

Tired though I was, I could laugh. Rinderpest made Natal cattle too costly for a missionary's purse. I never ceased hearing about my brother-in-law's obligation while living at Esidumbini, for the Zulus won't let a good joke die.

After breakfast the following morning, we settled chairs on the pounded dirt floor and Laura started her instruction. We had scarcely begun when a native clergyman, the Reverend Umvakwendhlu Syvetye, came in with patriarchial dignity to discuss the next Sunday's sermon. Joshua Mwandhla waited to discuss a disciplinary problem with Laura when the native pastor finished. And the Zulu lesson was barely under way again when bickering voices forced our instructor to step outside to settle a dispute between two natives about the boundaries of their gardens. These interruptions continued until Laura left to teach a class. Other problems required solving that afternoon; Laura had to prepare a sermon, plan meals with the cook, supervise the picking of winter oranges. This, we soon discovered, was typical of her days.

It was evident before long that despite her amazing energy, Laura's crowded hours allowed her little time to teach us Zulu. Margaret had spoken the tongue as fluently as English before leaving Africa at six, and it returned to her after she began supervising the kitchen girls. But I had such a poor ear for languages that I made little progress until I commenced treating patients, with the aid of an interpreter.

Zulu is a beautiful tongue, the soft, musical quality of native voices lending itself to the often poetical turn of its phrases. Mastering it demands absolute perfection of words and sounds, for a Zulu speaks precisely from childhood; no native mother ever uses "baby talk." The greatest stumbling block is that the language is intertwined with superstitions, social customs and primitive racial conceptions. A Zulu suffering from headache, for example, says, "I am ridden by the head and the load is heavy." With only a vague idea of the cause of illness, he describes a stomach ache as, "I am bitten by my stomach," or, if the nausea is severe, "My heart is black; it says, 'Vomit'!"

The speech is dominated by proverbs, some so ancient that no modern Zulu could give exact English translations of word combinations which are today meaning-less. I believe this dependence upon proverbs explains why they think in word-phrases rather than in single words.

Literal translation into Zulu is useless; and it was only when I had many of their word-phrases and prov-erbs fixed in mind that I was able to short-circuit my in-terpreter in dealing direct with a patient.

While Laura found little time to instruct us in the language, she would sometimes, at the end of a hard day, sit on the veranda and give us historical glimpses of the people. I had imagined the Zulus were a black-skinned race of primitives, living in isolated tribal villages. Laura corrected this misconception. Actually there is consider-able Zulu history, which reached its peak under a black Genghis Khan named Chaka.

Chaka's grandnephew was the nominal chief of the Zulus when I reached South Africa, but the British had stripped Zulu leaders of much of their old authority. Al-ready tribes which had fled in the warlike Chaka's day were returning to the territory. . . .

Life in many ways was idyllic at Esidumbini. The Christianized Zulus on the reserve lived in peace and con-tentment. Each day had sufficient work to give it interest, but not enough to cause it to be regarded with suspicion. Sundays were days of religious observance; and the natives looked forward all week to the sermons and hymns. They often had quaint misconceptions, however, about the words in sermon or song.

The mountains surrounding Esidumbini insulated it from the Boer War, though at times the wind carried the thunder of cannons bombarding Ladysmith. It was days before newspapers carrying reports of the battles reached

us; but we received accurate reports nightly by "Zulu telegraph." From hilltop to hilltop, news of the day's battles
were shouted by the natives.

In indirect ways, however, the Boer War pinched at
every meal. Beans and other vegetables were sometimes
purchasable from native gardeners, and the mission garden grew sweet potatoes, plantains and oranges. Canned
milk, meat and butter could be ordered when natives visited Tongaat, but the price was usually beyond a missionary's purse—butter, for example, costing a dollar a pound
can.

Fresh meat spoiled on the trip from Tongaat. The
salt beef that once came to Esidumbini now went to the
British army. Eggs appeared infrequently, and only once
during our seven months at the isolated mission could
Laura allow herself the luxury of sacrificing one of the
scrawny hens.

The war thus forced us to a starch-heavy diet. It was
serious enough in feeding two small girls, but really critical when Robert was born three months after our arrival.
Eggs, milk and other items of an infant diet were practically unobtainable.

Inadequate food forced us to shorten our stay at
Esidumbini, but I didn't regret leaving. I found I learned
Zulu fastest in practice, and with no dispensary at the
mission, there was little to encourage natives to make the
long, hard trip there. Obviously Adams Mission was a
better place both for language study and native practice.

Before I left Boston for Africa, my predecessor Dr.
Bridgeman informed me of a recent ruling of the Natal
Medical Council requiring a doctor to have a British medical degree. At Cape Town I verified the existence of this
ruling, but believed it might be waived for a practice limited to natives and missionaries. I attempted to register

when I landed at Durban. The secretary of the council doubted whether an exception would be made, but agreed to submit a statement of my training and experience at the next meeting.

A letter received at Esidumbini denied my request.

Still believing an exception was justified for a medical missionary, I stopped at Durban en route to ask for reconsideration. I was told I must make my request in writing. This I did, pointing out that American medical standards were not inferior to British, and were surely superior to the witch-doctor treatment upon which the natives then depended. I added that since the council had passed the ruling requiring a British degree, they could suspend it in special cases. My request was acknowledged, and prompt action was promised; but Dr. Maurice Pearson, a doctor sympathetic to the native cause, warned me:

"You have no chance without a British degree, old chap. So long as your practice is limited to Kaffirs, probably nothing will be said. Get on with your work, that's my advice. If you ever need a death certificate, I'll sign one myself."

A generous offer, certainly, but practicing without proper registration could at any time involve me in legal difficulties. Hoping the council might reverse itself, we continued on to Adams Mission to establish a home for the five McCords.

My appeal was denied shortly after I began dispensary work. Clearly the council could make any ruling it chose, but much as I begrudged time lost from practice to satisfy a technicality, I saw that my future in South Africa would be built upon quicksand unless I had a British medical degree.

My salary wouldn't permit five of us to live in England, so I sailed alone in June of 1901. Perhaps infected food or water taken in some native kraal was responsible, but I became ill after sailing—too ill to know or care whether I had dengue fever or typhoid. I probably owed my life to the faithful nursing of a steward.

I went to England not to study any special field, but to satisfy the requirements for a British medical degree. The climate of Natal is so similar to parts of the United States that such special studies as tropical medicine would be useless there. Therefore it was only necessary to study British texts, attend classes, and observe how British hospital methods differed from American. After a year of intensive study, I appeared before an examining board for written and oral examination and, upon passing, was given my degree.

When I returned to Adams, my family now felt quite at home in the large, airy bungalow known as Hilltop. I dug up the neglected garden plot of a former missionary and planted pawpaw trees, bananas, mulberry and mango trees, as well as packages of seed purchased in Durban. In our front yard, around the station church bell, I set in flowering trees and a profusion of flowers. One incredible night-blooming cereus vine in time gave us two hundred blooms to admire from the screened porch. My gardening was completed by the time native helpers had scrubbed and whitewashed the dispensary.

The path from the hills led past our door. On Sundays nearly naked Zulus went by with Sunday clothing in bundles on their heads, stopping, a few hundred yards farther, to slip on pants, shirts and dresses before continuing to the church. Later on the stream of travelers divided at the house, one branch flowing on to the mission, the other moving toward dispensary and hospital. During the first weeks after my return to Hilltop, however, my practice was confined to the boys of Jubilee Hall. Zulus, who are confirmed conservatives, always wait for someone braver to blaze the trail.

Jubilee Hall received its name because it was built on the fiftieth anniversary of the mission's founding, and the sixty boys living there seemed still to be celebrating the event. The large brick building resounded with talk, laughter and hymns whenever its occupants weren't in classes, in church or sleeping. The missionary teacher there needed stout nerves. Fifteen years separated the youngest and the oldest students, but the Zulus saw nothing unusual in a six-year-old and a twenty-one-year-old studying primary reading in the same class. It was established mission custom.

My first duty was to examine these students, beginning with those in evident need of medical attention. The serious impact of rinderpest, the plague which killed most of Natal's cattle, showed up in my examinations. The Zulus were in a transitional stage between hunting and pastoral herding when the contagion struck. Hunting skill had been largely lost; the wiping out of all but one per cent of their cattle deprived them of milk and meat. The disaster even prevented them from entering an agricultural stage on an equitable basis, for they lacked the means of plowing and the animals to transport excess products to market. The boys showed the effects of a deficiency diet in such poverty diseases as incipient tuberculosis, digestive troubles, children's diseases, and acute fever resulting from lowered resistance.

Boys in upper grades averaged better health than those just entering. Aside from the moral benefits from missionary work—and my observation led me to believe they were important—Adams Mission justified itself in the improved health of students who had lived for several years on the simple, balanced meals served there. I could relieve certain conditions, but only time and improved eating habits could remedy most of the boys' ills.

My work at Adams did not include preaching, but sometimes I helped in other phases of missionary work which might broadly be termed "preventive medicine," in that it prevented injuries. One day when most of the missionaries were at a meeting in Durban, I learned that the boys of the Makanya and Mapumulo tribes had got into an argument and were planning to fight after class dismissal. Since many of them were grown men, descendants of the two tribes from which came many of Chaka's warriors, and fights were with heavy sticks rather than fists, I had visions of a long list of injuries.

I called the leaders in one at a time, but they mistook my friendly attitude for weakness, and refused to call off the fight. Then, still smiling, I asked a native teacher to fetch a big, black *sjambok*—an ox whip which hung on the wall as an example of native handicraft. John Makanya, who was in my office at the time, stared at me in alarm, apparently deciding that a mild manner might be coupled with effective action.

"We will wait until Mr. LeRoy returns," he said hastily. Mr. LeRoy was head of the boys' school.

"All right, John," I said. "Will you give me your word not to fight until he returns?"

He promised—a promise I knew would be kept. One by one I called in the other leaders, and received their promises. What I would have done if the group had defied me, I don't know. But the fight was postponed until Reverend LeRoy returned, and after he had whipped the ringleaders, an armistice was declared.

Rolling his eyes, one of the boys later told me, "A reverend don't whip often, but he sure do whip hard."

Zulu schoolboys play at being warriors much as Amer-

ican boys play games. It's unwise to curb these games because in later life the boys must obtain part of their food
with an *assegai*—a stabbing spear. Missionaries allowed
these mock battles so long as they were in fun, but the
boys sometimes emulated warriors with such energy that
there were serious injuries.

Ntombiyensini, a Zulu debutante, brought her
younger brother, Mbangani, to the dispensary after one
such battle. She told me he had "died" the week before,
remaining "dead" two days before returning to life—the
Zulu word for "dead" and "unconscious" are identical.
The boy could not use his right arm or leg, and his body
burned with fever.

In my halting Zulu, I asked for more details. Ntombiyensini finally made me understand that after returning
from school Mbangani and his friends were having a
friendly battle with the boys of a neighboring kraal, using
reeds for throwing spears. When a spear flew at Mbangani
and he lacked time to step aside, he ducked, trying to stop
it with his head, a method that had previously proved
harmless. This time the heavy root penetrated his skull,
entering his brain. He lay unconscious for two days; now
the wound discharged a foul-smelling pus. Ntombiyensini
had carried her brother for many miles over rough trail,
her younger sister accompanying her to bring the food and
blankets needed in the hospital.

The boy sat motionless during my examination. The
root had been pulled out by one of Mbangani's companions, leaving dirt in the wound. The scalp had closed the
opening, clotted blood sealing in the infective dirt.

I would have to operate at once to save the boy's life.
After clearing the hospital waiting room of curious small
boys, I sent one boy off to find Reverend Bates, who ad-

ministered anesthesia in major operations, and another
to bring Margaret, now fast learning a nurse's duties.

By the time I had set up two small tables, end to end,
to serve as an operating table, and Mbangani was on it,
all the missionaries had come to watch; brain surgery was
something new for Adams Mission. Mr. William Cullen
Wilcox, teacher at the Inanda girls' school, had come by
bicycle to see Mr. Kilbon, and now he bustled around the
operating room in puttees, riding pants and tropical sun
helmet, looking like a condensed version of "Teddy"
Roosevelt. He was a man of considerable drive, but as his
energy was out of place in a surgery, I attempted to shackle
it by requesting him to watch Mbangani's pulse.

Margaret took instruments out to the kitchen hut to
be sterilized, and while we waited, Mr. Bates saturated the
cotton mask with chloroform to put over the boy's nose.
The whites of his sisters' eyes gleamed as they watched
from positions against the wall. Mbangani was unconscious by the time my wife returned with the instruments.

It was a serious operation, the first major operation I
had attempted without the guidance of an older surgeon,
but fortunately it was not really a difficult one. After removing the blood clot, I lifted out fragments of bone and
dirt, and cut away infected portions of the brain tissue.
After providing free drainage, my work was done.

During the operation Mr. Wilcox seriously fulfilled
his duties. Gravely he pronounced, "The pulse is getting
slower . . . slower . . . slower . . ." Puzzled, having
no reason to suspect a weak heart, I felt my patient's tem-
poral artery and found a strong pulse. But as it was better
to confine Mr. Wilcox's energy, I said nothing. His face
grew more solemn as the operation progressed, his tone
deepened. "The pulse is slower . . . slower . . ." Then

he started, cleared his throat, and announced in a sepul-
chral voice, "*It has stopped!*"

The missionaries regarded me apprehensively. Margaret's eyes were tragic. I winked, barely able to suppress a
grin. So great was her relief that she laughed, drawing
shocked glances from her fellow missionaries.

"Mr. Wilcox," I said, "you're pressing too hard—and
in the wrong place."

The boy made a good recovery in the hospital, his
two sisters caring for him until he could return home. The
infection had spread to the motor nerve cells, however,
and some of these cells were destroyed in removing diseased tissue. Mbangani dragged one leg badly and could
not use his right arm effectively for months. In time the
only evidence of his injury was a slight limp.

Cases such as his did more to break down the conservatism of the surrounding kraals than any amount of
persuasion. True, Dr. Adams had broken the first ground,
and Dr. Bridgeman tilled it after him. But to the Zulus
each new medical missionary must prove his magic. My
student patients were good propagandists, bringing many
new patients to the hospital and dispensary. It also helped
when I cleared up the kidney trouble of an influential
chief.

Margaret spent so much time helping as nurse and
general operating assistant that she had to find a girl to
relieve her of household duties. She chose Laura Nyuswa,
who, though she'd never before cooked for white people,
was soon a good American cook, and more than that introduced some delicious Zulu dishes to our table. She was
of such a happy disposition that missionary girls came calling when their work for other whites was done, sick girls
visited her on the way to the dispensary, and girls came
from neighboring kraals. The McCord kitchen was re-

garded as a community clubhouse, and often it sounded as if a suffragette meeting were in progress there.

Laura not only relieved the pressure on Margaret; she also found me a hospital assistant. He was her father, Umqibelo, who had been Dr. Bridgeman's assistant—a tall and dignified Zulu, with a sparse gray beard. Among other duties, Umqibelo was supposed to interpret for me, but he spoke little English; his handicap in this direction was my advantage, for I learned much of my Zulu from him. His father, Nyuswa, a great runner, had jogged along beside the horse of the Dick King of song and story on the three-hundred-mile ride that made King the South African Paul Revere; King went to Grahamstown to bring soldiers to relieve Durban when it was attacked by the Boers in the early part of the century. Umqibelo's story of his father's fame was accurate, but his claim that he'd been Dr. Bridgeman's anesthetist was not. The first time he administered chloroform was his last; with difficulty, I revived the patient. In other respects, however, he was a useful assistant. He washed bottles, kept the dispensary gleaming, served tea to patients who had sometimes walked as far as forty miles for treatment, and read the Bible and acted as a general evangelist in the waiting room, thus putting patients at their ease while they waited.

But finding a general female assistant and interpreter for the consulting and examination room was more difficult. After I had talked to several girls, Mr. Kilbon recommended Katie Makanya, then working for a British family about to leave South Africa. Katie came and looked around my consulting room with an almost proprietary air, then smiled at me with such good humor that I found myself smiling back. Both of us realized from that moment that the subsequent interview was needless formality; I was as determined to keep her as she was to stay.

Katie was a handsome woman of thirty, slim and tall and the color of honey from living indoors. Completely self-possessed, she answered my questions simply and without a trace of servility. Frequently her dark eyes gleamed with amusement, and her deep laugh was good to hear. She was one of a group of South African natives chosen to sing before royalty at Queen Victoria's Jubilee, and the account of her trip and her entertainment by royalty sparkled with humor and discerning observations. A Basuto, Katie learned Zulu when her husband found it too difficult to court her in her tongue. She was the teacher I'd so long sought—one who had learned Zulu and was aware of its shoals.

With Katie in my consulting room, my knowledge of Zulu rounded out. And the hospital was more cheerful for her presence. Often as she went about her work, she'd break spontaneously into song, her resonant contralto filling the building like organ music.

"You can trust me," Katie had promised when I engaged her.

This was true. For the first time since the stream of patients had been growing, the work bore superficial resemblance to a smoothly run clinic. Katie, developing into a trustworthy nurse, helped speed patients through the dispensary. Margaret was freed from this work for more exacting duties—preparing instruments and the operating room before surgery, assisting me in operations, and sometimes administering the anesthetic.

Even this additional help would not move patients through the hospital without adjustments. Natives needing longer convalescence often were discharged to give their space on the floor or veranda to more critical cases. I dreamed of enlarging the hospital, and sometimes when my wife and I sat on our porch evenings, we discussed these plans as we watched ships plying the Indian Ocean.

A death in the dispensary sent these dreams crashing.

The reason for that death was that Adams Mission was a back eddy of travel. Nearly two-thirds of my patients were heathen Zulu, who lived long distances from the mission. They had to journey ten to fifty miles afoot or by train. Three rail lines converged on Durban, and a dispensary there would best serve the Zulus. What drove that point home forcibly was having a native die of dysentery in the waiting room before I could see him. I inquired where he'd come from, and learned that he'd walked from a village twenty miles distant. That twenty miles may have cost him his life!

To me that was clear proof that it would be a mistake to enlarge the hospital at Adams. Yet Margaret and I hated to move. We loved Hilltop and its Elysian setting. We were happy, our hours filled with work worth doing. Even our human relationships were fortunate. True, the missionaries sometimes bickered as to whether Adams should be a theological school or should emphasize industrial training, but there was nothing selfish in this bickering. They were intelligent, sincere, united in a desire to help the natives. Margaret and I were not disturbed by debates about the purposes of Adams, for we were allowed to do our work without interference. And the missionaries, once they discovered that I was not a second Elder Weavers, had been good neighbors, kindly and considerate. We'd miss them.

That is, we expected to miss them when we made the decision to move to Durban. But we hadn't anticipated the storm of debate that proposal would let loose. There were many reasons why the move was opposed. The missionaries felt that as much missionary work as possible should be concentrated at Adams. They realized, too, that the medical work brought many Zulus to Adams, increasing its prestige among the natives. And if I left, there would be no doctor for the mission students. While there was a point in these arguments, the concern of the missionaries was in Christianizing the natives, mine was their health, whether they were Christian or heathen. So, with these opposite viewpoints, my request was always debated, and always turned down. But I continued to make the request at each meeting, until Mr. Kilbon the chairman, who always tried to weigh all decisions fairly, suggested that I allow the three members of the American Mission Board to decide the matter when they reached South Africa.

Late in 1903, Dr. Elnathan Strong, and Dr. and Mrs. Sidney Strong of the Board reached Natal in time for our annual meeting. I requested their permission to move from Adams, and they had no objections. Their interest was in the welfare of the missions as a whole, rather than in any one such as Adams, and after hearing my request, they advised my mission to allow me to move to Durban the following March.

That move, the opening of a dispensary in Durban, would be a step toward the Zulu hospital I hoped some day to build. But the hospital itself was still nebulous, an unformulated plan, unfixed in time, still clothed in the fragile substance of dreams, with no practical means of accomplishment that I could then foresee.

CHAPTER FOUR

KRAAL PRACTICE

IS DIFFERENT

SHORTLY BEFORE LEAVING ESIDUMBINI MISSION, MY wife, Laura Mellen and I were sitting on the bungalow veranda one afternoon when a native visitor appeared and Laura walked out to speak to him.

"He tells me that Chief Delewayo is very ill," she announced, upon her return.

On his visits to the mission, the tall chief's natural graciousness and dignity had impressed me. His emaciated appearance, however, and the flecks of blood on his lips after each spasm of coughing led me to suspect consumption.

Laura's slim, browned face was thoughtful and troubled. "Would you care to hike to his kraal to see whether you could help him, Jim?"

"My Zulu is still shaky," I said. "Would you help as interpreter?"

"Of course, if you need me," she said. "Let's go tomorrow."

Margaret had just given birth to Robert and could not accompany us when we started on foot the following

63

dawn on a course that crossed many streams and rivers flowing eastward to the ocean. Africa was so commonplace to Laura that she was amused when I stopped frequently beside a lacy waterfall or a brawling rapid to admire the high ferns and spidery palms, and orchids hanging from the treetops.

Upon reaching the Insuzi River, I looked at a scene which would have held the eye of a Gauguin. At a dark pool a crowd of Zulu women were filling enormous clay jars with water. It took two women to lift a filled jar—which must have held ten gallons—to the head of a water carrier, yet she would stiffen but slightly under the weight. Her slender body was nude except for her small beaded apron, and her flesh gleamed like black marble in the humid heat. She walked to join the single file of women marching uptrail through the forest to their kraal. Behind some of the water carriers walked naked little daughters, each with a stick or rock balanced on her head in conscious imitation of her mother.

Their supple grace seemed as natural a part of the forest as a faun you come upon unexpectedly, and I wasn't aware of the extent a black skin plays down awareness of sex until a white woman filled her jar. Her pale, pink-tinged, almost translucent flesh was such an obtrusive shock that I turned away, my cheeks burning.

Laura laughed. "She's just an albino, Jim. They're not uncommon among the Zulus."

We followed the procession through the forest and over a hill to Chief Delewayo's kraal. Shaped like two overlapping circles, it was surrounded by a stockade almost formidable enough to withstand an artillery assault. Man-high trees formed part of the walls, and a second row of equally high tree trunks buried in the earth made a second outside wall. Branches remaining on the trunks,

cut short and sharpened into spear points, were inter-
woven with vines.

This stockade, Laura enlightened me, guarded Delewayo's wives. His hut was beside the gate, those of his
number one and two favorites on either side, and his
other wives' dwellings following the walls in the order
of their descending popularity. Presumably any attack
would come from the rear, so that the least desirable
wives stood greatest risk of death or capture.

The number of huts in a chief's kraal is one measure
of his wealth, but there was an additional reason for
Delewayo's domestic arrangement. His wives' huts enclosed a smaller stockade, which held his cattle. A surprise attack thus might cost him some wives, who could
be replaced, but cattle, made scarce by rinderpest, were
priceless.

Now, at high noon, the cattle grazed on the golden-
yellow grass of the hillside, guarded by several of Delewayo's sons.

Opening the gate, we saw a dozen elderly men squat-
ting on their heels and drinking native beer. Wearing
only *umutshas* around their waists, their hair was arranged in a ring as if each Zulu had attempted to fashion
himself a halo. Laura had previously told me of this headdress of the *indunas*, the members of a chief's council,
achieved by rubbing a gummy substance mixed with soot
into the hair and allowing time to give it a high gloss.

These *indunas* ignored us as we sat down. Noticing a
visitor is considered discourteous, singling him out as different from the family, but this polite gesture grew embarrassing after many minutes of sitting like ghosts at a
banquet. Laura nudged me to call my attention to an
eerie figure wearing a fur cap and a necklace of antelope
hoofs and horns; it was the witch doctor approaching.

An *induna* called, "*Sa ku bona, Nyanga, Ungapi?*"

The witch doctor shook his head doubtfully at this question about his destination. "I go to make powerful medicine for the chief. I do not know if I can cure him. This sickness is very strong."

Half an hour later Delewayo walked slowly toward us, his gait suggesting the weakness following an emetic. After a respectable interval, he spoke, "We have seen you."

An *induna* then offered me an earthenware vessel of beer, but Laura spared me a refusal by explaining that I was not strong enough for beer after such a long walk, but that I was hungry. Smiles flitted across the councillors' faces, but Delewayo accepted this excuse with good grace, calling to a buxom young wife. She brought two delicious dishes, a fermented cottage cheese called *amasi* and roasted *amabele* meal.

Laura spoke casually about the weather, hunting and cattle prospects before mentioning my medical work among the Esidumbini natives. As if it were an afterthought, she expressed the hope that Chief Delewayo's health would soon be restored, and if I could help in any way I would be happy to do so—an indirect approach to spare his pride.

He sat thoughtfully sipping beer. "Since your brother-in-law is here, I would be glad if he would examine my chest."

We retired to his hut and he lay on a grass mat. Opening my bag to find my stethoscope, I felt a little insecure, for I was handling my first case without an interpreter. Laura had said nothing about accompanying us into the hut, apparently feeling that I could manage without her.

Pronouncing my words deliberately, I informed

Delewayo that the stethoscope would tell me what it saw in his chest. He nodded with reserve. After an instrument examination I thumped his chest, trying not only to get a clear idea of his condition but also to impress him. Inevitably his judgment would be largely based on my diagnostic ritual; I didn't want to suffer by comparison with the witch doctor.

Laura had known Delewayo for years, and what she'd told me confirmed my own prognosis that the chief suffered from an advanced case of pulmonary tuberculosis. After my long examination, I placed a finger over the spot where I'd discovered a cavity.

"This is where the disease started and where it is strongest."

Speaking slowly in the unfamiliar tongue, I said that he had started coughing a year before and soon felt pain in the cavity. His cough then brought up a very bad sputum, and he became short of breath. Though merely describing the usual steps in a rapid case of consumption, Delewayo's patrician face expressed his amazement. I had asked no questions!

"You see truly," he said. "My doctor tells me I am bewitched. Do you believe so?"

I hesitated, knowing that to ridicule Delewayo's beliefs would only bring distrust.

"I know your sickness because my instrument tells me about it. In my own country I studied this malady, for many white people grow sick in the same way. With them, it's not caused by witchcraft." I paused, allowing this point to sink in. "But I know little about your witchcraft or witch doctors. If you were a white man, I'd say the disease came by itself and that you are not bewitched."

He nodded, and asked quietly, "Will I get well?"

"Some people get well from this sickness if they are strong. But it's a powerful disease, and if your doctor cannot cure you, you must not blame him."

Only hospital treatment at an early stage of the disease could have saved the chief. Instead, his witch doctor's ignorance had allowed it to progress to a hopeless point. Yet I couldn't destroy Delewayo's faith in his only doctor. Advising nourishing food, rest and open air, I promised to send medicine. His courteous manner remained unchanged, but his shrewd old eyes told me as I departed that he guessed my verdict: he had only months to live.

In visiting heathen kraals I often had to diagnose without asking questions, simply because the witch doctors did and the Zulus were accustomed to the method. Having little idea of the nature of disease, they thought sickness was caused by magic. Powerful countermagic was needed to counteract it, and when I first came to the country, they saw no difference between my medicine and the charms and concoctions of the witch doctor. If his powerful magic didn't work, mine might, was the way they reasoned.

To be classed with a witch doctor is deflating to a white doctor's pride. But failure to understand the native viewpoint could make the most skilled physician useless in Zulu practice. When they knew me better, I questioned patients as much as I pleased, and if a stranger objected, I'd say, "I'm not a witch doctor." Perhaps the native attitude is not so strange, considering the preference of many white patients for a doctor with a good bedside manner.

When I first came to Africa, I imagined that the work of other white doctors would have smoothed my way. And to a degree, this was true. Dr. Bridgeman's work at Adams, for example, made my own work there much easier because he had gained the Zulus' confidence. Beyond the radius he had reached, however, I was on my own. Every witch doctor must prove his magic; so must every white practitioner. And the Zulus' natural conservatism makes it difficult to prove you can help. After overcoming this handicap, on the other hand, the Zulus are ideal patients, following directions in cases where white patients would backslide.

My call on Chief Delewayo introduced me to practice in native kraals, an introduction to be followed by many other such visits after I moved to Adams Mission. True, I visited only patients too ill to reach the mission, but the total over the years ran high, particularly in childbirth cases. At times I felt like a journeyman medical corps, and Margaret was part of that corps, when she could accompany me. Travel was by every means offered in South Africa at the beginning of the century. A journey started by train might be completed by oxcart, boat, rickety buggy, horseback or afoot.

The hardship of that sort of travel mattered little in view of the knowledge I was gaining of how the Zulus lived, ate, and what medical treatment they received from witch doctors. This knowledge helped materially when I started practice in Durban, for I knew the setting from which my patients had come, knew what habits of eating or living might have precipitated their illnesses.

The call on Chief Delewayo opened no doors because soon afterward I moved to Adams, and I might have waited there a long time before a like opportunity arose if it had not been for Willie Shabane.

Willie, a lay preacher at an out-station church, made regular trips to Adams. He was an intense and dignified little man, as black as the overlarge missionary's coat

which bagged from his lean frame and dangled to his
knees. A soft wart, hanging from his left eyelid, caused it
to droop, and one day he asked if I could remove it.
Willie, I knew, had no intention of an immediate operation, for though he was a Christian, he was as reluctant as
another Zulu about trying a new doctor. Before he had
time to take alarm, I laid him on the operating table, gave
him a local anesthetic, and within a few minutes the wart
was gone and I had applied dressings.

When he returned, and the dressings were removed,
he studied himself from every angle in the mirror. His
wide mouth was curved in a delighted smile as he departed.

Not long afterward, he rode up and tethered two
scrawny horses outside my house. He came into the house
to tell me that he'd visited Chief Tim Ogle, and that
Chief Tim had pronounced him now a handsome man
and was amazed that there was no scar.

"Chief Tim asks that you come to see him," Willie
added. "He is very sick man from drinking too much."

Now, I knew Chief Tim by reputation. He was a de-
scendant of a British pioneer who added colorful pages
to South African history by following the custom of
marrying numerous native women; he had left a host of
half-caste children. Tim himself sympathized with missionary work; had, in fact, married but once to leave the
door open in case he decided to become a Christian.
However, that meant giving up native beer, no easy denial
for a man who drank *utshwala* by the gallon. So he'd remained a heathen.

To improve the health of this influential chief would
undoubtedly win confidence among the Zulus. But how
could I improve the health of a dipsomaniac, whose ill
health resulted from his immense thirst?

I didn't know, but nevertheless I mounted Chief Tim's big horse and let Willie Shabane lead the way through the bush and over open veld, his coattails flying before me. At last we came to a kraal, smaller than Chief Delewayo's, but with a large house, with many windows, built for comfort. Inside, in a tremendous oxhide chair that sagged beneath his massive body, sat Chief Tim. His legs were so swollen he couldn't rise to greet us. He looked like a man of indefinable race, gone tropical beachcomber. When we refused *utshwala,* he asked his wife to bring food, which he regretfully watched us eat.

I examined him and found that his heart was labored, that his inflamed kidneys weren't working. As with Chief Delewayo, I showed that I was familiar with his symptoms by my questions.

"This sickness," I told him, "comes from too much *utshwala.* It irritates your kidneys." And I explained their location, their function.

"Will they lose their sickness?"

"That depends. Continue drinking and you'll soon die. But if you give up *utshwala,* you might live years without further trouble."

He didn't seem to hear. His eyes strayed to his children playing in the kraal, beyond them to the wind-stirred cornfield, and then lifted toward the wild tangle of green hills across the valley. He gazed abstractedly through a gap at the blue expanse of distant ocean, sighing as if he found all this too good to leave.

"I'll give up *utshwala.*"

I thought of my brilliant young colleague, who had died in delirium tremens at 33. If Dr. Cavett was unable to overcome his addiction, what chance had a naked black man like Chief Tim?

Tim proved that strength of will doesn't depend

upon the color of a man's skin. He kept his pledge. After
a year of temperance, he became a Christian and with the
zeal of a new convert preached the benefits of abstinence
to all his former drinking companions. He was well advanced in years when he died, and never once was he
known to take another drink.

Treating Chief Tim's kidney trouble consisted
merely of giving obvious advice, but curing such an influential man proved to the native mind that I had strong
magic, and before long I was making many trips from
Adams to see patients.

At first these journeys were afoot, not an easy mode
of travel because Natal is all aslant, the mountains sweeping like waves from the interior and receding as they approach the Indian Ocean. Yet walking at a steady four
miles an hour was usually the fastest method of reaching a
patient. You might be delayed days if you waited until
you found a bedraggled horse or an ox team spared by
rinderpest, and then the chances were you'd have to climb
the hills.

Vacations from increasingly heavy dispensary and
hospital duties were commonly spent hiking through the
backcountry alone or with friends. On these "postman's
holidays" I studied health conditions in remote parts of
Natal and Zululand. But I still remained a journeyman
medicine man, treating sick natives along the way, and
finding welcome in any native kraal where night over-
took me.

The sick would be waiting in a group at each kraal,
having learned by "Zulu telegraph" that I was coming.
Even though I'd become acquainted with the Zulu
method of shouting news from the hilltops when living
at Esidumbini, it continually amazed me to come upon a

kraal I might never have seen or known existed, and have patients awaiting treatment.

I tried to avoid surgical field work by sending ambulatory cases to Durban after I moved there. And when medicine was required (sometimes I'd write a score of prescriptions in a single large kraal), each patient's name was jotted down on his prescription and later on the label of his bottle of medicine. This medicine I myself compounded, until I could employ a man to do it. The medicine was then sent to the nearest missionary, teacher or magistrate, to be distributed in a kraal. I made sure my patients took it by collecting a fee at the time of examination. No Zulu who has paid for medicine will fail to take it!

Collecting fees is important. The Zulu expects it because his witch doctor's first question is, "How much money do you carry in your bag?" The natives are frugal, hiding coins saved from menial work in the city, in the mines, or from the sale of cattle or such handicrafts as spears or beadwork. This hoarded money is for emergencies. The Zulus regard free treatment or medicine as worthless—a commendable view I never tried to change, for I had but a small salary and little money to carry on my work among them.

Fees were, however, kept low. When Dr. Bridgeman was at Adams Mission, he had charged sixty cents for an ordinary examination and a dollar for internal examinations. And he put up medicine in large bottles to save his patients excessive travel. His total fee for examination and medicine usually ranged from $1.25 to $2.60. I charged the same fees, and the Zulus never complained. Anything above the cost of medicine and other expenses went back into the work—to care for charity cases, to build a dispen-

sary, and in future years to promote an even more ambitious Zulu project of which I'll speak later.

Walking tours confirmed my findings at Esidumbini
and Adams regarding the impact of rinderpest on native
health. In kraals I found the same deficiency diseases, digestive troubles and acute fevers common among my dispensary patients. Younger Zulus suffered from all manner
of children's diseases.

Though most of my cases in kraals were of this nature, "field hospital" work was sometimes unavoidable.
Once, for example, I was approaching a hillside kraal
when I heard shouts. Running toward the group of huts, I
found the kraal empty but upon rounding the last hut, I
saw a group of women leaning over a man writhing on the
ground, while small boys threw sticks and stones at two
bulls lumbering across the slope. I pushed through the
circle. Perspiration and blood glistened on the man's
body, and his bowels were exposed by an abdominal
wound.

By questioning one wife, I learned that the two bulls
had been fighting. Small boys tending the herd tried to
separate them by throwing rocks, but when this failed,
their father rushed out to help. One bull turned, gored
him with a horn, and flung him fifteen feet.

When I examined the man, who was groaning and
twisting in pain, I found that he had been extremely fortunate, for though the horn had pierced the abdominal
wall, the intestines were untouched, and a fold of the
peritoneum had pressed into the wound, almost sealing it
against dirt. The only antiseptic I had was a bottle of lysol,
so I used this full-strength, saturating some gauze and
cleaning out the wound. All that remained to be done
was to pack the opening with iodoform gauze.

This treatment proved so fascinating to the wives

that they appeared to forget they had nearly lost a husband. When I'd finished, they carried him back to his hut. The wound closed with no additional treatment except the changing of dressings on later visits.

When starting my African practice, I had no funds to pay helpers, so my wife filled this need. Margaret had never taken a full nursing course, but she had studied nursing, and was soon performing the duties of nurse, assistant and even anesthetist, helping with so many cases that she acquired much practical medical knowledge. This was invaluable at times when appeals for help came while I was away on other cases, and though I tried to discourage her emergency medical calls because of the risks she ran, it was not in her nature to consider personal risk if a patient was suffering. Frequently when I was treating a sick native in one kraal and thinking that Margaret was safely at home, she was actually as far from home as myself, caring for an injured Zulu.

One night, for example, when frightened natives knocked at our door and found me away, they begged Margaret to accompany them. A young man had received a bullet wound at a wedding party where *utshwala* flowed too freely.

My wife hastily packed a medical kit and followed the natives as they hurried single file through the bush. Though their flaming torches showered sparks on the brittle, head-high grass, Margaret was less concerned about fire than snakes. Black *imambas* slither through high grass, rearing and striking as high as a man's face, and their venom brings death within ten minutes. The less deadly but more numerous puff adders and night adders also made night travel dangerous.

Following the sputtering torches for ten miles, she came at last to a kraal and was shown to a hut where a native lay moaning. He was seriously wounded, but the bullet had passed through his body. So with no need for probing for the leaden slug, Margaret cleansed the openings, took sutures, dressed the wound, and remained a guest of the kraal until her patient made an uneventful recovery.

On another emergency call, she sewed up the severed tendons in a native boy's hand, doing such neat surgery that the boy was using his hand before I had a chance to examine it.

Once when Margaret was visiting her sister during my absence, a native father came to Esidumbini Mission so badly frightened and incoherent with grief that my wife imagined the man's son was either badly injured or dying. She was afraid it might be too late if she awaited my return, so she packed a bag with medical supplies and accompanied the father.

A recent cloudburst, slacking off as she started, had almost obliterated the treacherous trail through the mountains, and Margaret had visions of slipping down one of the deep gorges it skirted.

Breathless from the climb, she came to a hut suspened on stiltlike poles above a roaring chasm. The father had grown calm enough by now to describe his son's accident. His son Ndayisi and an older brother were playfully tussling in the hut. Ndayisi ran out but, when turning at the corner of the hut, he slipped on the narrow, muddy walk, and rolled fifty feet down the chasm wall, landing on the sharp rocks of the river bed.

Inside the hut Margaret found the mother and the boy's uncle hovering over Ndayisi. My wife directed the mother to start boiling water, while she made a preliminary examination. The boy had a compound fracture of the right arm, bones piercing the skin in two places. The father had fallen many times carrying the boy up the steep slope, so that dirt was embedded in the wounds. Since this could be a seat of infection, Margaret first washed the arm with soap and water, then followed with a second washing, using a five per cent solution of carbolic acid.

After she had removed the dirt, she explained to the men how they were to help. The uncle held the boy, while the father pulled the arm. Ndayisi had watched with the whites of his eyes showing until the pulling started, but now he kicked, bit and fought with such fury that the uncle could scarcely hold him. Margaret manipulated the bones until they slipped back into position, and packed the arm in a splint.

She dressed the arm daily until I returned to Esidumbini. I found the bone set properly, the flesh healthy. Her care prevented the sepsis complications which sometimes follow in compound fracture cases—which *did* follow, in fact, in a parallel case two months later when another native boy broke his arm, and there was no journeyman medicine man to give it prompt attention.

In the second case the bone protruded from the boy's flesh in one rather than two places, and the wound was also packed with dirt. The father had once watched a white doctor set a broken arm, so he set the bones in apposition, but failed to cleanse the wound.

The accident happened only twenty miles from Durban, but train service was slow and father and son did not reach my office until the next morning. By then the boy's wrist was badly swollen, the discolored flesh crackling when I touched it because of the air pressure beneath. A virulent form of blood poisoning known as gasedema had already set in, and I could advise nothing better than amputation at the wrist to halt spread of the infection.

The father, disgruntled, went away to consult other

doctors, but they gave him the same advice. It was twenty-four hours before he called at my office for a second examination, and by then oedema extended to the boy's elbow. I realized that further vacillation would result in the boy's death, so I gave the father a blunt verdict:

"Either let me take the arm off at the shoulder, or order a coffin. Tomorrow will be too late to save your son's life."

The operation was performed, but I couldn't help wishing when the boy was discharged from the hospital that Margaret might have been able to treat the second boy's arm as well as Ndayisi's.

Improved roads made the life of a journeyman medicine man far easier. In time I sped by car over smooth macadam to settlements once reached only after hours by bicycle or afoot. Extended bus service allowed sick natives to ride comfortably to Durban, but many preferred home treatment until my growing practice forced me to raise fees on out-calls. I charged three pounds when going out on a confinement case, for example, a pound more than it cost a Zulu mother to have her baby in the hospital, where she would have good nursing, good food and every other care. (If operative procedure was necessary, fees were slightly higher.) Zulu women love a bargain as much as their white sisters, and after these fees were established, few babies were born under primitive kraal conditions.

But there remained cases like that of Bafinani Mapumulo which always required tires and legs.

Bafinani was an exceptional Zulu. Most young men work in the Johannesburg gold mines to buy enough cattle to pay for a wife, or to attain some other limited goal, and then quit. Bafinani was already married when he went to work in the mines. He was ambitious to rise more quickly to prominence in the Odidini district than by the slow accumulation of cattle to buy wives, and the raising of marriageable daughters to trade for cattle.

He was erecting supporting timbers in a new tunnel when he slipped from a scaffolding and fell astride a sharp rock. The fall numbed him but, feeling little pain, he soon resumed work on the scaffolding. Not until hours later, when a desire to urinate brought acute distress and he was unable to pass water, did he suspect serious injury. Sharp pain was followed by sickness and dizziness, but it never entered his black head to consult the mine doctor.

A Zulu hurt in a strange locale thinks only of reaching his home kraal, so Bafinani boarded a train leaving Johannesburg. His impressions from then on were blurred by nausea and swift stabs of pain, and the next thing he remembered clearly was stumbling up to his own kraal.

His wife, alarmed by his moans and sickly appearance, called their witch doctor. The old fellow had recently undergone a grilling by a white magistrate because several of his patients had died under peculiar circumstances; his professional confidence was badly shaken and he could not afford to lose another case just then. So, after a glance satisfied him that Bafinani was dying, he went away.

The wife sent a runner to Adams Mission and a missionary called me from there late that afternoon. I set out immediately in my machine.

The first twenty miles to Adams was smooth driving, and there I picked up the runner. Beyond Adams any car not hardened to African travel might have rebelled. My Zulu guide bounced on the seat and showed symptoms of mounting alarm as I drove down steep banks, forded streams, scraped off paint on the narrow flanks of forest roads, and shook loose nuts bouncing over rocks. I stopped in the bush when the car could push on no farther, and we completed the last two miles on foot.

Bafinani lay on a mat outside his hut, his face a ghastly gray. In a voice thickened by suffering, he described the accident, but he couldn't precisely locate the pain. The nature of his injury suggested an obstructed bladder, even though it was not greatly distended. I expected to find on percussion a dullness to his navel, but when I tapped with my hand, there was only normal resonance.

Then, noticing a swelling in the lower part of the abdomen, the inside of the thighs and the genito-urinary organ, I suspected what had happened: the sharp rock had ruptured the urethra. For three days urine had seeped into the subcutaneous tissue and decomposed there. Those poisoned tissues were now in a gangrenous condition. This prognosis could be confirmed only by an operation, but to bolster the evidence, I pressed on the distended tissue and found that it formed an edematous mass, hard enough to retain the impression of my fingers.

"Bafinani," I said, "I must operate within a few hours to save your life."

He nodded weakly.

"But I can't operate here," I went on, knowing that if surgery confirmed my diagnosis supplementary operations must follow. "I must take you to the hospital where nurses can care for you and I can watch this sickness."

"I will do what you say," he whispered.

I described to the youth who had accompanied me how to construct a light stretcher of sticks, and asked him to find men to help carry Bafinani to the road. Then I hurried back to the car and turned it around with great difficulty. But I had a long wait. It had grown dark before eight men staggered through the brush bearing Bafinani

on a stretcher of heavy poles that would unquestioningly
have supported a baby elephant.

My patient was placed in the back seat and then
began a wild ride along a narrow, rutted road that was just
what oxcarts and nature had made it. The big rocks in the
road were seldom visible in the bobbing headlight beams,
and I missed so few that Bafinani spent as much time in
the air as on the seat. His grunts and groans, which he was
gamely trying to stifle, set my teeth on edge, but there was
nothing I could do but keep the throttle down and hope
for the best.

At the hospital, I sent a nurse to awaken my associate, Dr. Alan B. Taylor, and he entered the operating
room as Bafinani was being lifted from a stretcher. Dr.
Taylor agreed with my diagnosis and to the advisability
of an immediate operation. Our patient was in acute discomfort, so I slipped a Clover inhaler over his nose to
anesthetize him.

The first step was to make an opening by which urine
could escape from the bladder, for it was causing gangrene
of the tissues. A catheter or tube was then placed in the
bladder to allow urine to escape freely afterward. The next
step was to drain the swollen mass of toxic fluids by surgery. After this was done, Dr. Taylor flushed out the tissues with normal saline solution, and then shook his head
doubtfully.

"The damage is already done."

He meant that three days of delay had allowed escaping fluids to destroy skin tissue and the area beneath, and
much plastic surgery might be necessary. But that could
be undertaken if Bafinani rallied. Now, at least, he had
some chance of recovery.

I felt more optimistic on my morning visit. Bafinani's
eyes were brighter, and he felt less discomfort, though still

in some pain. There was little decrease in the swelling of his abdomen or thighs, but surgery could partly explain that. I gave him an opiate, and asked the nurse to change his dressings frequently.

Assisted by youth and fine physical condition, Bafinani improved rapidly, so that I was soon able to undertake the slow process of transplanting and grafting skin to restore it to normal. There's considerable confusion about these terms, but their meaning is simple. Transplanting is covering a wound with a flap of skin moored at one point to its original anchorage, and is more likely to be successful than a skin graft, where the skin is actually detached before being placed on the wound. In transplanting, the blood still circulates through the attached pedicle, while that is not possible in skin grafting. Both methods were necessary in this case.

When weeks of plastic surgery had restored Bafinani's skin, it was a simple matter to remove the catheter. He was able to pass urine as well as before his injury, but his domestic life, I regret to say, would never again be satisfactory.

His dream of many wives and a large brood of children was no longer attainable, certainly a bitter reward for what a Zulu young man would consider a laudable ambition.

What kept me in country practice even after work in the Durban dispensary and hospital required all my time was the marriage of our native nurses. These nurses, settling in many parts of Natal and responsive to their people's medical needs, constituted a medical frontier where only the ignorant superstition of witch doctors previously existed. They cared for sick neighbors after marriage and often while carrying a child. They fought epi-

demics singlehanded, sometimes dying victims of diseases
they combated. Respecting their loyalty and courage, I
helped them with cases beyond their skill.

One of the most capable of these nurses was Constance Makanya, who married Jonathan Makanya and
settled near Imbumbulu. She established a dispensary in
her kraal, and twice a month I drove there to help her
with difficult cases.

Passing the kraal of my friend Nykanya on one trip,
I was stopped by numerous natives crossing the road, and
before I could drive on, Nykanya approached my car. His
courtesy was none the less patrician for the fact that he
wore only his monkey tails, and he misunderstood my
presence and thanked me warmly for coming to his son's
wedding.

Ordinarily I avoided weddings because the natives
attend them less to watch the marriage or the dancing
than to celebrate afterward with *utshwala*. This strong
beer (made from finely ground corn meal and allowed to
ferment) leads to arguments. Though the Zulus "check"
their clublike knob-kerrys and *assegais* in the bushes when
at a wedding, they bring them forth to settle heated con-
troversies. Nykanya was so pleased to see me and had been
so helpful in assembling native handicraft for my collection, however, that I drove toward his kraal rather than
disappoint him.

There was the usual wedding confusion, with natives milling about waiting for something to happen. The
bride's party, Nykanya informed me, had spent the night
in huts assigned to them and were now at the river bathing the bride and dressing her in her wedding finery—a
new beadwork apron, bangles, and bracelets of sticks and
stones to rattle during the dancing. Bride and bridesmaids
soon approached the dancing ground outside the kraal

stockade, while stalwarts from the bridegroom's kraal walked to meet them.

When the group reached the dancing ground, a native policeman stopped the bride to ask whether she was being forced into marriage. Her flashing smile as she answered the policeman's questions made no secret of her happiness, so he was soon satisfied. Nykanya then left me to meet the bride's father on the dancing space and arrange the transfer of cattle to pay for the bride.

Afterward the ceremonial dancing began. Mixed dancing is unknown among Zulus. The bride walked onto the dance space and sang to her bridesmaids. They closed a circle about her until she was screened from view, before beginning a dance which was enthusiastically applauded by the spectators.

When the bridal party withdrew, young men ornamented with beadwork and feathers sprang into the dancing space. Their dancing was a vivid pantomime of battle. The principal step was a stomping of feet in time to the rapid beat of drums as the phalanx challenged another tribe to combat. Though they gestured with real spears, they danced with courting shields rather than the larger shields of war. Working themselves into simulated fury, their furs and feathers bobbing, their bracelets making a rattling din, they stomped harder and finally leapt and jumped and made throwing motions with their spears to kill imaginary enemies. The cries and expressions were so convincing that you expected spears to begin flying. This phantom battle, like many others I had witnessed, ended in overwhelming victory for the dancers.

Zulu dances play a large part in courtship. The men applaud a particular girl dancer to show their approval and also to draw attention to themselves. For the same reason the girls gazed with shining eyes when Somveli

Mapumulo passed before them, applauding with fervor to catch his eye. He leapt highest and stomped most wildly, and his expression of savage hatred caused me a chill of uneasiness. Presumably the unmarried women felt his exhibition proved him a good hunter and a brave warrior—a man worth attracting although he already had three wives.

The dancing ended at an outcry from the crowd. The bride ran as fleet as a deer toward her father's kraal, which was hidden from us, a mile beyond the crest of the hill. A black shadow darted behind her; the bridegroom's effortless lope soon brought him within a hundred yards of the girl. Capture by pursuit is the high point of a Zulu wedding, and a maiden would be thought brazen if she failed to pretend to avoid capture; pursuit meant her mate found her too charming to lose. But neither bride nor groom really extended themselves. The bride would be disappointed if her husband failed to catch her before she reached her father's kraal, for he would then forfeit one more head of cattle to reclaim her. At the summit of the hill, the two shadows merged, and the properly "captured" bride, now breathless and laughing, was brought back to the party.

Afterward, guests danced or drank *utshwala*, and as soon as I could decently leave, I said good-bye to Nykanya and drove on.

Constance Makanya had half a dozen stubborn cases awaiting me, and a confinement which kept me at Imbumbulu most of the day. Upon my return, the native policeman waved me to a stop at Nykanya's kraal, and, after explaining that a guest had been injured in a fight, led me to the dancing ground.

Most of the guests had departed. Nykanya attempted to greet me with dignity. But his voice was uncertain, his face stricken with anxiety. Unsteadily he walked toward a little knot of natives hovering over a man on ground damp with blood.

The man lying there was familiar. His chocolate-colored body had rippled with the play of his muscles as he had danced that morning. Now the flesh of his abdomen was torn. A bloody *assegai* beside the man told an ugly story of drink and fighting.

I made a quick examination; my stomach tightened with a feeling of helplessness. The man's intestines had been pierced in numerous places, and the bowel contents had emptied into the peritoneum. His pulse was scarcely perceptible, his heartbeat weak. It was barely possible he would survive the trip to the hospital, but at least I must attempt to get him there. I asked the natives to lift him into my car.

Before they could do so, a voice halted them. It was a native sergeant of police, who had just reached the kraal. He reprimanded me for moving the wounded man before he could get a statement. Rather than risk lost time in argument, I told him the wounded man was unable to speak, and that I must take him immediately to the hospital, but that I would report to the magistrate on the way.

The natives started to lift their fallen companion. Then they hesitated, looking at me with rounded eyes. I glanced at the man on the ground, then stooped to examine him. He was already dead.

I spoke a few comforting words to Nykanya, for the man had been his friend, and then got into my car.

Over the purr of my motor, as I drove away, the rising and falling cadences of the death wail reached me—the cry with which the Zulus mourn their dead. I could never hear that cry without an uneasy, clammy sensation. Forever it remains in the memory of anyone who has once heard it. And a journeyman medicine man hears it many times in his Zulu practice, particularly if he attends many wedding ceremonies.

CHAPTER FIVE

ZULU

PHARMACOPOEIA

LONG BEFORE I SAILED FOR AFRICA, MARGARET HAD TOLD me of her father's experiences with Zulu witch doctors, of their ignorant surgery and of the horrible brews they concocted as "medicine." Mr. Mellen respected the truth too greatly to have invented these incidents, yet I could not believe that the ignorant practices he was familiar with were universally true.

My first contacts with witch doctors' methods as a consequence came with the shock of personal discovery. Mr. Mellen had if anything conservatively understated his case. The sheer ignorance of witch doctors about anatomy and the drugs they brew does an enormous amount of mischief and unquestionably results in many deaths. But the mere passing of laws to deny them the right to practice will not end the evil, for a medical need can't be treated by a vacuum. If the Zulus cannot receive competent treatment from doctors, either white or black, or from native medical aides or trained nurses, they will inevitably turn to the practicer of witchcraft—regardless of what laws are passed.

My acquaintanceship with witch doctors' methods began with my first African practice, and continued for forty years. Undoing the damage they did constituted a large part of my work, and it was the native belief in witchcraft which made my practice so different from that of a medical man in the United States. It might, for that reason, be well to describe some of the witch doctor's drugs and methods, for until this background is sketched in, it is difficult to understand the peculiar problems of a white medical man whose patients are Zulus.

Demonstrating one of our problems was the case of an unconscious Zulu brought to my hospital in a rickshaw. My native assistant was puzzled by the sick man's appearance and called me. After glancing at him, I had him taken to the isolation ward for a thorough examination.

The rickshaw boy standing between the traces, rubbing one long whitewashed leg against the other to brush off flies was Gavana, whose infected foot I had recently treated. The large horns on his head bobbed when I asked if he knew the sick man.

"He is Makuba, a laborer on the docks. He asked me to take him to the train, but when I reached the station, he was dead, so I brought him here. He will come to life." This statement didn't surprise me because the Zulus use the same word for *dead* as for *unconscious*, though they naturally know the difference.

I asked if Makuba had been going home to see his witch doctor.

"Yes," Gavana answered. "He said his doctor knew more of the diseases of black men than a white doctor."

An examination proved that Makuba suffered from bacillary dysentery, which strikes with greater severity among natives than the amoebic type, often causing death within a few days. I promptly instituted treatment with such old-fashioned remedies as Epsom salts, aromatic sulphuric acid with bismuth, and opiates. But I was really depending on monsonia avata to effect the cure. It was a drug that a Boer doctor had told me a colleague in South Africa had found most effective for bacillary dysentery. Though it had never been mentioned for the cure of this disease in medical textbooks, I had found it useful in almost every case. In all probability, Makuba owed his life to the drug.

Monsonia avata did not bring about any miraculous recovery. But it got such a grip on the disease that Makuba was soon sitting up, conscious yet hazy minded. Like many other natives, he had imagined that hospitals resembled Dante's Inferno, and the pretty native nurses, in their crisp uniforms, were so far removed from this picture that he apparently believed himself in the Zulu equivalent of Heaven. The morning that he was clearheaded enough to realize that he was in a hospital, and not dead, he greeted me with a flashing smile. Thereafter he made a steady recovery. And to a greater extent than other patients, he was deeply grateful for every attention.

The reasons for his gratitude were not clear until the day he was leaving the hospital, and stopped at my office. His voice broke when he tried to speak, and at last, shrugging helplessly, and with tears glistening in his eyes, he turned to go.

"You wished to say good-bye?" I asked.

Makuba shook his head. "Why didn't I know about this place before? If my father and brothers had come here, they'd still be alive."

Sensing my sympathy, he told me how his older brother came to Durban to work as a wharf roustabout and lived in a dormitory-type slum building where food and sanitary conditions were inexcusably bad. When the brother fell sick, he returned home to be treated and to die at the hands of the family witch doctor. A second brother contracted dysentery and also died after taking the witch doctor's "powerful medicine," and before long the third brother and the father passed away in the same manner.

Makuba must have contracted dysentery nursing his father, for he fell ill only a few days after starting work in Durban. Since four men died within a few hours after taking the witch doctor's medicine, it seemed probable the medicine rather than dysentery was responsible.

I spoke to my friend, the district surgeon at Port Shepstone, near Makuba's kraal, but he had already exhumed the bodies of the father and the last brother to perform postmortem examinations. He told me they died not of dysentery but from a strong corrosive poison which burned away the lining of their alimentary canals. The district surgeon reported the case to the local magistrate, and steps were being taken to bring the witch doctor to trial on manslaughter charges when my medical colleague died. By then it was too late for a second postmortem, so the case was dropped.

An isolated instance of a witch doctor's administering a deadly brew through ignorance would deserve no more than passing mention, but this was but one of many similar cases with which I'm familiar. Zulu witch doctors have many strong medicines, some harmless purgatives and emetics, others highly poisonous, which they use with little idea whether they are safe or deadly. My encounters with their drugs have brought this home impressively.

One day, for instance, a gray and very shaky middle-aged native appeared at the hospital, his salivary glands flowing so freely that he had to swallow constantly as he spoke. He was constipated and his witch doctor gave him medicine which affected him like a strong poison, but acted in the end as a purgative, clearing itself from his system. He needed no further treatment, so I put him to bed for observation; and then examined a stalk which he said had gone into the "medicine."

Usually a witch doctor compounds his concoctions in private, but in this case he mixed the medicine before his patient. My patient recognized one of the stalks going into it, and after his seizure cut a short section to bring with him to the hospital.

I'm no botanist, but I doubted whether the stalk was poisonous, for it resembled sugar cane. To identify it, I touched my tongue to the raw core, instantly recognizing my mistake. It caused a biting sensation, though it had no flavor. Quickly spitting to avoid being poisoned, I laid the stalk aside and called my next patient.

A pungent sensation spread over my tongue and down into my throat, accompanied by a heavy mucus discharge so irritating that swallowing was difficult. Saliva no longer able to pass down my throat accumulated until it flowed from my mouth. Since I was unable to question my patients in this condition, I was obliged to go home.

The biting sensation in my tongue and mouth grew sharper, and the rapidly flowing mucus became thicker. Eating or sleeping was out of the question, so I spent the night with my head on a chair beside my bed, with my mouth over a bucket and drooling like a baby. These novel and alarming symptoms had abated by morning so that I suffered from nothing worse than a sleepless night.

I threw the stalk into a waste receptacle to prevent anyone from repeating the experience. I've since regretted not having it identified, for I know of no drug producing such an effect. The use of unfamiliar drugs by witch doctors, however, isn't uncommon.

One afternoon, when a native girl was carrying my baby daughter Laura out to her play pen under a blue jacaranda, a young Zulu stepped from behind a bush and blew a powder into the nurse's face. Recognizing him as a boy who had twice tried to speak to her, she guessed that the powder was a love philtre he'd bought in the native market to affect a change in her indifference. After recovering from her start, the nurse upbraided the boy sharply, for the natives fear any "medicine" thrown on them, and then she came running to the house.

The nurse girl and Laura soon ran high temperatures and had to be put to bed. Margaret secured a description of the boy, and I asked the police to find him, but, warned by friends, he had fled from the city. Then I sought the herbalist who sold the love potion, hoping to learn what it contained so that I could give an antidote. This attempt also failed.

I had no idea what caused the girls' illness. It's doubtful if the routine measures I took to reduce their fevers explained why their temperatures dropped two days later. The drug-induced fever had probably run its course. To this day I know of no powder which can raise temperature merely by being breathed.

However, I did learn what went into another love philtre brought to our kitchen door by a Zulu boy. He handed the bottle to our kitchen girl Nyesa, describing it as a charm mixed by a herbalist and asking her to mix it with the food of another kitchen girl who had spurned his attentions.

Fresh in Nyesa's memory was the previous experience, so she gave the bottle to my wife, and Margaret sent it to a Durban chemist for analysis. The chemist reported that the "love potion" contained sufficient poison to kill twenty-five people. The boy, when told of this analysis, was horrified to learn how close he'd come to killing the girl he loved.

Now love charms are not "medicines," though prepared by a herbalist who mixes medicine. He's ignorant of the nature of the drugs going into either. Zulus find nothing incongruous in asking herbalists to prepare concoctions for aching hearts as well as ailing bodies. They believe magic will cure both. Herbalists' preparations may or may not contain poison; with practically no pharmaceutical knowledge, these drug-mixers would have no way of knowing. They use formulae learned from other herbalists equally unacquainted with the properties of drugs, adding whatever leaves, barks or roots strike their fancy.

Many cases of fatal poisonings come before the white magistrates of Natal and the Native High Court, sometimes within an hour or less after a patient has taken a herbalist's or witch doctor's "medicine." There are few convictions. The native medicine man pleads that he was doing the best he knew. And this, lamentably, is true. Natives seldom hold it against a witch doctor whose concoction kills a relative. They believe the witchcraft causing the sickness was stronger than the medicine.

Medical missionaries are familiar with many cases of this nature which never come to trial because of the small chance of conviction. My friend Reverend Johannes Astrup asked me to examine a boy whose ears had been filled with poison by a witch doctor hoping to cure brain fever. But I could do nothing for the little fellow. Part of the ear had been destroyed by a strong corrosive, and the child was permanently deaf.

Supposedly the herbalist deals solely with the preparation of medicine, the witch doctor with the satanic forces of magic, and the "smeller-out" with the art of smelling members of a kraal until he detects the "scent of evil."

A herbalist is licensed by the government to deal in medicinal herbs and roots. Granting such a license is in my opinion a grave mistake, since it gives quasi-legal sanction to the drug-dispenser without requiring from him any knowledge of drugs or training in their preparation. Moreover, a true Zulu herbalist doesn't exist outside the pages of fiction. Though he compounds medicines, he shares the native belief that sickness results from witchcraft, magic or poison, so he is also something of a smeller-out and witch doctor.

Before the coming of white men to South Africa, the smeller-out possessed life and death power over a tribe, smelling out and accusing any person as the witch or wizard causing sickness. The accused one was speedily put to death, without any chance of appeal.

A smeller-out still sniffs the members of a kraal to discover who has "bewitched" his patient, before attempting a cure by countermagic or medicinal means. But I was amused to find that these charlatans often prefer white doctors when there is illness in their own family.

Among the patients in my consulting room one day was a woman wearing the distinctive dress of the smeller-out. Black clay was rubbed into her hair and it straggled about her face in hard ringlets. Across her chest hung her badge of office: two bands of goat skin, hair side out, and crossed in front.

I said, "*Sa ku bona, Sangoma.*" (Good morning, witch doctor.)

She smiled with pleasure at having her profession recognized, and told me her little girl was ill. After examining the child and giving the mother medicine for her, I asked the woman how she "smelled out" those practicing witchcraft and causing sickness. She declared that she grew nervous and hysterical if the guilty man or woman appeared before her.

"But," the old wretch added, "in the old days if there was anyone who had done me an injury or whom I disliked, I accused that person."

And she laughed heartily, believing it a great joke to have condemned to death enemies innocent of any wrongdoing.

White man's law deprives the smeller-out of the power of sending supposed witches to their death, forcing the smeller-out to branch out into compounding medicine and to become something of a witch doctor.

This worthy works with charms and spells, performs surgery, and also makes medicines. In addition to the herbs and roots commonly used in medicine, the witch doctor formerly found the parts of the human body effective, particularly if his victim was killed by twisting the neck until it broke. In an article *Native Superstition in Its Relation to Crime*, Justice C. G. Jackson of the Native High Court cites six murders committed in recent years by witch doctors requiring the parts of the human body to prepare strong medicine. Unsympathetic courts, however, are causing the practice to disappear.

Today herbalist, witch doctor and smeller-out are one; all are witch doctors dealing in the black arts and compounding medicine. Where strong medicine is not needed, the witch doctor is sometimes roughly effective with enemeta to clean out the system and emetics to produce vomiting. Unfortunately, he treats tuberculosis and diphtheria in an identical manner.

The witch doctor leans heavily on counterirritants, curing a headache, for example, by cutting through the scalp and applying an irritating drug which causes such distress that the headache is forgotten. Incisions for the introduction of counterirritants may be made anywhere in the body.

Primitive logic is applied in preparing native medicines. A witch doctor believes the fat of the more powerful beasts will cure severe illness, lion fat being especially favored because of the lion's strength.

A patient bleeding from nose or mouth is given medicine compounded from the bark of the Umdlebe tree (which has a blood-red sap), the parts of an animal which bleeds freely when touched and the flesh of any animal having a considerable amount of blood, such as a lion or an ox. After the mixture is burned, the powdery ash is divided into three parts, to be taken internally, on the tongue, or by introduction into cuts.

Nervousness and fear are treated with medicine made from the heart and eyes of a lion, an animal supposedly devoid of fear. A python's flesh is believed to prevent spread of disease by holding anything together with its constrictive power. A small bone from a dog is strapped on a broken leg to mend it. Twitching of the flesh and spasms are treated with a medicine composed of a small beetle known as the *imfingezi*, which curls into a small ball if touched; and of sea-anemones, worms and leaves that fold at night.

The witch doctor carries his preparations in the antelope horns and gourds hanging from his neck, serving both as his medicine bottles and the sign of his calling.

At one time while writing a paper on native remedies for the Durban Medical Society, I purchased numerous medicines at the native market for study. In the bottles were pieces of crocodile skin, the feathers and skin of vultures, powdered cuttlefish, powdered dried flesh of snakes, horse hair, porcupine quills, bits of bark, insects, and partially burned lizards.

A. A. Dalton Francis, a registered chemist and Fellow of the Chemical Society of Great Britain, made a report of the remedies sold by one Mafukuke Ngcobo, who modernized the Zulu pharmaceutical business by the introduction of European drugs. Francis found upon analysis that Ngcobo's medicine claimed to cure coughs, chest trouble and colds contained only oil of eucalyptus and glycerine. A medicine to expel worms was a mixture of oil of cloves and an oily substance similar to castor oil, but with red coloring added. Ngcobo's most remarkable panacea, advertised in his circular as UZifonzonke, "hunted in the blood, and fought there were it found any trouble." The medicine seller asserted that it cured chest troubles, swellings, pains in the bones, stitches in the stomach and between the shoulder blades, and other ailments. Francis found it was simple iodine and water.

Undoubtedly the witch doctor relies partially upon tricks like those of a stage magician to convince his patients of the efficacy of his treatment and medicines. I'm certain they strengthen their hold on native credulity by such tricks as hiding articles and then "smelling out" their location. Often sickness is attributed to swallowing a snake. Witch doctors sometimes verify this diagnosis by cutting a small incision and releasing a small snake concealed in one hand, the patient believing the snake came from his own body.

Once, unwittingly, I assisted in such deception. A native came to the hospital complaining of pain in the lower right abdomen. Although appendicitis is rare among Zulus, an extreme tenderness to probing indicated it might be present in this case. The patient was given bismuth and an X-ray taken. I showed him the plate, explaining that his appendix was normal—the tenderness must be the result of a fall he'd mentioned. The man stared at the plate intently for minutes, at last nodding in apparent satisfaction.

Later I learned that his witch doctor told him before coming to the hospital that a snake had entered his body while he slept. The colon on the X-ray plate, clearly outlined by bismuth, looked like a snake. He returned to his kraal and his witch doctor "removed" the reptile, probably by sleight-of-hand.

Despite such hocus-pocus, I'm certain witch doctors possess certain psychic powers. When I opened my first small hospital in Durban I treated the child of a witch doctor late one afternoon. She and her child were placed in the women's ward, and a male witch doctor, who just happened in and had no place to stay, was placed in the men's ward. Neither was informed of the other's presence, but nevertheless they rolled and tossed and were unable to sleep. Finally the man grew so restless that he dragged his blankets outside.

"There is an evil presence in the hospital," he explained, when I found him lying in the yard the next morning. "I could not sleep there."

Shaking his head, he went away. I stepped into the women's ward to ask the female witch doctor how she and her child had spent the night.

The child had slept well, she told me, and then added, "But I rested poorly at first. After a man left during the night, I felt at peace. He must have been very evil."

They may both have been right.

CHAPTER SIX

I OPEN
A ZULU DISPENSARY

ON THE FIRST OF MARCH IN 1904, AN OXCART DRAWN
by a span of sixteen oxen, drew up before a small cottage
in the Greyville section of Durban, a polyglot slum district
where the Zulus, Indians and half-castes of all nations
met on an equal footing. My tall and dignified assistant
Umqibelo climbed from the back, and helped the driver
unload boxes of dressings, bottles and my few instruments. My other assistant, Katie Makanya, folded plump
arms across her broad bosom and gazed raptly at the new
dispensary.

"It looks mighty fine, Doctor," she said approvingly.

Katie always made the best of things, for the truth
was that this little building at 76 Beatrice Street was a
poor affair even by comparison with the dispensary we'd
left at Adams Mission. Divided into three sections, with
a gate, a door and a window for each, we were to occupy
only the left third, consisting of two small rooms, the
front room for examination and consultation, the back
room for drugs. Bottles would have to be stored in the

coal shed behind, and the sandy street in front must serve as waiting room.

Nevertheless, I shared Katie's optimism. The long months of uncertainty lay behind us with this move; we were planting roots in Durban where greater numbers of Zulu patients could reach us, with far less difficulty than by the laborious road to Adams.

It took but a short while to place the bench, the two chairs and the examination table in the front room of the dispensary; to stow away drugs and bottles. And then my assistants climbed into the oxcart again, to help unload the household goods at our house on Montpelier Road, half a mile farther on.

When the oxen stopped before our modest little cottage, Katie jumped out and went ahead with the children. She opened windows to air the house, and when I appeared with a box, she was struggling with the back door. It yielded to her efforts at that moment, and, hearing a startled gasp, I went to see what was wrong.

A native couple sat on the steps of the back veranda. The woman's hair, stiff with dried red clay, stood out in stiff strands like Medusa's snakes. A blanket wrapped close around her body swelled over the abdomen, warning me that she was with child. The spasms of her body as well as the perspiration on her smooth young face made it appear that she was already beginning labor.

The husband rose, awkward and ill at ease as he explained that his wife had had three stillborn babies; now that she was to have another, he wished me to deliver it. They knew of my work in confinement cases at Adams, and by Zulu grapevine had learned that we were to move that day to Montpelier Road.

"But I have no hospital," I explained. "And my dispensary is only to treat sickness and to give medicines."

The husband shifted uneasily. "I want my wife to live," he said, with deep concern. "I will not take her to the Government hospital."

There was reason for his feeling . . . and for the farewell celebrations often given Zulus obliged to enter the Government hospital. The white nurses there felt it beneath their dignity to tend Zulus, and some doctors shared the feeling of a number of white South Africans of that day that "it will be a decent country when the Kaffirs have died off." Zulus dreaded the Government hospital.

Katie watched me, her usually cheerful face now expressive of her troubled thoughts. Though herself a Basuto, she had married a Zulu, and their troubles were hers. Glancing toward the yard, her face suddenly brightened.

"We could put her in the coal shed, Doctor!"

"But, Katie," I protested, "I can't deliver a baby in—"

The relieved smiles of the Zulu couple stopped me. They didn't consider Katie's proposal outrageous. So, while we moved in household effects, Katie swept out the small amount of coal remaining in the shed, and the husband placed blankets on the floor. As dusk settled, he laid a fire, and over the crackling sticks prepared a meal for his wife and himself. Like all traveling Zulus, the couple carried both food and blankets, being thus prepared to camp anywhere.

I made an examination, discovering that the woman had a narrow pelvis, which might explain her stillborn children. But not anticipating any trouble, I went to my own dinner. Early in the morning the husband called me, and I delivered, with forceps, their first living child.

The happy father departed to find some friends with whom to share the good news. It was not until later, when I was examining my first patients in the dispensary, that he reappeared there, accompanied by a group of natives bearing a man on a crude stretcher. The face and hands of the sick man twitched as though with epilepsy.

The new father beamed at me. "They were taking Dabula to the Government hospital," he explained. "I told them he would die if they did. I said that here he would surely get well."

I didn't thank him for his missionary work. It was a hospital, rather than a dispensary case, but nevertheless I made a brief examination. Everything the sick man's friends told me about his symptoms sounded like Jacksonian epilepsy. I was convinced that his twitching resulted from a depressed skull fracture, caused by a falling stone while Dabula was working in a mine. I explained the nature of a dispensary, informed the natives that I had neither operating room nor hospital, and advised them to take Dabula to another doctor.

They understood better than I did at the time that few white doctors would accept native patients, and their only alternative was the Government hospital. And, knowing this, they refused to leave. At length, my resolve not to handle the case being weakened by Dabula's palsied twitching, I inquired whether he would mind sharing our coal shed with my confinement case. When his friends eagerly agreed, I directed natives to carry Dabula to Montpelier Road, promising to be along as soon as I had seen my remaining patients.

By the time I reached the house, Margaret had moved a kitchen table to the latticed back veranda, where there would at least be semiprivacy, and Dabula was lying on it. Instruments were already boiling in the sterilizer on the stove.

As my wife prepared to give ether, Dabula murmured, "I want a big scraping."

His head was scarred where Zulu witch doctors had cut through the skin and periosteum to scrape the bone, and he thought that scraping a wider area would stop his headaches and epileptic seizures. There was a well-substantiated theory that irritations of the motor surfaces of the brain caused the Jacksonian type of epilepsy; if true, the cicatrices adherent to the depressed portion of bone might increase the irritation. An operation could certainly make his condition no worse.

As soon as Dabula lost consciousness, I raised the scalp and periosteum, trepined a small "button" of bone with a ring-saw, and after removing it nipped off the irregular bits of depressed bone pressing on his brain. The button of bone meanwhile lay on a sterile bandage, ready for replacement, but fearing that it might act as a foreign body and cause complications, I decided in the end not to use it. I covered the hole with the periosteum and a flap of skin, trusting that the periosteum would in time regenerate any needed bone.

A sheet was hung from the center beam of the coal shed, and my unconscious patient was placed opposite the mother and her newborn babe, in what was now the "male ward" of my primitive hospital. Both patients returned home a week later. Dabula visited the dispensary regularly for several years. His epileptic symptoms had ceased, and in time the small opening in his skull filled in with what answered for normal bone.

A doctor's best-laid plans are likely to go astray when his patients are Zulus. Though I hoped to limit my practice to dispensary cases until the dispensary was solidly established, this beginning with two institutional cases made it impossible to convince the natives that I was not also running a hospital. Well, they won their point—and quickly, too. For only a few days after opening the dispensary, I was obliged to rent a cottage to serve as a hospital unit. It stood behind the mission chapel on Beatrice Street, and could be reached by crossing a yard from the back door of the dispensary.

From then on, the demarkation line between dispensary and hospital was blurred. Prenatal cases that began with examinations in the former, would end, when they promised complications, in the latter. The same thing happened when surgery was required. So it is difficult to write of dispensary work without at times overlapping on that of the hospital, for the two units, though separated, were parts of a whole. The hospital was primarily for operations and such confinement cases as could not safely be taken care of in kraals, and opening it when I had scarcely money enough for the first month's rent, and none at all for nurses, beds, or hospital food, raised a host of new problems which I will treat in a subsequent chapter. But one effect of the new unit might be mentioned here.

I had felt the dispensary could do the most good in pediatric and maternity cases, and progress could be made in both directions by teaching Zulu mothers the advisability of prenatal care. This was a matter of slow education, because they seldom gave the subject so much as passing thought. Even the problem of delivery was one they frequently neglected to consider until labor pains started. In the past when finding themselves in such straits in Durban, they had landed in the Government hospital. But now, with the opening of the cottage hospital, they would climb into a rickshaw and the rickshaw boy would start a wild dash for the dispensary. Sometimes these races ended in a dead heat, the baby being born as the mother was helped onto the table, but at other times the stork won in a walk.

The precipitate nature of some of these births is indicated by the names of babies I would have delivered, given more time. The natives of Natal often name their babies after an event concerned with its birth, prefacing the descriptive word by *U* in the case of boys, or by *No* or *Noma* if the baby is female.

One mother brought a newborn girl to the dispensary, explaining that she intended to arrive earlier, but her husband took her to the races and she withstood labor pains because she wished to watch all the horses run. In the climax of the final race, her baby was born and promptly named "Nomaracetrack." Two babies born in rickshaws en route to the dispensary were named "Urickshaw" and "Nomarickshaw." Another native woman fell on the front steps and before I could reach her gave birth to a girl who was obliged to go through life named "Nomasteppes." In another losing race with the stork, a mother requested a rickshaw boy to stop and after being helped to the ground crawled part way through a hedge and gave birth to a boy. The hedge surrounded the building in which the matriculation examinations (equivalent to the finals in American high schools) were being given. This circumstance led the disappointed father, whose six previous children were all boys and therefore worthless for the purpose of trading at maturity for cattle, to christen his latest son "Matriculation Examination No-Girl."

It was my hope in opening the dispensary not only to make childbirth easier for Zulu mothers but also to do something about high infant mortality. Largely to blame for the extreme death rate among native babies were incorrect feeding habits. Infants in the heathen kraals farthest from civilized centers had the least chance of survival, the northwest coast of Natal, formerly Zululand, being particularly bad in this respect. My first chance to encourage mothers from that region to bring their babies to me came shortly after starting practice on Beatrice Street.

My patients always lay basking in the warm sand of the hundred-foot-wide street while awaiting their turns. Umqibelo served tea and bread to make the wait easier, and the Zulus liked the custom for many of them had walked since daybreak without pausing for food. My assistant quoted scripture while the others sipped their tea, and being an able lay preacher, he often put on his glasses and read long passages from the Zulu Bible, and then, closing his Bible, would preach a sermon.

Stepping to the window of the consulting room one day to see how many patients were waiting outside, I spied a woman with a crying baby on her back. The red tablecloth she wore instead of a blanket marked her as a heathen woman from Zululand. Years ago an enterprising Britisher imported a stock of red tablecloths which were eagerly bought by Zululand women, remaining their distinctive dress. She stood a little apart, timid and seemingly undecided whether to stay.

"Katie," I said, "bring that woman in before she changes her mind."

Katie had proved a valued assistant during the year she had been with me, and she didn't fail me now. I watched her approach the stranger, and though I couldn't hear what she said, her good nature had its effect, for the woman smilingly followed my assistant inside.

She was clothed as the law requires for the street, from neck to knee, but no more than any other Zulu did she connect this legal technicality with modesty. After seating herself, she removed with dignity her red tablecloth, folded it and laid it on the chair beside her.

Her other clothing was negligible: beaded necklaces,

copper bangles, on wrists and ankles, and an oxhide petticoat attached by leather thongs about her waist—the petticoat a bridegroom rubs with grease and black clay to present to his bride at marriage, much as we give a wedding ring. And, usually, it too must last a lifetime.

Patience and skill had gone into her high coiffure. The problem with a Zulu woman is not waving the hair but removing the kinkiness by liberal use of grease and red clay. When the hair is straight, several strands are tied in a topknot and other hair sewn around the knot in spirals until it stands up six to eighteen inches from the head, somewhat resembling the headdress once in vogue in the French court. It takes two women an entire day thus to dress another woman's hair, and she must sleep on a brick or curved piece of wood during the year between dressings to avoid disturbing its shape.

The mother lifted the crying baby from her back. Its stomach was distended. An examination showed that the child suffered from nothing worse than digestive trouble, and when I described its symptoms the mother anxiously nodded. Knowing how Zulu babies were fed, I said:

"When your baby was born, you gave it a corn mash. When the milk flowed, you fed it from your breast. Now when you eat, you sometimes give it meat or beans or other food from your bowl."

The mother glanced up in astonishment, wondering how I knew these things. She nodded, sure now that I had strong magic.

I wasn't as sure. Past experience taught me that most Zulu mothers suckle their babies while eating, thoughtlessly thrusting heavy foods into an infant's mouth any time it ceases nursing. Digestive troubles originating in this way often result in sickness or death. Advising against the practice convinced few mothers for they pointed out that *their* mothers had done likewise. Probably this was true, for stomach trouble is fairly common among the Zulus.

Placing the baby in the mother's arms, I stepped into the dispensary to prepare a medicine containing pepsin. Though it would relieve the baby's immediate distress, I was troubled, knowing it would do no good if the infant continued eating adult foods. As I corked the bottle, I saw that the error in my approach was that it ignored Zulu mental processes. They believed medicine contained magic properties. How could eating meat or beans weaken its magic? Another course was advisable.

"This is strong medicine," I told the mother, handing her the bottle. I explained she must buy a spoon and give the infant a spoonful whenever it nursed. "But this medicine loses its strength," I added emphatically, "if your baby is fed on anything but mother's milk. Bring the child back in six weeks."

The baby gained four pounds in that time. The mother's eyes were shining as she described how the magic properties of the medicine had driven away the sickness. Not once, she informed me, had she ignored my warning and fed the baby anything to weaken the medicine's strength.

I had discovered a point of Zulu psychology which worked well with other babies from Zululand and elsewhere, and with adults as well.

Many of my male patients came to the dispensary after company physicians pronounced them unfit to work in the mines. They hoped I would reverse the verdict of the mine doctors but I never found reason to do this, though sometimes a minor operation or treatment of a disease enabled a worker to pass a second examination.

Kidney trouble caused by drink was a common cause

for rejection. Few workers were as rock-willed as Chief Tim, and they couldn't be trusted to remain temperate until their trouble cleared up. But the method used with the baby from Zululand achieved the same effect.

I compounded a medicine consisting of the most bitter drugs available for kidney ailment. Witch doctors' medicines are vile tasting, and the Zulus are convinced that the potency of a drug increases with its repugnance. After giving a patient a bottle of this mouth-puckering stuff, I'd warn him that powerful though it was, it cured kidney trouble only if he avoided liquor while taking it. While the medicine itself helped, abstinence from liquor really did more to clear up kidney troubles, when the disorders weren't too long standing. Having sampled the medicine during its preparation, I wasn't surprised at the number of patients who became teetotalers rather than face a second course of treatment.

The aftermath of rinderpest showed itself in the Durban dispensary, as it had in my previous practice among the Zulus. Malnutrition diseases such as tuberculosis and rickets were common, as was scrofula, a tuberculosis of the lymphatic glands of the neck.

Medical schools of that day taught students that tuberculosis of the lymphatic glands spread to the lungs, the distinction between bovine and human tuberculosis not having yet been made. I didn't suspect Natal's tubercular cattle of causing scrofula, but I began questioning my teaching, for scrofulous patients rarely developed tubercular lungs. I failed to make what now seems the next obvious step: noting the relation between rinderpest and scrofula. Quite by accident, however, I learned of a cure for lymphatic tuberculosis.

A mother and father one day appeared with a child who looked deathly ill. The mother had carried the child three miles on her back, not a great burden at that, for when she removed the support-blanket, the little girl's body was so thin it reminded me of pictures of children in famine lands. Nomapupo was the child's name, a word meaning "a dream"—a bad dream in this case, for Nomapupo's neck was swollen enormously and pus oozed from open sinuses. It was an ugly case of scrofula, its ravages showing in the bony little legs circling the mother's waist, and in the tight skin outlining every rib.

My expression of dismay was correctly interpreted by the father, and his disgruntled expression grew more marked. He remarked grumblingly as he sat down that he knew it was useless to bring his child to a white doctor who knew nothing of witchcraft.

What moved me to take what seemed a hopeless case was the child's expression. She had never before seen a white man, yet her large eyes regarded me with the same trust I'd once seen in the eyes of a pet dog when it laid an injured paw on my knee.

I'll do what I can, I thought.

The mother's face was anxious. "Has she been bewitched?"

Before answering, I inquired the length of the child's illness and what her treatment had been. The mother said the swellings appeared two years earlier; for the past year Nomapupo had been confined to her mother's hut while the witch doctor gave her such witchcraft antidotes as emetics and purgatives, and scratched the swellings to rub other medicines into her skin. On the whole this was encouraging. If Nomapupo was tough enough to survive such treatment, she was stronger than she looked.

"We are afraid it is *umzimba omubi,*" the mother concluded. The term "the body which is bad" is used by Zulus for scrofula.

The father's skepticism changed to gratification when I lifted Nomapupo to a table to listen to her chest with a stethoscope. A few old stethoscopes have fallen into the hands of witch doctors, and while most of them are so clogged with dirt that no sound could pass through them, they have convinced the natives that these instruments possess strong magic. . . . Finding the child's lungs clear, I gave a routine percussion, palpation and prodding, to satisfy the parents.

Again the mother asked, "Has she *umzimba omubi?*"

"Yes," I said, "the disease is strong."

The mother drew a sharp breath. "Have you any medicine which will cure her?"

I nodded, smiling at the child. "Nomapupo, I am going to make you well so that you can play again in the fields with your friends."

The large brown eyes trustfully regarding me danced with excitement and a radiant smile lighted the small, thin face.

It was a rash promise, but the child needed courage and hope. The success of my hastily conceived plan depended on Margaret, upon whom the burden of treatment would fall, so now I called her in from the next room. Halfway through my explanation, she interrupted.

"You want me to fatten up the child?" she guessed; and when I nodded, she laughed. "You didn't need to ask that, Jim!"

The last obstacle was persuading the mother to bring the child every day to the dispensary because "I could allow no one else to give the medicine." Witch doctors frequently make the same request, so she readily agreed; but, surprisingly, hesitated when I added that Nomapupo must eat at our house. The parents argued over this condition, but in the end consented.

In truth I knew of no medicine then in use which had any effect on scrofula. I applied peroxide and dressings, and the effervescent bubbling of the peroxide impressed Zulu mothers as powerful magic, but I had no faith in it, except as an antiseptic measure. The only effective measure I knew was air, sunlight, rest and good food. As long as Nomapupo was brought regularly to the dispensary, she'd spend part of each day in the open. And I trusted Margaret's cooking to put flesh on the wasted little body. You could never convince a native that anything so simple as building up resistance would cure scrofula, but it had worked in other cases.

Now as it happened, my sister-in-law Laura Mellen paid us a visit as Nomapupo's parents left with the child.

"A bad case of scrofula," Laura observed, as I started to examine another patient. "Dr. Bridgeman used to cure it with iodine, and his father had used it for years before him."

I rose so quickly I almost upset my patient. "*Iodine!* You mean he put it on the sinuses?"

"Oh, no—he gave it in medicine. I have the formula somewhere."

At Adams I had seen patients with puzzling scars on their necks. The natives insisted that Dr. Bridgeman, my predecessor at the mission, had not operated. All gave the curious explanation that he'd given them a blood-red medicine to clear up scrofula. Zulu medical testimony is so often inaccurate that I doubted this. But now Laura Mellen confirmed their stories!

A few days after returning to Esidumbini, she sent me the formula by mail. It was very simple—a quarter grain of iodine, and half a grain of potassium iodide in water twice daily for an adult. Harmless certainly in that quantity, but how effective?

Halving the proportions, I gave the medicine to Nomapupo. Neither this formula, cod liver oil, fresh air and sunlight, nor Margaret's cooking did much good during the first three months, though the child added some weight. The sinuses weren't as foul, it's true, but the treatment was on the whole disappointing. Particularly so because the little girl accepted with such profound child faith my promise to cure her.

I reminded myself that Nomapupo had looked like death; it was probably miraculous enough that she showed any improvement. The treatment was continued without change, and in the second three months there was marked improvement. At the end of the year her neck was of normal size, and only puckered scars remained where there had been open sinuses. The child was as healthy as any Zulu girl of eleven, and perhaps a little heavier.

"Now," I said, on her last visit, "you can play with your friends."

Nomapupo nodded very gravely, but there were imps of mischief in her bright eyes.

I couldn't determine whether better food or Dr. Bridgeman's formula cured Nomapupo; but proof was forthcoming in other cases where patients took the medicine but lived at home and continued their normal diet. In time I was willing to promise to clear up a case of scrofula if a patient took the "blood-red medicine" for a whole year, and never in forty years do I remember a case which failed to respond to this simple but effective remedy.

When I opened my dispensary, the Government hospital was regarded fearfully by the natives. Zulu patients did sometimes receive indifferent or careless treatment there. But the hospital often received blame that should have been directed against witch doctors who allowed disease or a surgical condition to progress until little could be done.

The word *dispensary*, on the other hand, held no such terrifying connotation. Patients who would have died before entering a hospital came without hesitation to the dispensary, and if they needed surgical treatment, they were shuttled over to the cottage hospital, which had none of the cold, formal atmosphere of such institutions. I was glad to have a part in breaking down the prejudice against operations.

I had performed a good many operations at Adams Mission, and some difficult operations among them, but it was really the dispensary, bringing me patients I would never have seen in a hospital, which made me a surgeon. In time I was doing surgical work for the natives that the whites of Durban were having to go to England to get, and for the skill I acquired in that line, I owe a great debt to that small Beatrice Street dispensary.

Some of the patients who came to the dispensary and later went to the cottage hospital were typically South African cases. One day, for example, four natives appeared carrying a young girl. When her brothers unwrapped dirty bandages from her right leg, I saw that it had rotted away in ghastly fashion, only the stump of her tibia and bare bone being left below the knee.

Another brother unwrapped a dirty cloth to display a decomposing lower portion of his sister's leg.

"We want the leg sewn together again," he said.

The girl informed me that while going to a pool for water, a puff adder had bitten her. Instead of coming to me when I might have prevented infection, she allowed her witch doctor to treat the leg until it had slowly rotted off. Now infection was spreading upward from the stump.

The girl had been afraid to go to the Government hospital. "I would die there," she stated emphatically. "And I don't want my leg taken off."

I told her I knew of no way to graft on a leg, and advised her to have the stump amputated before the infection spread further. Her eyes rolled in alarm, and she shook her head vigorously.

Argument proving useless, I cleaned up the unhealthy flesh as much as possible, asking her brothers to bring her again the next day. For three days I treated the leg, each time advising the girl of the need for amputation. By the fourth day the infection had spread so far that further delay would be fatal. I refused to touch the leg because that would only delay a sane decision.

"If you wish your sister to live," I informed the brothers, "she must be operated on today."

Evidently the matter had been discussed. The brothers shifted uneasily, looking at their sister. Her lips were compressed, but seeing that none of them wished to be spokesman, she made the decision.

"I'll have it taken off, Doctor—if you'll do it in the little house." The cottage hospital held none of the terrors for her that the larger Government hospital did.

I removed the infected stump, and the leg healed without incident.

A year after the dispensary was opened, my third daughter Laura was born, and that year my parents came to South Africa to see their grandchildren. My younger brother, Rob, then an attorney and today an Iowa judge, accompanied our parents to relieve father, then seventy-five, of the burdensome details of travel. As a result of this visit my parents became so interested in Zulu medical work that my mother and her brother, the Honorable

A. W. Hopkins, for many years a member of the Illinois Legislature, later jointly loaned me $10,000 to build a native hospital, thus laying a solid cornerstone in what had heretofore been a nebulous dream. The money was in effect a gift, and was later made one. But hospitals being a precarious financial risk, they sought to protect this gift from a possible swarm of creditors should the institution fail to pay its way.

The hospital, however, would have to wait. My most pressing need was for greater dispensary space, for the dispensary, which was serving the most patients, was bulging from its two small rooms. It lacked space for ailing Zulus, let alone that required for drugs, files, equipment and its small staff. So I used half of this loan to build a large and modern dispensary at 86 Beatrice Street, next door to the mission chapel, knowing that in time this $5,000 could be repaid from dispensary fees.

The new building, which was to be my headquarters for thirty-five years, had a large waiting room—used also as a small chapel, where Umqibelo could preach his sermons at ten o'clock—a consultation room to serve both dispensary and hospital, and a large drug room. To say that the Zulus liked the new waiting room better than the old would be stretching the truth, for the warm sand of Beatrice Street had suited them perfectly. However, it was easier for them to wait there than to adjust to the idea that each patient was to be received in the order of his or her arrival. To the Zulus, accustomed to respect status, the daughter of a chief, a witch doctor or a smeller-out should take precedence over more humble patients.

This idea received a rough jarring one day when Chief Mandhlakayise strode into the crowded waiting room and saw several members of his tribe awaiting their turns. As a prince, the chief had been sent by his father to receive an American education, and though he'd acquired a fluent English tongue he had also acquired a taste for liquor, so that he returned to his tribal kraal and his *umutsha* of monkey tails somewhat the worse for the experience. His self-esteem was bolstered on this occasion by considerable drink, a khaki riding suit and a heavy black whip known as a *sjambok*.

Katie Makanya opened the door of the consultation room at that moment to admit the next patient. Chief Mandhlakayise brushed her aside roughly and, confronting me, demanded, "Here, McCord, what do you mean by keeping my people waiting?"

At my desk, jotting down notes on the last case, I glanced up in surprise and then paused before answering. Clearly it was time to establish the principal that there was to be no favoritism in dispensary or hospital. With an edge on my voice, I said, "Get out!"

The chief, not accustomed to being spoken to in this manner, blinked at my harsh tone. As he remained frozen with indecision, too dazed to move, I repeated sternly, "Get out!"

When he still stood paralyzed with bewilderment, I sprang up and started toward him, repeating the same order in Zulu: "*Suka!*" I hadn't lost my temper, but I pretended that I had. The startled chief watched me coming a moment longer and then, seeming to realize that I was somewhat the bigger man, he backed from the room, still looking bewildered at this brusque treatment of a chief.

I grinned at Katie as I dropped into my chair, and Katie, who had become somewhat alarmed, smiled back. "Who's next?" I asked.

The Reverend John Dube came later to apologize for the behavior of his cousin; explaining that the chief was drunk, he said that he hoped I would understand. John Dube's father would have been chief of Mandhla-kayise's tribe had he not relinquished his royal rights to become a Christian and a preacher. His son, following in his steps, had became an able preacher and without question was the most influential Zulu in Natal. I laughed off the incident, explaining to John Dube that in my practice all Zulus were equals. Something far more important than my personal dignity had been at stake. Never again was the complicating question of social status to arise among my incoming patients. However that problem was to reappear, in another guise, in later years.

As minor and sometimes major surgical work was added to the growing dispensary practice, I needed the help of a younger and more adaptable man. Umqibelo could serve tea, quote scripture, and keep the dispensary immaculate, but that exhausted his possibilities. Margaret was raising a family as well as performing the work of nurse, anesthetist and operating assistant, and there simply weren't enough hours in the day for her to help with other dispensary work—such as changing dressings, for example. Katie Makanya faithfully carried out any work assigned to her, but her knowledge of six native dialects made her so invaluable as interpreter that I kept her much of the time in the consulting room. A long time after the need of another assistant arose, I was without one because I could not find a qualified man.

One afternoon Joseph Gobezi appeared. Joseph was a handsome young man, rather too flashily dressed and too sure of himself, but well qualified by intelligence and training for the work. He came well recommended . . . by himself . . . saying that he'd been a male nurse serving under Dr. MacVicar in the Victoria Hospital in

Cape Province. This recommendation should have been checked, but I was afraid that if I delayed Joseph might find other work.

In time Dr. MacVicar answered my inquiry: he knew no Joseph Gobezi, nor had he ever had a male nurse. By then I knew Joseph well enough to realize that facing him with his deception would only result in a bland admission of guilt and a more fanciful story. The truth and Joseph were scarcely on speaking terms, but somewhere he'd picked up much useful knowledge. Few doctors could apply a dressing in awkward places more skillfully than Joseph, and his familiarity with drugs (acquired in a variety of ways, depending upon which of his stories you believed) made him invaluable in mixing prescriptions. His bump of integrity was a dimple, but despite this handicap he learned so quickly and was so useful that I was grateful to have him.

For months I tolerated the competent rogue until I discovered that my bills for drugs were mounting. I watched Joseph but his measurements were always exact; he wasted nothing. The explanation came when I smelled brandy on his breath; I discovered that my supply of medicinal brandy was almost gone. Additional investigation disclosed that Joseph practiced medicine on the side, stealing what drugs he needed from the dispensary. Faced with the evidence, Joseph cheerfully admitted his guilt and departed.

According to the schoolbook maxims, he should have come to a bad end, but Joseph knew nothing of those rules and in any case wouldn't have believed them. Securing a herbalist's license to avoid legal entanglements, he set himself up as a native practitioner. He convinced his patients, which included some whites, that he had the same medical education as Dr. McCord, and that he had the advantage of additional post-graduate study in Japan. When he could have received this education, since he had never been outside South Africa, none of his patients troubled to ask. He developed a large practice, even performing minor operations, but he was clever enough not to attempt major surgical work which might cause deaths and involve him with the law.

I imagined that I was well rid of Joseph, but one day an old woman with a shriveled hand visited the dispensary with her grandson Gershim, my former assistant's son. Nomabotwi explained that her daughter had married Joseph years before, but following his rise in the world as a "doctor," he found her a social handicap and refused to support either his wife or son. Now her grandson's left arm was diseased. Joseph, for all his professed skill, refused to treat it. Gershim, a thin, listless boy with uneager eyes, lifted his arm indifferently for me to examine it. Two tumors four inches apart had broken and suppurating sinuses discharged a foul-smelling pus. I believed Nomabotwi when she said the odor was offensive to everyone in her kraal. The infection, sapping the boy's health and strength, might partially explain his listlessness.

After giving Gershim a whiff of anesthetic, I examined the holes and found that a channel along the middle of the bone connected them. With an older patient I would have operated to remove the diseased bone, leaving an opening for free access and drainage, but I disliked depriving a boy of the use of his arm for the time that would require. Nomabotwi misunderstood my hesitation.

"I have no money," she said; "but I do not want my grandson to go to the Government hospital. I will work for you—"

I smiled, for the frail little grandmother could use only one arm. "Gershim can pay his way working in the yard," I said. "I'll have to keep him here, anyway, in order to treat his arm every day."

Halfway measures are usually a mistake. I first tried passing antiseptics down the suppurating channel, and after that performed several minor operations. But in the end it was necessary to remove the diseased bone. This proved successful, for the bone in time thickened where the diseased portion had been chipped away, and the arm grew fully as strong as a normal one.

His listlessness was apparently the result of the infection, for he later acquired an excellent reading and speaking knowledge of English. This fitted him for a position with a large mercantile house in Durban, where he served as interpreter and intermediary between his white employers and their Zulu boys and workmen. Competent and thoroughly honest, he was well suited to this position.

During the time Gershim was my yard boy, however, he gave no indications of future promise. The only time when he showed conspicuous energy was when I called him, and then he'd come running, with a broad grin, happy to drop whatever work he had halfheartedly been doing. His allergy to work in any form did not extend to delivering messages, at which he was good, and it was on an occasion when he was acting as messenger that he drew the attention of a leading Durban banker.

The banker noticed Gershim's bandaged arm. By asking questions, he learned that the boy suffered from the same infection as his own son. However, by then the native boy's arm was almost well, while the banker's son had undergone treatment for months and his arm was no better. The banker asked me to treat his son, and was incensed at my refusal.

"But you take missionaries as patients!" he protested.

"My salary is paid by the American Missionary Board," I reminded him.

"But if you bother with Kaffirs, I don't see why you can't help a white boy," he growled.

"There are dozens of doctors for white people. The Zulus have only one doctor they can call their own."

I appreciated the incongruity of giving medical treatment to a native boy who, at that time, showed neither ambition nor ability, and denying it to a white boy. But I had come to South Africa to fill a need. Too often doctors settle in foreign lands, resolving to give their time to a primitive people, and then find their white practice so profitable that natives no longer are welcome in their offices. I was determined not to begin that. You can't take one white patient and refuse another without making enemies.

Native patients were already giving me all the work I could handle. That might not have been true if my practice had been limited to the dispensary. But the cottage hospital was by then proving itself a surprisingly lusty infant.

CHAPTER SEVEN

MY COTTAGE HOSPITAL

WITHIN ONLY A FEW DAYS AFTER STARTING PRACTICE in the Durban dispensary, I had discovered so many long-neglected conditions needing surgical attention that I felt the opening of a hospital could not be postponed. Youthful optimism made me overlook some weighty obstacles to the establishment of a hospital. Not the least of these was the fact that I had but $50, saved from small dispensary fees, to accomplish this purpose.

The only house which would fit my limited budget was a small cottage, but twenty-four feet square, which I rented for $40 a month. It stood on the next street, and from the back door of the dispensary, it was but a short walk across the bare yard behind the mission chapel to the cottage. A row of pickets served both as porch rail and front fence, the roof was of corrugated sheet iron, and the cottage had but three small rooms, the largest fortunately being divided by a partition to make four small cubicles.

One cubicle was immediately made into an examination room and surgery. For a dollar and a quarter I bought enough lumber and nails to knock together within an hour and a quarter an operating table more suitable for

my height than more elaborate tables, costing hundreds
of dollars, which were to serve me in later years. Dressings,
antiseptics and a few other hospital supplies exhausted
my remaining funds. Luckily I had surgical instruments
brought from Adams or acquired in England or America.

But what of beds, blankets, nurses or a proper hospital kitchen? These refinements I couldn't afford, nor
was their absence as great a handicap as might be supposed. A Zulu usually came to the hospital with anywhere
from one to a dozen relatives or friends, and they always
carried their own food when traveling. These relatives or
friends gave medicine, and also nursed the patient and
prepared food in the cottage kitchen. Lack of beds was
regarded by the Zulus as a blessing, for, accustomed as
they were to sleeping on the floor of a hut, nothing made
them more nervous than sleeping in a bed raised from
the ground. It was unnecessary to supply blankets because the patients always brought their own. And while
they were sometimes lice-infested, that, to a Zulu, was a
characteristic of blankets. For a time, it's true, either
Margaret, who was acting as head nurse, or I had to change
all dressings—until Joseph Gobezi and others could be
trained in this work.

By these expedients I hoped to make the cottage
hospital self-sustaining on fees ranging from $10 for
an ordinary delivery or minor surgery up to $25 for a
major operation or a confinement involving complications. This hope was realized from the first month, despite
the fact that the hospital would hold but twelve patients.
Most of these patients were recovering from operations
ranging from the removal of a wart to the removal of an
abdominal tumor. Maternity cases were in the minority;
insufficient space in the cottage still made it necessary
to travel sometimes twenty or more miles to deliver a

child. Nevertheless there were always a few Zulu mothers whose confinements required hospital care. To avoid contagion which might imperil their lives, patients with communicable diseases were given medicine and sent home, a course they entirely approved of, their prejudice against hospitals being strong.

At night, when visiting the hospital, I had to switch on a flashlight before entering the crowded little cottage, for mothers and babies and patients convalescing from operations occupied almost every foot of floor space.

A young Durban doctor who called at the new hospital was shocked by its crudities. He was a practitioner who, though but twenty-four, already had a luxuriant red beard and a ready opinion on almost anything. Pointing out its many shortcomings he expressed strong disapproval of my intention of operating there.

Since Zulus then in need of surgery had a choice between dying or chronic illness, and an operation in the only hospital I had the means to give them, the criticism nettled.

"The operating room doesn't make the surgeon," I said, somewhat testily. "A surgeon makes the operating room. Given enough instruments, he should be able to operate on a kitchen table."

My red-bearded colleague refrained from asking whether I was a surgeon. That would have been embarrassing. I'd had no surgical experience in America, and during my four years at Adams, I'd undertaken only small operations in maternity cases, to remove fatty tumors, or to clean out wounds and sew up lacerations. And none of this could be called operative surgery.

Now, the naturally cautious Zulus did not beat a path to the door of the new little hospital. They came instead to the dispensary, which seemed less formidable than the Government hospital they dreaded. If a condition demanded surgical treatment, they seldom objected to entering the cottage hospital. It lacked the institutional atmosphere and the formality associated in their minds with a hospital, and I'm sure many of them thought of it as a convalescent home. Yet there were exceptions, patients who full well knew the nature of the cottage unit, but distinguished between governmental and private care.

One of these was a self-possessed Zulu woman nearing middle age who appeared at first glance, but only at first glance, to be in a family way. She had a larger fibroid tumor than I'd ever seen, for it had grown to pumpkin size and filled her abdominal cavity. Placing her in the hospital, I went to my textbooks to read everything they had to say on uterine fibroids. The pitfalls in such operations were alarming; the heavy percentage of fatalities quoted even more so.

I was not a venturesome surgeon, and by choice I employed a scalpel only when the odds favored its use or when it might save a life. Calling my patient into the consulting room, I explained the great risks, and advised her against an operation. "While you're uncomfortable, you can live with your tumor. But if I try to remove it, you may die."

She looked at me calmly. "I am already dead. Go ahead and operate."

Her steady, determined expression showed no intention of yielding.

"Very well," I said, after a pause. "But I'll need time to prepare."

The preparation was more for me than my patient. For several days I mentally rehearsed each step of the operation, planned for every foreseeable contingency. Preparing for a new and difficult operation has always been a nightmare for me . . . a mental bracing that is largely accomplished when I've learned everything I can beforehand about the surgery I'm undertaking. And as an additional precaution in this case, since the operation would be extremely hard for an unaided surgeon, I asked the help of two young colleagues, Dr. Pearson and Dr. Bray. Though they were but little more experienced than myself, both had the interests of the Zulus at heart.

The operation itself proved ridiculously simple, in spite of all my forebodings. With no adhesions whatever to complicate matters, I lifted out a fifteen-pound tumor, and took sutures to close the incision. Within a week the woman made an uneventful recovery and left the cottage hospital.

But that was not, by any means, an end of the affair. My patient, now possessing a slender figure of which she was inordinately proud, wore only a skin petticoat reaching from her waist nearly to her knees, and this left her abdomen and its surgical scar exposed. Other Zulus noticed this scar when she was on the road in Zululand, and would stop her to ask, "What is that you have over your stomach?"

Pleased at this attention, no less prone to discuss her operation than her white sisters, the Zulu woman would sit down and describe in detail her former condition and how she had acquired a wasp waist. She was thus a walking advertisement both for the hospital and for tumor operations, and the publicity she gave both was responsible for the large number of abdominal operations I performed in the following years.

The second operation of this kind, however, forever dispelled the idea that the texts had overstated the hazards. The woman we were operating on also had a large tumor, and it adhered to almost every organ it touched, thus demanding slow and tedious dissection. Bray kept Pearson and me in a state of nervous tension by his constant reminders that if we didn't hurry, we'd lose our patient. While this did not happen, the operation lasted four painfully trying hours.

We worked so well as a team that I frequently called upon Bray to administer chloroform and upon Pearson to assist me in difficult operations. It was curious that we could work so smoothly together because our differences were pronounced.

Dr. Maurice Pearson was then Assistant Surgeon of the Umalzi District south of Durban, and had been a friend since my early days at Adams. It was in those days, in fact, that he'd offered to write a death certificate whenever needed at any time my right to practice might be questioned for lack of a British medical degree. Tall, slim and rather sharp of face, he had the pleasant, polished manners of an English gentleman. And whether in the hinterland or the city, he was always faultlessly dressed, even to the monocle in his left eye. His formality in speech and dress was in marked contrast to his humble approach to medicine, for he was always eager to learn. This latter trait was to win him renown for his femur operations in the Richmond Hospital in England during the First World War.

Best illustrating the human qualities of the man was an experience several years before I moved to Durban. Margaret and I were at a missionary meeting, forty miles from Adams, when my son Robert fell ill with what I suspected was laryngeal diphtheria. Having never seen or treated the disease, I wasn't sure of my diagnosis. So my wife and I started with our small son for Durban. A broken buggy harness made us miss the first train, and by the time we reached the city, Robert's condition was serious.

No hospital or nursing home would admit him, and his condition was becoming critical when I turned in desperation to Dr. Pearson. He'd had considerable experience with diphtheria, and at once verified my suspicion. Without a moment's hesitation, he made a room in his home into a hospital ward, with Margaret in charge, despite the fact that his own son, who was Robert's age, was in the house. Dr. Pearson gave the sick boy an antitoxin shot and was prepared to undertake an intubation operation if Robert's breath was shut off. When the white membrane in my son's throat broke away the following morning, this proved unnecessary.

One afternoon, shortly after opening the Durban dispensary, I dropped into Pearson's office to ask if he could recommend a doctor to take over the dispensary for two hours a day, at a pound a day, while I was on vacation. A plump, jovial little Irish physician, Dr. Ernest Bray, dropped in while we were speaking, and Pearson mentioned my request.

"Think I'll take it on myself," Bray said with a smile.

This was unexpected good fortune. Bray already had a wide and successful practice, and for the small pay I could offer, I had no reason to expect the services of such an able physician. Both his generosity and his complete indifference to money were responsible for his acceptance of the offer. He would come to the dispensary in the middle of the day to take my more pressing cases, earning the confidence of Zulu patients both by his competence and his good nature. It was a very happy arrangement which was to be repeated in future years whenever I was absent from Durban.

Bray, then in his late thirties, was an Australian-born Irishman who had received his medical training in an Edinburgh medical school. Rather short and quite fat, he had hair as white as an octogenarian's and black and bushy brows which gave his round face a genial expression. He was not, however, invariably good natured. At times his black brows were like warning storm clouds over his deep and piercing eyes and his explosive temper would quickly reach its low boiling point. On one such occasion his Indian boy fell asleep when he should have been holding Bray's horses; Bray nearly felled him with a cuff on the ear.

Durbanites were either for or against, but never indifferent, to the plump little physician. Generally his patients were unswervingly loyal, even though he might give them a tongue-lashing if they neglected his instructions. His rich patients cheerfully paid high fees, feeling his services worth them, while his poorer patients frequently received no bills at all. Bray was a Roman Catholic, on Sundays a very devout man who never missed his mass, but on the other six days he felt entitled to gamble, drink or use the "forceful" language which many regarded as profanity. Brusque at times to the point of rudeness, making not the slightest social pretense of friendship for anyone he disliked, he was as much a rough diamond as Pearson was a polished one.

After Pearson, Bray and I had worked together on several operations, we decided that it would improve our ability at diagnosis to state in advance what we expected to find. At first this was done verbally. But we soon discovered that each doctor, perhaps due to the stress of the operation, would incorrectly remember his own diagnosis. This resulted in some heated arguments after our patient had been carried to his ward. Bray would use his most "forceful" language to convince us that Pearson and I had changed to his diagnosis after the operation had proved him right. Pearson, with precise and clipped diction, would argue that while Bray was correct in stating that McCord had changed his mind after discovering his error, Bray had done likewise, both of us having reverted to his, Pearson's, original opinion. Naturally I contended that both men were trying to claim credit for my prognosis. To end these postoperative arguments, Pearson suggested that each man write his diagnosis on the white-washed wall of the surgery. This gave the first man to write on the wall a decided advantage, because the other two felt impelled to disagree. And there were times, I recall, when all three of us were wrong.

On one such occasion a Zulu woman came to the dispensary in failing health, after having suffered almost constant pain for fifteen months. To me it seemed a clear case of a soft fibroid tumor, which should be removed; and that was the diagnosis I wrote boldly on the surgery wall before scrubbing up for the operation. With a pitying glance at me, Pearson wrote below my prognosis, "Ovarian cyst." Bray shook his head at such denseness and scribbled with a flourish, "Dermoid cyst."

After making the incision, I was shocked to find a baby's leg. Having detected no sign of pregnancy, I was too stunned for several moments to say anything to the two doctors staring inquiringly at me. Then, as an explanation of what I had uncovered was borne home, I composed my face and managed to say casually, "Pearson, tell me what you think."

Pearson found the baby's leg, and his face blanched so rapidly that I thought he'd faint, "Oh, I say, how could we have missed it?"

I removed the child, and when Pearson saw that it

had been dead for some time, the color slowly returned to his face. It was a case of an extrauterine pregnancy in which a cell, instead of passing along to the uterus, reached partial development in the Fallopian tube and then had burst into the abdomen. Protected by its body sack, the unborn baby had lived there until its ninth month, when it had died. In such a case among civilized races, a mother would have been rushed to the hospital for removal of the baby. But Zulu women, before the turn of the century, were obliged to carry their burden throughout life. If the mother's body was healthy, no infection resulted, but the dead baby might in time calcify, becoming an uncomfortable and disfiguring millstone. Extrauterine pregnancies of this type are more common among the Zulus than among white women.

Goiter is also comparatively common among the Zulus, and while a goiter operation is usually not anything to worry an experienced surgeon, my first case of this kind was an ordeal. It happened to be the worst case I was to encounter in my entire practice. The patient was a man who had a goiter extending from ear to ear, shutting off air to such an extent that every breath was a shrill whistle. The texts were as pessimistic concerning goiter as about abdominal-tumor operations, but as there was no Durban surgeon any better qualified to do the work, I was faced with the bleak choice between undertaking the surgery myself or allowing the poor man to return to his kraal to await the day when he'd strangle to death for lack of air.

Before I had finished the operation, I felt that even the most gloomy medical writers had made light of the difficulties, for the array of arteries and nerves in the neck are pushed from their normal positions by a goiter and all of them resemble it in color.

However, my patient knew nothing of the risks he'd run. Delighted to be able once more to breathe normally, he went home in high spirits to assure his friends that the removal of a goiter was like a brief sleep. Perhaps it was as well that I'd started with my most trying operation of this type, because I had a great many goiters to remove after that, and all seemed, by comparison, relatively easy.

On one such operation, when Dr. Bray was giving the anesthetic, a woman patient lost consciousness slowly, and while she remained conscious, she fairly bellowed a Zulu song of a nature that was, to state it mildly, earthy. Katie Makanya was acting as dirty nurse (the nurse who serves as general helper and therefore does not have to sterilize her hands), and understanding the words perfectly, her lips tightened with disapproval.

Noticing her grimace, Dr. Bray sought to tease her by asking, "What's she singing, Katie? One of your hymns?"

Katie, who never permitted her religion to be treated lightly, glanced up with steady eyes. "No, Dr. Bray. She's singing the *Ave Maria*."

Dr. Bray gulped. For the remainder of the operation, he had nothing to say, though afterward he accused Margaret of putting the idea into Katie's head. . . .

I had hoped some day to repay, at least in part, Dr. Bray's generous help, but when that day came, I was placed in an awkward position, for the help he desired was for a white patient.

A Catholic woman, the mother of six children, had developed a large goiter which not only made it difficult for her to breathe but was undermining her health. Two Durban doctors she consulted advised her that no surgeon "this side of London" could remove the goiter, and they advised her to sail at once for England to have this done before her condition grew worse. Certainly this was most impractical advice for a woman too poor to pay for the trip, let alone the operation.

Then the woman consulted Dr. Bray, explaining the advice her previous doctors had given her.

Bray snorted. "Traipse clear to London? Poppycock! We've taken out plenty of goiters as large or larger than yours for the Zulus. I'll see what can be done."

Bray came at once to see me. He'd never removed a goiter, but he had assisted many times when I had. Knowing that on occasions I operated on missionaries, he thought I might make another exception to my rule against taking white patients in the case of the poor Catholic woman. Surely I'd have liked to, for judging from his description of his patient's condition, six children would lose their mother unless the operation were performed. But by that time I was regularly operating on the Zulus for conditions which required a trip to England for white residents of Durban similarly afflicted. If I accepted the case, how could I refuse a like favor to my other colleagues? The Zulus, like the Catholic mother, could not afford to travel to London, and I was at the time doing most of their surgical work.

An alternative plan occurred to me. "I'm operating on Johanna Nonkontole in the morning, Bray. Her goiter appears to be identical to the one you describe. Suppose you remove it, while I assist. Then I'll assist again when you operate on your patient. That way, the operation will be performed in your name."

Bray agreed. In the operation in the cottage hospital to remove Johanna's goiter, he proceeded slowly, tying off the supplying arteries, dissecting carefully and with considerable skill, while I made suggestions when needed.

At no point was it necessary for me to give active assistance, but Bray was nevertheless relieved when he brought the operation to a successful conclusion. Later, at the Catholic Sanitarium, he undertook the operation on his own patient. Her goiter, as it turned out, was a little larger and more difficult to remove, but the chief difference lay in the greater amount of time involved.

Characteristically, Bray did more than remove the goiter. To persuade his patient to take the convalescence she needed, he hired a woman to care for her six children, paid all her expenses at the Catholic Sanitarium, and found her husband a better-paying job. The bill the woman received, upon leaving the sanitarium, bore no figures and only three words: *"Paid in full."* And knowing Bray, I feel sure he brushed off any attempts his patient made to thank him.

After Katie Makanya had acted as dirty nurse at many an operation, she began questioning me about her sister, Marian Makanya who had lost her nose due to a syphilitic infection. This infection, Katie insisted, was not due to any lack of virtue on her sister's part but was the result of the vaccination required by law.

Now, this was not ingenuousness on Katie's part. Seventy years ago, when less was known of such things, it was common practice even in America to use the scar from a successful vaccination in vaccinating a second patient. No harm resulted if the scar came from a healthy donor, but syphilis and other infectious diseases were transmitted in other cases. The same method was common in South Africa fifty years ago. So, thinking Katie might be right, I asked her to bring Marian to the dispensary.

It took some urging, but Marian finally appeared,

shy and self-effacing because of her disfigurement, and wearing a cloth below her fine eyes to conceal her lack of a nose. When with great reluctance she removed this cloth there was revealed, where her nose should have been, only two small holes, her nostrils. Syphilis had eaten away the bones of her nose, but aside from this disfiguring handicap, Marian Makanya was an exceptionally handsome girl, though she carried herself so humbly in an effort to avoid attention that this was not immediately apparent.

"Before I can do anything about your nose," I explained, after my examination, "the disease must be cured."

With downcast eyes, and her voice shaded to a whisper, Marian said, "Can I start treatment now, Doctor?"

I administered the potassium iodide and mercury used in that day for syphilis. And during the months Marian underwent this treatment, I worried considerably about how to rebuild her nose. Margaret suggested that if the children of Israel could build bricks without straw, I should be able to build a nose without tissue. Perhaps so; but little was then known about plastic surgery, and I had to devise the method. At the end of a year, when Marian's face sores had healed and her tissues were once more healthy, I had worked out a procedure which might work.

In brief, this required two operations to repair the ravages of the disease, and dressings had to remain on the girl's face for a month after each operation. The first operation was to "borrow" bone and flesh from her forehead to construct a new nose, and the second was to cover the part of the forehead from which it had been borrowed.

When the second set of dressings was removed, Katie's anxious expression changed to a broad smile. She nodded approvingly as I handed a mirror to her sister.

Marian studied her face full view for a long time, then tilted her head first to one side and then the other. Her new nose could hardly be distinguished from a normal one, but as she continued to examine herself with the glass in silence, I began wondering whether it displeased her. At last she sprang up, her eyes shining, and cried, "I'm going down town and buy myself a new dress!"

She made a very handsome figure as she left, her shoulders erect, her head held proudly.

When she was brought back only a short while later in the custody of a policeman, however, her hair and dress were disheveled, and her eyes flashed in anger.

"This girl was disturbing the peace," the policeman said. "I can't get the straight of it, but she said she came from here."

Marian was too enraged for several minutes to tell a coherent story. It appeared that she had walked along the road toward town in the same manner as she had left my office, with pride in her changed appearance giving her a beauty that caught the eye of every male Zulu. Presently young men made provocative remarks, and tried to make love to her. Zulu love-making is not distinguished by its subtlety, and Marian, who had heretofore been ignored by men, was incensed by what she regarded as bad behavior. Picking up rocks, she pelted her would-be suitors until the policeman intervened.

"You shouldn't have done that, Marian," I scolded her.

"But they were rude to me," she sputtered. "To *me*! To me, myself!"

She was as indignant as a medieval queen would have been if a rustic had made her the object of his rough horseplay.

I laughed, and after explaining the girl's background, promised the policeman that my patient would give no further trouble, but I suggested to him that men would now have to show greater restraint in the way they treated a girl with a new nose.

It was somewhat more difficult to convince Marian that having a nose was scarcely a unique attainment, and certainly no reason to attract attention to herself. To play down beauty, especially when suddenly acquired, is probably not easy for any girl, but Marian managed to do so after that. . . .

Another case of a syphilitic infection innocently acquired was that of a woman named Nomasonto.

Nomasonto, when acting as nursegirl for a white magistrate's two children, fell in love with the native police chief whose duty it was to bring accused natives into court and stand behind the magistrate's chair while the trial was being conducted. This young man, who was favored not only by his good position but also by fine physique, had led a promiscuous life and unknown to Nomasonto he had contracted syphilis.

After their engagement, the police chief insisted on a native wedding, with beer and dancing. Nomasonto, who had picked up fragments of South-African law while living in the magistrate's home, was equally insistent upon a civil ceremony. In the end, however, she pretended to bow to his wishes. In high spirits from this victory, her fiancé was in no mood to oppose her when she suggested, on the way to the native wedding, that they stop at the magistrate's for a civil ceremony. This ceremony gave Nomasonto a secret weapon that she kept hidden for years.

Because she contracted syphilis from her husband, her first child was stillborn, and her next nine children were either stillborn or died shortly after birth. Her husband, furious at having no daughters that he could sell for cattle, threatened to find another wife. It was then that Nomasonto first revealed her reasons for insisting upon a civil ceremony; by that marriage her husband was prevented from taking another wife. Bitterly angry at having been thus tricked, he told her that if she once more failed to produce a living child, he'd take another woman, whether in marriage or otherwise.

Nomasonto, then pregnant again, came to the dispensary to see if I could do anything for her condition. Prompt treatment cleared up the venereal disease; and later, in the cottage hospital, she gave birth to a healthy daughter which she called Daughter of the King. Her husband was so delighted to become a father after so many disappointments that he remained drunk for days. Nomasonto did odd jobs around the dispensary for three months to pay for her board, while she learned how to feed and care for her baby.

A year later, while I was on furlough in America, she again became pregnant. Nearing her childbearing time, she learned of my return and tried to reach the hospital. Nightfall found her at the station, with no train until morning, and before it arrived, twin boys were born. She appeared with these boys a few days later, anxious to have my assurance that they were healthy, which they certainly were. Nomasonto was then approaching the end of her childbearing years and was not likely to have more children, so she decided to keep both. Her Christian training made it possible for her to overcome the repugnance so many natives feel toward allowing both twins to live.

And her husband, true to form, went on another extended spree to celebrate his twice-proven manhood.

Nomasonto lived near a church, and after her children were old enough to walk, she made rather a nuisance of herself by hurrying from her kraal with her daughter and her two little sons any time the church door was opened, even if only to be swept out. The pastor was able to overlook this idiosyncrasy, however, because she did an immense amount of good for the native women of the district. She'd learned enough about simple nursing while working in the dispensary and hospital to become more than a passable nurse, and she was willing to help any woman of the district who was ill. . . .

Healthy twins were born to another Zulu mother in the hospital, and though they appeared equally strong at birth, the baby girl gained rapidly while the boy steadily grew weaker. The reason, Margaret discovered, was that the woman felt the daughter would one day bring her husband ten cattle while the boy would be a burden. So, in native fashion, she intended to let the boy die.

Coincidence saved that little boy's life. The mother's sister was in the hospital at the same time for a hysterectomy, and in extremely low spirits because the operation made it impossible for her to bear other children. Margaret asked if she'd like to have her sister's little boy, and her dark eyes lighted eagerly at the suggestion. The mother was not only amenable to the adoption, but she was then willing to nurse the boy twin until it could be cared for by the sister.

It is commonly believed that primitive mothers have an easier time in childbirth than their white sisters, but my experience in Zulu confinement cases indicates quite the opposite. The mischief done by witch doctors when a native mother has difficulty delivering her child explains part of the trouble, but only part, for witch doctors would not be called upon so often for assistance were it not for the fact that a narrow pelvis is more common among Zulu women than white. It was the frequency of difficult deliveries among my patients that made me consider taking a child with a Caesarian section, at a time when the mortality for this operation was extremely high and it was attempted only as a last resort.

The Caesarian section is one of the oldest operations known to medicine. Legend holds that Julius Caesar was delivered in this way, and whether or not this is true, Roman law made it mandatory for physicians to take a child from a mother dying in advanced pregnancy. Not until 1500 was the operation performed on a living woman, and the results thereafter, in the days before antiseptics, were almost always fatal, the mother dying of either sepsis or hemorrhage. Even at the turn of the century, mortality in such cases was nearly fifty per cent. Several experiences in my cottage hospital nevertheless made me conclude that even against such odds, Caesarian operations should at times be undertaken.

The first of these cases was a mother who had a constricted vagina as a result of scar tissue formed after she was badly torn in a previous childbirth. Dr. Bray and I labored for hours before we were able eventually to take her baby with forceps, and as a result of its delivery through such a narrow passage, it was dead.

In a second case, normal delivery was impossible because of the mother's narrow pelvis. She'd come to the hospital with relatives, and they stubbornly refused to permit me to take the baby by Caesarian section (the only possibility of saving mother and child), until the husband would agree. He was in the distant hills buying goats, and after word was sent to him hour after hour slipped by, while my patient grew weaker and weaker. She died before the husband reached the hospital.

Surely, I reasoned, a Caesarian could have no more tragic result. So the next time I was faced with such a case, I wasted no time, but operated when labor began. The operation proved ridiculously simple; and in a short time the happy mother was able to leave the hospital with a bright-eyed baby girl, whom she named Caesarina.

These operations became commonplace in my hospital, and the mortality was extremely low. The mother ran very little more risk than in a normal birth. The reason for this surprising contradiction of the statistics in time became apparent. Caesarian operations had not been resorted to in the past except as a last resort, when the mother was weakened from prolonged labor and the case was well nigh hopeless. Naturally the mortality under such conditions would be high!

Almost every operation undertaken in a large American hospital was performed in my little cottage hospital, and they were generally of the same type, though there were notable exceptions. Vesicovaginal fistulas such as Nolaka's were far more common in my practice because of the ignorant "surgery" of witch doctors. This operation gave me more satisfaction than any other, both because it relieved a distressing condition and because it often allowed a Zulu woman once more to become a mother. Operations for abdominal tumors, requiring either a hysterectomy or an ovariotomy, were our most common cases of major surgery. While spectacular, they were in reality easy operations in which the mortality was very nearly zero. Appendectomies, for reasons some future medical researcher may discover, were almost unheard of among the Zulus. Cancer was also decidedly rare.

A few cases of cancer, such as those more common in America, nevertheless did occur. Once a very pleasant young native woman of twenty-five came to me with a lump in her left breast, which I removed and sent to a pathologist. Though his report indicated it was a benign tumor, the young woman was back within six months, her breast enlarged with a growth that was definitely cancerous. It was necessary to remove the breast and all suspicious tissue leading into the abdomen and arm. Yet even after this thorough job, the right breast had later to be removed, and the case ran into a typical sarcoma involvement which caused the girl's death.

A more difficult case of this kind was that of a young girl who had sarcoma in the right side of her upper jaw. She was a very pretty girl, so pretty in fact that she had a suitor quite willing to overlook the swelling in her face, caused by the disease. The boy's father, who was less tolerant, refused to pay the regulation ten cattle for the girl until this defect was removed.

So the girl's father brought his daughter to me. His reasoning might appear cold-blooded, but it was scarcely more so than a calculating Frenchman trying to find a daughter-in-law who would bring a fat dowry. He knew I'd operate on his daughter for $10 or $15, while the girl would bring cattle worth from $200 to $300, so his gain beyond the cost of the operation would be considerable.

There was, unfortunately, no South African surgeon better qualified than I was to undertake this particular operation. I wished most heartily there had been, for I recognized the risks of hemorrhage. For days I went through my usual uneasy preparation for a new and difficult operation, until I was familiar with each step that must be taken.

The operation itself was a relief after the mental turmoil that preceded it. Everything went as planned. As soon as my patient was unconscious, I inserted a tracheotomy tube, both for breathing and for administering the anesthesia; tied off all bleeding vessels; controlled the carotid artery with a ligature; and within a relatively brief time the diseased bone was out.

Surprisingly enough, the girl's appearance was afterward little marred. Only by looking at her from the right side would you notice the slight depression of her cheek. Since she was an intelligent girl, and anxious to marry, she faced her prospective father-in-law squarely when he came to inspect her, and she kept her mouth closed so that he would not notice the missing teeth on one side. Well pleased with the girl, he willingly paid ten cattle to her father.

The girl and her sweetheart were married a short time later, and a very happy marriage it was. Nor was there any reoccurrence of the sarcoma, so far as I know, to trouble the couple in after years.

The cottage hospital, originally intended as a temporary expedient, was to serve the Zulus for five years in such difficult childbirth and surgical cases as I have described. All during those years, it was so crowded that it was usually necessary to discharge one patient before another could be admitted. Long before there were any means to build the larger Zulu hospital I dreamed of, the cottage hospital had been outgrown. But it had played an important rôle, filling a medical gap as the first native hospital in Natal, teaching the Zulus that a hospital was not a place they need fear.

It's human habit to imagine that mere enlargement

of our earlier efforts will necessarily bring greater happiness. Years and sobering experience dispel this notion. I know now that some of my best years were spent in the little cottage hospital, serving my apprenticeship as a surgeon. There the problems of surgery, of Zulu psychology, of hospital management all had the fresh, untrammeled quality of an unfamiliar road you are discovering for the first time; each new piece of equipment, bought by scrimping and planning, was unwrapped upon its arrival with feverish excitement.

In time every turn, every view on the road was to become familiar; it was to lose its unexplored quality, and when that time came the delivery of crates of equipment left us untouched by the zest we'd felt when a single new and badly needed instrument reached the cottage hospital. Yet there were new problems ahead, many of them, and so part of the happiness of traveling that new road was undoubtedly due to the period of our lives in which the journey was made.

Youth was with us on that journey.

CHAPTER EIGHT

BAMBATA'S REBELLION

THE YEAR AFTER I OPENED MY COTTAGE HOSPITAL, the Natal Government, in seeking new sources of revenue, enacted a poll tax to make the Zulus bear part of the cost of being governed. Normally a law-abiding people, they were more puzzled than annoyed by this taxation. In one district a small group went to the local magistrate to inquire the meaning of a poll tax, and he, most unfortunately, informed them it was a "head tax," an explanation the natives took literally.

The Zulus would not have objected to a tax on their huts, on their cattle, or even on their possessions, but they were outraged at having their heads taxed. And when the delegation reported to their chief on what they conceived to be the nature of the tax, he was equally indignant and called a council of other chiefs. From a consideration of the new tax, discussion ran to other grievances against the whites until feeling reached an explosive stage.

This feeling spread from tribe to tribe, from kraal to kraal, until the natives of large parts of Natal and Zululand were in an excitable state. At Henley a magistrate trying to collect the poll tax was met by twenty-seven armed Zulus who not only refused payment but dared the few police accompanying the magistrate to attempt collection. Chief Gobisembe and a thousand of his warriors arrived at Mapumulo on the day appointed for payment of the tax and, after refusing to comply, threatened both the magistrate and the Government. Similar incidents occurred in all parts of the province, strong indication that only a spark was needed to ignite the countryside.

This spark was provided a year later by a tribe known as the Zondis, The Haters. Chief of the Zondis was the quarrelsome Bambata, a man of uncontrollable temper who fought constantly with his neighbors and frequently stole their cattle. The Natal Government decided there was already too much unrest without the trouble he stirred up, so they deposed him and made his uncle chief. Bambata, not a man to take calmly this loss of face, held a secret meeting of the most hotheaded younger warriors of his tribe one night, and persuaded them to help him regain his former power. They surprised the sleeping uncle, kidnaped him, and held him under heavy guard.

When word of this reached the Government at Pietermaritzburg, a magistrate and several policemen were sent to Keat's Drift to investigate. They were stopped just short of their destination by Bambata and his warriors. The latter fired a few shots, but apparently without intent to kill, for no one was injured. The reason for their halfhearted attack may be explained by the Zulu respect for the law. The magistrate had only enough policemen to enforce an ordinary arrest, thus making his party appear to the natives to be nothing more than a law-enforcement body, and hence claiming their begrudging respect.

The large cordon of police sent out in charge of Colonel Mansel a few days later, however, they viewed in quite a different light. Both the presence of an officer and the size of the force convinced them that this was a military and not a civilian body, and a hostile army was always fair prey. Bambata's men attacked fiercely, only their erratic marksmanship sparing the smaller Government contingent from heavy losses as it fell back in an orderly rear-guard action. To the native warriors, unfamiliar with the finer points of military tactics, this looked like a hurried retreat. They sought to make it even more so by pressing their attack, causing a number of casualties among Mansel's force before it eventually escaped.

Such a skirmish could not have occurred at a less favorable time. The account of Bambata's defeat of a Government "army" lost nothing in the telling as it spread among tribes already inflamed by the injustice of "taxing a man's head." Though older men advised caution, younger Zulus drifted away from their home districts in small groups to join Bambata's growing army. Made bold by so much support, Bambata now defied the Government. And his warriors hunted for stray white soldiers, believing their blood could be made by the witch doctors into a "medicine" which, when applied to Zulu bodies, would turn aside the bullets of the whites. Thus began the uprising known as Bambata's Rebellion.

The white settlers of Natal are of the same British and Dutch blood lines as the early American colonists, and their descendants are remarkably like Americans in many ways, particularly in their spirit of independence. It was this independent spirit which made the Natal Government desirous of putting down Bambata's Rebellion without help from the mother country. To eliminate

the need for such assistance, there were organized the
Natal Mounted Rifles, the Zululand Mounted Rifles,
the Durban Light Infantry, the Natal Rangers, the Natal
Field Artillery and numerous other regiments, including a modest one composed largely of loyal natives,
both heathen and Christian, known as the Natal Native
Horse.

Since a medical corps was needed, Dr. Hyslop of
the Government hospital at Pietermaritzburg was made
surgeon general of the citizen army, with power to enlist a staff and to purchase needed medical supplies and
equipment. Dr. Pearson, who promptly enlisted and was
made a captain, suggested to Surgeon-General Hyslop that
I might prove useful because of my knowledge of and
interest in the Zulus. He warned his superior, however,
that as an American, I would refuse to swear allegiance
to the king. Choosing to overlook this detail in his need
for medical officers, Hyslop offered me a commission.

True, I couldn't have sworn allegiance to the king,
but an even more troublesome question was whether a
missionary doctor should take sides in a conflict against
the rebellious Zulus. I was as deeply concerned for their
welfare as for that of the loyal natives. What eventually
decided me were rumors of inhumane treatment received
by the first rebels captured. Feeling I might make their
lot easier, I enlisted and was commissioned a captain in
the Natal Native Horse.

Margaret and our four children were at the time
visiting Norwegian missionaries, our friends the Astrups
at Untunjambili Mission, within sight of Bambata's
kraal. Writing her of the step I'd taken, I advised her to
remain there, because the countryside was overrun by
Zulu war parties. She disregarded this advice. Like any
other woman whose man is going to war, she wished to

see her husband for what she feared might be the last
time.

Bishop Johannes Astrup could not accompany Margaret because he felt it his duty to protect the mission
property. Nor did he think it necessary to leave. He and
his wife were then in their seventies, and because of
their years of service and their awe-inspiring size and that
of their son and three daughters, they were venerated
by the Zulus. The Astrups were all giants, ranging from
Caroline, who was five-feet-eight and the midget of the
family, up to the son and father, who were both six-feet-
three. Bambata had promised that they would not be
molested if they stayed at the mission, and the Astrups
believed he'd keep his word. Bishop Astrup, in fact, sometimes sat on his veranda watching parties of Zulu warriors passing by. None either bothered him or touched
any mission property.

Lack of an escort, however, failed to discourage
Margaret. She bundled the children into an oxcart, and
with an old native driver started for Greytown. Not far
on their way, they were surrounded by warriors decorated
with feathers and reed bracelets, carrying large war-
shields, and armed with *assegais* and large headed clubs
known as knob-kerries. These weapons, more effective in
native hands than guns, they used to threaten the terri-
fied old driver, until he stopped. A thorough search was
then made of the oxcart. The Zulus appeared disappointed to find neither soldiers nor policemen hidden under the blankets, for their warriors' pride made it impossible for them to fight women or children or a harmless
old man.

When Margaret explained that she was the wife of
Dr. McCord, the Zulus, who knew the name, nodded
understandingly, and bidding her a courteous *"Salani*

kahle"—"Stay well"—they waved their weapons and
went on their way.

The oxcart was stopped numerous times by roving
war parties, but never once did my family receive anything but courteous treatment.

They found Greytown in *laager*—a Boer term originally meaning the drawing of wagons into a circle in defense against native attack, before the word gained
broader usage. A circular barrier of barbed wire replaced
the wagons in Greytown, this entanglement enclosing
the church and a central portion of the city. Women and
children had gone into *laager* in the church, but the
townsmen went about their business beyond the entanglements, assured that the scouts on the outskirts
would warn them in time should there be an attack.

An engine with one empty coach was about to attempt the run to Durban, but all our Greytown friends
advised Margaret not to take it. They were certain that
Bambata's warriors would roll rocks onto the tracks to
wreck the train, and then kill anyone who survived. Margaret, ignoring this good advice, went to the railroad
station to talk to the engineer. He also tried to dissuade
her from making the trip, pointing out that he could
offer her and the children no protection because the
train's single guard must ride on the cowcatcher to watch
for rocks.

"You can lock us in the coach, can't you?" Margaret
suggested.

That he could do, the engineer agreed glumly, but
of what value were locks when the coach had windows?

"Please lock the doors, then," Margaret said firmly.
"We're going with you."

And so my family were aboard when the train pulled
out of Greytown. It was extremely slow because the en-

gineer never knew when he might have to stop because of a wrecked bridge or an obstruction on the track. Here and there, from the windows, Margaret saw war parties moving single file along hillside trails. But none of these warriors did more than pause to stare at the slowly moving train; it reached Durban unmolested.

Thus I had a few days to spend with my family before the Natal Native Horse moved northward by train to Dundee for several weeks of badly needed training.

There, on the outskirts of the town, which then had a population of less than 3,000, our native regiment had an encampment. None of our natives saw anything incongruous in fighting their own people, for the Zulus have always practiced intertribal warfare. So eager were they to fight, in fact, that it was difficult to persuade them of the necessity for training in drill, in shooting their breech-loading carbines, in learning horsemanship. Very raw troops, they could more correctly be called "mounted infantry" than "cavalrymen," but they were only a little more green than most of their officers.

Officers were selected for our regiment on the basis of their knowledge of the Zulu language and people rather than for military experience. Our commander, Major Moe, son of a missionary, was however a captain in the regular army. Speaking Zulu as if it were his native tongue, he was a dashing figure of a soldier . . . wearing his hat at a rakish angle, riding like a cavalryman, and impressing the Zulus no end by his military bearing.

Second in command was Captain R. C. A. Samuelson, likewise the son of a missionary and an officer who had served in other campaigns. Samuelson was a heavy, phlegmatic Pietermaritzburg lawyer, who sat in his saddle with scarcely more grace than a sack of cement. From sore experience in previous Zulu wars, he had none of

Major Moe's confidence in an easy victory, and he had deep respect for the Zulu both as a fighter and a military strategist. Samuelson drove the three white lieutenants under him unmercifully until the men of the Natal Native Horse could drill, ride and shoot with at least passable skill. He also bore down on the quartermaster when supplies were short or likely to be; and at times when there was a slight delay in building latrines, his comments to me were more than a gentle reminder. Samuelson was not a picturesque soldier, but he was a good one, both his military experience and his civilian viewpoint making him an invaluable officer for such a regiment as ours.

Our companies were all led by native chiefs, and the leader of the mission Zulus' company was Chief Stephen Mini, a tall and serious native who spoke English with the utmost precision. Chief Mini held that the rebellion was against the king and not the Natal Government. For that reason, he believed redcoats should do the fighting, maintaining that Bambata's warriors would lay down their arms and flee at sight of a British regular's red jacket. Captain Samuelson scoffed at this view, and could prove his point by describing the Zulu War of 1879, in which he had engaged—a campaign where redcoats had been liberally represented, and had not discouraged Zulus who had taken the warpath.

Reports on the progress of the war reached us at Dundee. Here and there our forces fought pitched battles with Bambata's. The Zulu rebels, certain that medicine made from white men's blood and rubbed on their bodies would protect them from bullets, unhesitatingly charged Government riflemen and machine gunners, to fall by the hundreds. Many such engagements were fought before the rebels began to question the protection offered by their witch doctors' medicine.

The men of the Natal Native Horse were impatient to join this fighting. At last several companies of our heathen troops—who were least tractable to training and most anxious to do battle—were called into service. They engaged in some active fighting. By the time the mission Zulus were called up, several weeks later, little was left to do but round up the remnants of the rebel forces, still roaming the countryside in small bands.

Through an oversight so common, apparently, to any army, I was not ordered forward with my regiment, and so the last of the Natal Native Horse went into action without a medical officer. I had to await an order from the Medical Corps, and it was necessary to jog the memory of the Surgeon-General several times before it was given.

This time was not, however, spent in idleness. I had a chance to visit Dundee friends, and both before and after the departure of my regiment, I was assigned to other regiments on occasions to replace a medical officer who was ill or away on other duties.

Among these assignments was a period of three days spent as medical officer of Royston's Horse, a white regiment. Royston's Horse was composed largely of hard-riding, hard-drinking young troopers who looked upon war as a pleasant interlude from the restrictions of civilian life. They were eager to get back into battle in order to shoot "Kaffirs," for they regarded the ugly business of war about as a duck hunter regards the shooting of ducks. Tales I heard while among them sickened me. Many of the prisoners taken, whether warriors or non-combatants, were brought up at the rear on a march, and irresistible opportunities were offered for their escape.

Guards would then, with enthusiasm, shoot the escapees. None ever got away.

This was in sharp contrast to the treatment Bambata's rebels had accorded my family and missionaries remaining in the war zone. No missionary or his property was touched while he was at his station. And though there was looting in some cases where missionaries were ordered to go into *laager* in cities, considerable doubt existed as to whether this was done by rebels. Probably one reason missionaries were ordered to leave the fighting zone as the war progressed was their strong protests against the inhumane treatment of prisoners. These protests, winning them no sympathy from Natal's white residents, were termed calumny against the defenders of the province. Headquarters, of course, did not countenance the shooting of prisoners. But the top officers found it difficult to enforce regulations in an undisciplined, nonprofessional army.

Assignments to regiments in which there was a large proportion of youthful Colonial rowdies made me realize that the Zulus of the Natal Native Horse were, by comparison, essentially gentle and kindly men. So it was with a feeling of relief that I received my orders to report to my regiment, then fifty miles away in the Qudeni Mountains.

Since only my small native orderly, Alfred, was accompanying me, and much of our way was through hostile country, we traveled light. By hard riding and stops only to allow our horses to drink, we covered half the distance by dark and spent the night at Helpmakaar base camp. The second day's journey was through mountainous terrain, heavily wooded in places and with giant boulders along the slopes to provide possible ambushes. The rebels, determined to resist to the last, were still numerous in this country. Not caring to have my blood used to "doctor" any of Bambata's men, I forced my horse to run whenever we approached clumps of trees, boulders, rocky ledges or any cover that might hide rebel warriors. Alfred ignored my horse's dust to ride close behind.

We were still far from our destination when the shadows of the mountains spread across the rolling veld. Presently, as we entered a deep gorge, the light began to fail. We urged our tired horses into a gallop, not wishing to be overtaken by darkness in a location so ideal for ambush. The thud of our mounts' hooves echoed eerily in the stillness. Occasionally, as the dust thickened, we were badly startled by the whir of night birds. And then at last we saw Madhlozi Mountain, the legendary "Mountain of the Spirits" which natives believe is the home of the dead. At its base we spied, like a host of fireflies, the flickering lights of many campfires.

We soon stopped our weary horses at the command of a sentry. Recognizing me, he ordered us to pass on. Without regret, I turned my horse over to Alfred to tether, and limped to a rock to eat my supper. It consisted of two ship's biscuits, biscuits so hard that I had to pulverize them between rocks before they could be eaten. But no meal before or since ever tasted better. By the time I'd finished, most of the men had rolled up in their blankets beside the glowing embers of dying campfires to escape the needling cold. I chose a deeply worn cattle trail instead, hoping that its high sides would afford greater protection from the brisk wind. And then, after being comfortably settled, I wondered whether to trust the common belief that cattle stepped over anything in their path. The deep dust felt so soothing to my saddle-sore and aching body, however, that I decided to take the risk, and fell at once into the drugged sleep of exhaustion.

Orders came the next day to fall back to Rorke's Drift, within the Natal border, the rebellion by then being so well under control that headquarters felt the services of the Natal Native Horse would not be needed. After another long day's ride, we reached an encampment enclosed by barbed wire. It offered sufficient protection so that Alfred could erect a seven-by-three-foot tent and I could afford the luxury of removing my shoes before crawling into it.

I must have slept five or six hours before being awakened by running men. An excited voice near my tent was shouting, "Wake up, you beggars, the Zulus are attacking!" I found my small, cramped tent much easier to get out of than it had been to enter.

Around me stood shadowy figures. Rifles rattled as men loaded their pieces. Here and there a soldier flitted by, gun in hand, as he hurried toward the gate of the enclosure.

"What did the sentry fire at?" a soldier near me called to a man running in the opposite direction.

The man replied in Zulu. "He saw rebels creeping up on our camp."

The soldiers near-by started toward the trenches, close to the gate, and I followed. We tumbled into a trench and waited. I began to long for my shoes and blanket, for it was bitterly chill. As I stood there, shivering, I thought of what the passing native had said. It seemed strange that Bambata's men would creep stealthily up to our camp like American Indians. From all I'd heard, Zulus tried to terrify their enemies with war whoops in making an assault.

After a long period of waiting, a lieutenant went out with a mounted patrol to reconnoitre. Occasionally their figures were visible as they rode around the *laager*. They

circled the entire barbed wire enclosure without finding
any enemies, then grew bolder and made a wider circle,
and still another, even more distant from the encampment. Still they found no lurking rebels.

Enboldened by this and by the first light of dawn,
a few soldiers ventured out through the gate. Suddenly a
man shouted, and a group soon surrounded him. The
man had found the tracks of an ant bear, which had
been digging for white ants. It had been the cause of the
nervous sentry's shot, and he was not likely to hear the
last of it so long as he lived.

Because the men of the regiment were for the most
part young and healthy, my medical duties were light.
I directed the building of latrines, pulled infected teeth,
treated diarrhea and dysentery, and gave cathartics to
relieve the distress caused by the rough camp fare. I also
treated a number of cases of bilharziasis, which had resulted from bathing in water infected by pollution.

Bilharziasis is relatively common in South Africa, and
I'd frequently encountered the disease at Adams Mission and in my Durban dispensary. It is caused by parasitic
flukes which pass one phase of their lives in the human
body, another in any one of several types of fresh-water
snails.

The microscopic bilharzia larvae have an affinity for
human skin and mucous membranes and, after penetrat-
ing the body of a bather, are carried by the blood stream
to the lungs and eventually to the liver, where they mature. Some crawl down the abdominal veins to the bladder wall and there lay their eggs, which then enlarge and
burst into the bladder, causing bleeding and extreme pain.
Painful elimination and the passing of blood are, in fact,
the principal symptoms of the disease. If a river or stream

is polluted by an infected person, the eggs hatch into embryos in the water, find their way to snails, and then develop into larvae which in time rupture the snail and are then ready once more to attack any human taking a dip.

At Adams I had studied the flukes under my microscope, but without discovering anything useful in treating the disease. Medicine then given for bilharziasis had not the slightest effect on it, but having nothing better, I felt obliged to use it. Once in preparing it, however, I added methylene blue, which would make my patient pass blue water and convince him that he was taking powerful medicine. To my astonishment, the patient returned a month later to report that the medicine had indeed great power. All his symptoms of bilharziasis had disappeared.

To determine whether this was mere chance, I tried the dosage on other patients, always with the same result. Then I eliminated the medicine entirely, using only methylene blue. The patient would pass blue urine for a while, and invariably all symptoms of the disease would vanish, usually within a month. I know of no reason why anything as mild as methylene blue should be so effective. But since it cleared up every case of bilharziasis that I treated, I was able in time to promise a cure for anyone so afflicted.

So when our native troops came to my hospital tent, complaining that they found it painful to pass water, and that it contained blood, I would make an examination for bilharziasis. If a soldier was suffering from the disease, I gave him a bottle of the "blue medicine." In every case it brought about recovery in the usual period of a month. . . .

One day a patrol was sent to a near-by village where

a few rebel stragglers had been seen. I rode with the patrol to care for any men who might be wounded. We found nothing but several empty kraals dotting the steep hillside, showing no signs of recent occupation. Though it seemed rather pointless, the lieutenant in charge insisted on burning the huts to prevent their use.

Among the mounted natives was a thin, stooped Zulu who coughed constantly as we rode along. Upon our return, I asked him to come to my tent. After tethering his horse, he did so. By questioning, I learned that he was Ushumela (Shoe-Mender), a Greytown cobbler. Prosperous by native standards, he owned a small house, with an open porch. An examination disclosed that he was running a temperature, and his lungs showed the first stage of tuberculosis. Recovery was unlikely while he led the active life of a soldier, so I arranged for his discharge and sent him home. Ushumela promised me that he would follow a prescribed diet and screen his porch and sleep there until his lungs healed.

Not long thereafter Bambata was killed, and his thousands of followers were either shot or captured. Punishment of the rebels was severe; their homes were burned and their cattle confiscated. The Natal Native Horse and other regiments organized to put down the rebellion were then disbanded, and I returned to my practice.

But years later I was to have a curious reminder of my part in Bambata's Rebellion when a native woman brought her sick daughter to my dispensary. While examining the girl, I asked the mother her name, and the name and occupation of her husband. Her answer to the latter question surprised me, recalling a patient I'd forgotten. She seemed a little astonished when I inquired about her husband's health.

"He is a strong man, and a good provider," she assured me.

I nodded, and put my instruments away.

"Your daughter has tuberculosis—a sickness of the lungs. Though it is a strong disease, it will leave your daughter if you feed her the food I recommend, and have her sleep on your porch."

The woman offered no objection to the diet suggested, but she was shocked at the idea of her daughter sleeping on the porch. "My husband would never hear of it. He knows, as I do, that night air is dangerous."

I smiled. "I don't believe he'll object. And it's the only way your daughter can be made well."

"My husband would never permit it," the woman insisted.

"I'm sure he will," I said, smiling. "You ask him."

"I will," said the mother, shaking her head. "But it will do no good. I know!"

Months later she brought back her daughter for an examination. The girl's lungs showed noticeable improvement.

"Your daughter has been sleeping on the porch, I see."

The mother nodded, giving me an odd glance. "But how did you know my husband would permit this strange thing? He made no objection—no objection whatever— which is hard to understand."

I smiled but offered no explanation, since it would have revealed a secret the woman's husband apparently wished to keep. Ushumela, I'd felt certain, was one native father who wouldn't jeopardize his daughter's chances by the usual Zulu prejudice against night air.

CHAPTER NINE

DURBAN FIGHTS
MY ZULU HOSPITAL

AN OLDER AND MORE EXPERIENCED MAN THAN MYSELF might have foreseen the strong opposition that would be aroused by an attempt to build a Zulu hospital in a part of Durban reserved for the white community. While I never took the step with the intent of challenging the practice of segregation, the effect was the same. The strong prejudices of an influential section of Durban were stirred up, and the hospital became the storm center of a long and bitter controversy.

If this "teapot tempest" failed to reach heights that could be called sublime, it did on occasions approach the ridiculous. Interspersed between legal maneuvers, courtroom trials and protest meetings were incidents reminiscent of the back yard bickering of bad neighbors. Certain of these incidents might have seemed amusing if the outcome of the controversy had been less serious.

Underlying the conflict were circumstances beyond my control. One of these was Durban's place on the map. By being more accessible to the Zulus than any other Natal city, it was the ideal location for a native hospital.

And the Greyville section of Durban, perhaps the logical place to build, was already congested with Zulus, Indians and half-castes, giving the property of that section an artificially high value. To buy enough land there for a hospital and allow for future expansion, I would have to purchase and demolish existing buildings, an extravagance I couldn't afford.

So when the cottage hospital proved too small for Zulu needs, and my mother and her brother providentially loaned me money to erect the first unit of a permanent building, Margaret and I began to look for less expensive property in other parts of the city. We thought we'd be able to buy, at a modest figure, enough land on which to erect our own home and a hospital as well. We had saved $2,000 earned in practice at Lake City and now intended to apply it as a down payment on our home. The hospital could be started when the new dispensary had paid for itself. But when we went property-hunting, these plans were given a chill reception.

Oh, there were sites a-plenty, even spacious sites with beautiful outlooks of the harbor and the Indian Ocean. For in Durban, rising from tidewater to 3,000 feet at the crest of Berea Hill, views are the rule rather than the exception. But to possess these scenic advantages, we were asked a price dear for those days. Property sufficient for our needs would cost $10,000 to $15,000. This was disheartening, for if I paid so much just for land, there would be nothing left or worse, an actual deficit, before even the foundation of a hospital was laid.

In the hope of finding a more reasonable site, we then looked at property outside the city limits. At last we located a piece, slightly less than an acre in size, which seemed exactly right. And although we were not insistent upon a view, this property had a magnificent one. It looked down upon the city and a broad sweep of the ocean. At night, when the hospital was built, we could visualize convalescing patients lying in their beds and watching the lighthouse at the point of the harbor blinking its warning to ships at sea. The price would fit our budget, and we didn't think there would be any objection to a hospital in the neighborhood since there was already a nursing home for whites but a hundred yards farther up the slope.

Still, there might be another objection. On the few occasions when we'd found property within our means, the owners had refused to sell after we explained how we intended to use it. So now again I explained my plans for building a home and a Zulu hospital on the land. The agent, who in this case was also the partner of the owner, offered no objection. More than that, he assured us the site was well suited to our purposes. Of that we were already convinced!

Papers were signed, money changed hands, and a friend loaned me $4,000 which, added to our money in hand, gave us enough to build a comfortable home on the property. In the closing months of the same year of 1906, work was started on the hospital. Construction was only well begun, however, when an influential group of Durbanites mobilized forces to oppose my plans.

Leading the opposition was J. Ellis-Brown, a wealthy coffee merchant and the mayor of Durban. At a meeting he called, and to which I was not invited, many of my prominent neighbors lent their wholehearted support. Foremost among them was Dr. Samuel Campbell and Dr. Archibald McKenzie, who ran the nursing home for whites and did not wish a Zulu hospital located near it; two of Natal's outstanding lawyers, Messrs. A. D. Millar and W. Kimber; and a brother-in-law of a Justice of the

Supreme Court. Likewise attending, upon request and to explain his action, was the former owner of the property.

This latter gentleman, whose partner had been fully informed of my reasons for buying the piece, now attempted to squirm out of the responsibility for his act by denying that he'd known I intended to erect a Zulu hospital. This explanation was accepted, and the meeting went on to consider the means to prevent me from carrying out my plans. The proposal which met with the most general approval was for the influential citizens at the meeting to bring pressure on the Town Council to refuse my application when I applied for water connections with the city mains. When it was suggested that I might fight this measure, a woman rose to reassure the gathering. She was sure that a missionary wouldn't fight. A committee was then formed to draw up a paper to be termed "A Timely Warning."

Of all this I knew nothing until several mornings later, when I was inspecting the construction work. Two neighbors, Dr. Sam Campbell and Mr. Butcher, appeared while I was walking through the partially constructed building. With stiff dignity and in a manner soberly reproving, they spoke of the protest meeting and of the timely warning I was about to receive. I must stop work at once, they advised me, and if I ignored their neighborly advice, they would take legal steps to see that I did.

I've never taken kindly to coercion. My Irish blood grew exceedingly warm, and my Scotch stubbornness planted its heels. Yet with something of an effort, I explained without heat that I'd already received legal advice to the effect that I was acting within my rights. Why, I asked, had they waited so long to make this protest, when my intentions had never been a secret? Now that my home was built and the hospital under way, I was going to continue with my plans. To stop now would end my usefulness, my whole program of laying a solid foundation for Zulu medical care.

Calmly and with a politeness that bristled, we discussed the matter, in the end bowing and smiling at the gate, but without having come any closer to agreement.

Shortly after this visit, the opposition requested my plans. Having nothing to hide, I allowed my architect to send them a copy. These plans were for a hospital with two wings and forty-eight beds, ambitious plans I'd had my architect draw as a goal toward which to work. The much smaller single unit we were then building was marked off from the proposed structure by red lines. Troubled by the problem of sewage disposal after viewing the finished blueprints, I'd taken them to the Durban Health Officer to ask his advice, and he'd drawn a rough sketch of a septic tank which he said would satisfactorily dispose of sewage.

These plans, showing a large structure and a crude sketch of a small septic tank, were ammunition in the opposition's hands. And on the misleading points, they based their plea to the Supreme Court of Natal for an injunction to stop work on the hospital. Numerous objections were raised in the plea. The opposition claimed that the hospital would obstruct the view; block the cool ocean breeze; jeopardize the health of the community (the patients in the white nursing home up the hill presumably subjecting it to no such risk); be a nuisance because of noisy native patients; spread contagion because I had no water connections and could not keep patients or hospital clean; and menace health because of inadequate sewage disposal.

The Supreme Court promptly served me with an injunction restraining me from any further construction

work until those opposing the hospital had time to prepare a case. The hearing was scheduled for six months
later, and even if I won, that meant a long delay in finish-
ing the work.

I went at once to my lawyer, and suggested that since
the injunction was based on plans for a larger building
than I was constructing and on a crude sketch of a septic
tank for a smaller building, that it might be well to have
new plans made of the actual structure and of a septic
tank designed by a specialist. With such blueprints, I
could explain to the opposition that I had no intention of
taking more patients than could properly be handled.
Lack of running water was, of course, the opposition's
fault and not mine.

My lawyer listened with set face, and then brusquely
informed me that I'd already done too much talking. In
the future, he advised me coldly, it would be wiser to let
him do the talking and to handle the case in his own way.
He added that the injunction forebade the construction
of a hospital, regardless of plans, and that the opposition
must defend its request for a permanent injunction on the
basis of any plans we submitted. This seemed like a pre-
carious assumption, but assuming that my lawyer knew
his way around in legal matters, I let it rest there.

Before the hearing could be held, Bambata's Rebellion broke out, and I left Durban to serve with the Natal
Native Horse. But I was allowed leave to attend the hearing. A specialist in septic tanks was brought from Johannesburg to testify, and because one of the justices felt
indisposed, and the hearing was postponed several weeks,
it cost me several hundred dollars to pay for the travel
and wasted time of this expert.

Another leave was granted me when the case actually

came to trial. Dr. Bray, undaunted by the calibre of the citizens opposing me, appeared to testify. He, as well as Margaret, our lawyer and other witnesses, sat at the defendant's table.

Witness after witness took the stand and, in the British manner, addressed the Chief Justice with a respectful, "M'Lord," before launching into testimony that became more tiresome and repetitious as the hearing progressed. When it was my turn to testify, I omitted the formal salutation—until the shocked faces in the courtroom reminded me of my error. Then, with my face burning, I corrected myself with a flurry of embarrassment, "Oh, *my* Lord!"

Dr. Bray's chortle broke upon the suddenly still courtroom, and with his sides quaking, he turned to murmur audibly to Margaret: "I never expected to hear Dr. McCord swear."

Everyone was laughing by then at my discomfiture, the most hearty laughter of all coming from the Chief Justice. Turning to me, he said with amusement, "I see your American tongue does not easily adapt to our formal mode of address, so we will excuse you, Doctor."

This was the only light interlude in a drab trial. The plaintiffs hammered away at the health menace of a forty-eight-bed native hospital in the community. My lawyer based his defense on the fact that the opposition complained of a hospital built according to one set of plans while I was building with an entirely different set, and as a consequence, he told the court, he had no intention of defending the plans of which the plaintiffs complained.

At last the Chief Justice said, "We seem to be talking at cross-purposes. The plaintiffs are speaking of one set of plans; the defendants of another. Court will be recessed while it gives the matter consideration."

No judgment was passed for several days. Then one morning, while still on leave from my regiment, I read the Chief Justice's decision in my morning paper. Briefly the decision was that since the plaintiffs based their case on plans drawn by Dr. McCord's architect and these plans were not defended, judgment was rendered to the plaintiffs and the injunction against the hospital was made permanent.

Until you become involved in litigation, you're likely to think of justice as a fair decision based on law. Actually, the human factor may influence justice as it does our other affairs. In this, my first experience with the courts, I had failed to attach any importance to the fact that the Chief Justice was a close personal friend of Mayor J. Ellis-Brown and also of Doctors Campbell and McKenzie. Another justice was the brother-in-law of one of my most determined opponents. Whether these relationships were significant may be judged by the refusal of the third justice to have any part in the decision rendered.

I was still simmering at what I considered an injustice when the evening paper reached my home. Splashed across the front page was a remarkably good caricature of J. Ellis-Brown sweeping a hospital from the summit of Berea Hill. Below the cartoon was a limerick:

> A bold doctor of Durban one day
> Did a home for sick niggers essay
>   On Berea expected
>   To have it erected
> Now his plans are all swept away.

Was it true that my plans were all swept away?

I sat down with the paper to study the full decision of the Chief Justice, which consisted of two parts, the judgment of the court and its restraining order. The first part referred to the plans furnished by my architect, and only to those plans. The second part, the order of the court, forebade me from erecting any building whatsoever that might be used for a Zulu hospital. It required no judicial mind to see that the judgment and the order of the court referred to quite different things.

Although loss of the trial would force me to pay $4,500 in court and legal costs, and I'd never had confidence in my lawyer's plan of defense, I said nothing of this when I took the paper to his office in the morning to show him the discrepancy in the decision. Seeing my point at once, he said that our remaining recourse was an appeal to the Privy Council in England, in effect the Supreme Court of the British Empire. I asked him to make this appeal through a King's Counsel in England, and there for a time matters rested.

Throughout the long controversy, Margaret and I lived in outwardly friendly relations with our neighbors, though in minor ways we were made to feel their displeasure.

The attorney Mr. Kimber, whose property adjoined ours, had taken an active part in opposing the hospital, and in spite of his frigidly courteous manner, he never left us in doubt of his attitude. Shortly after the first opposition meeting, he suggested that since we saw matters in a different light, it might prevent conflict if we built a high cyclone fence on the survey line to prevent encroachment on one another's property. To this, I agreed.

One morning, when I went out to see how this fence was progressing, I found Mr. Kimber in pajamas making a similar inspection. We greeted each other courteously, if not warmly, and when his cook boy brought his morning cup of tea, he sent the boy back to the house for another cup for me.

As we stood sipping our tea and discussing the day's news, two of my children, Jessie and Robert, came scampering to join us. They smiled up warmly at Mr. Kimber, for to them all neighbors were friends. Thawed by this sweet childhood trust, Mr. Kimber asked the youngsters if they liked dogs. They said that they did.

"I have some new puppies. Why not take a run up to my place to look at them?"

The children needed no further urging. After a time they returned, bright eyed and bubbling with enthusism.

"Would you like a puppy?" Mr. Kimber surprised me by asking. His dogs were thoroughbreds, of which he was very proud, and for which he usually exacted a good price.

Jessie seized one of my hands, and Robert the other. "Oh, can we have one, Daddy?" they clamored.

Knowing that my neighbor entertained no genuine feeling of kindliness for us, I wished to accept no such favor. So I thanked him for his thoughtfulness and declined the dog.

Later a friend heard Kimber express his disappointment that the children could not accept, for he had intended to bill me $25 for the puppy, realizing that it would weaken to that small extent my already shaky financial foundations. . . .

Fresh eggs were not easily found in Durban at the time, and to insure an adequate supply, we, like nearly all our neighbors, kept chickens. These fowl are notoriously disdainful of man-made boundaries, but their trespassing had been looked upon with a lenient eye until the hospital issue made the poor creatures unwitting participants in the dispute. Both Mr. Kimber, the neighbor on one side, and Mr. Jennings, on the other, found the straying tendencies of our chickens trying and warned me that they'd take measures to prevent it.

Presumably the cyclone fence would end the complaints from Mr. Kimber, but before it was finished, Margaret stepped outside one morning to find several of his boys chasing a number of our squawking hens toward their employer's property. When my wife demanded an explanation of this unneighborly act, the boys sheepishly confessed that Mr. Kimber had told them they could eat any of our chickens that strayed onto his property. They were merely making certain that the hens would stray. . . .

Another morning Margaret called me, and I went out to find her near the Jennings' property line, holding a limp chicken. Mr. Jennings had warned us that he'd kill and throw onto our property any of our chickens that wandered onto his grounds, but it seemed a bitter commentary on human relationships that this beautiful rooster would no longer strut proudly among our flock of hens, no longer eat from the children's hands, or crow with the awakening day because of a quarrel that had never concerned it.

Sadly I cut off the head of the rooster, which was still warm, and it appeared, fricasseed, on our table that night. A few hours afterward, when Margaret closed the chicken coop for the night, she found our rooster on his accustomed perch.

Mr. Jennings had wrung the neck of, and we had eaten, Mr. Kimber's prize Rhode Island Red!

One morning my lawyer sent word that he'd heard from the King's Counsel in London, so I called at his office. The King's Counsel had written that our case could not be placed before the Privy Council until we had applied to the Supreme Court of Natal to rectify its mistake in failing to make its order of court agree with the judgment. Until the Natal court had admitted this mistake, and had refused to rectify it, nothing could be done.

My lawyer laughed ironically at the suggestion. "Imagine the Supreme Court admitting such a mistake, which would be an acknowledgment of its own incompetence."

"Even so," I said, "we'll have to try it."

"It will be throwing good money after bad," my attorney warned me.

"Probably true," I agreed. "But my future in Africa depends on winning this case."

Few things are less predictable than legal justice. When our appeal came before the Supreme Court of Natal, the Chief Justice handed down a wordy decision which in effect declared: "Our previous decision having worked a hardship on Dr. McCord, preventing him from building his hospital, we will of course amend our order of court so that he may proceed with the work, but not in accordance with the plans submitted by the plaintiffs in this case." Appended was a somewhat galling afterthought: "And I am sure that if Dr. McCord does erect this hospital, that he will submit his plans to his neighbors for their approval."

My attorney assured the court that I would gladly do so, and while this was not the adverb I'd have chosen, I allowed the point to pass. At least, no hearing before the Privy Council would be necessary.

Having won my fight, I was now at liberty to build a Zulu hospital. The legal battle, however, had taken the entire amount with which I'd hoped to construct it, and more. I was worse off than penniless; I was deeply in debt.

When I first considered building a Zulu hospital, I discussed the project at a meeting of the Natal Mission. Informing my fellow missionaries that I was using private funds, I explained that the hospital would be in my name and that I would assume entire responsibility for the work. I asked permission, however, to deduct five per cent from the funds of the Medical Department of the Mission (of which I was the head) to cover rent, maintenance and other charges, and also to reimburse myself, when the department had funds to spare, for the private capital invested. After the cost of the hospital was repaid, I proposed to turn it over to the Mission, free of all encumbrances.

Pleased at the prospect of acquiring a substantial property at no expenditure of its own funds, the Mission readily assented to these conditions, but made it plain that I must personally be responsible for all sums required by the hospital either during or after construction.

Three years of legal entanglements had undermined my plans.

In searching for a way out of my financial troubles, I thought of $3,000 that the new dispensary had accumulated from patients' fees. Usually, as head of the Medical Department, I spent dispensary funds for instruments, rent, or any other expenses at my own discretion. But now, because of the amount involved, I placed the disposal of these savings before the Mission at its next meeting.

My own capital, I pointed out, had been exhausted in a fight to build the hospital. It was a fight waged for the right to enlarge the medical services available to the Zulus, the same general purpose for which any profits from the dispensary had always been used. Would the Mission therefore approve the use of the $3,000 to meet part of the litigation costs? In return, I would offer it an equity of an equal amount in the hospital.

The missionaries exchanged doubtful glances. A committee was named to consider the proposal, a committee that included every member except myself, and it left the room. Judging by the time it was absent, the matter wasn't easily resolved. The missionaries at last filed in, their faces grave, and sat down. They would not accept my offer, their spokesman told me, because they feared the Mission might become involved in further litigation. They would, however, allow me to apply the $3,000 in dispensary funds against my past litigation expenses providing I abandoned the plan for building a hospital on Berea Hill.

"How in the world," I asked with some warmth, "can I build elsewhere when every cent I possess is tied up in the Berea property?"

Why not, someone suggested, ask the American Board for $10,000 to erect a hospital in another location? The suggestion scarcely deserved a serious answer. The hospital at Adams Missions had proved how impractical it was to run such an institution away from the main channels of travel. And my fellow missionaries should have been as well aware as I was that the American Board could not provide such a sum without stinting missions in other parts of the world; there wasn't a shadow of a chance it would be granted us.

I'm afraid I looked upon my fellow missionaries as timid and disloyal, whereas they were really trying to guard the interests of the Mission and still offer some crumbs of comfort to what they must have regarded as a stubborn and hotheaded young doctor. Rather bluntly, I told them that I would build the Zulu hospital where it had been started. And I added that if I could complete it and continue my work as a member of the Mission, I'd do so, but if not, I would carry on the same medical work for the natives privately.

Once more the missionaries withdrew, leaving me alone long enough for my temperature to decline somewhat. Upon their return, they said that I was at liberty to use the dispensary funds to meet half of the litigation expenses. But the Mission would accept no equity in the hospital. Any further litigation, they warned me, must come from my own pocket. To these terms, I agreed.

The dispensary funds and $2,000 loaned me by a friend in America cleared up the last of the legal expenses. And by obtaining a $4,000 mortgage on the property, we were at last ready to complete the hospital. In plans submitted to my neighbors, however, it was termed a dwelling. The subterfuge, which did not and was not intended to deceive anyone, gave my neighbors, if they so chose, a chance to drop their opposition without loss of face. Apparently they decided to do so, for none raised any objections, and the hospital was completed. For a short time, it was rented, but when my tenant left, I notified my neighbors that I intended to take a few patients. If the patients caused any disturbance, I promised to remedy matters quickly.

The opposition made no issue of this. However, Mr. Kimber watched the hospital closely to make sure that I lived up to my agreement.

One Sunday he called me on the 'phone and, with a triumphant note in his voice, told me that an evil odor came from a shed on my property. He threatened legal steps unless the unsanitary conditions were at once corrected.

I couldn't imagine what there could be in the shed to cause any smell, but rather than dispute the point, I asked my neighbor if he'd meet me at our boundary fence so that we could locate the source of the offensive odor. Gruffly he agreed. After leaving my home and starting toward the fence, I noticed the direction of the wind, and returned to my house for a box of matches.

Mr. Kimber awaited me at the fence. With a smile, I struck a match. The jet of flame flickered toward me because the breeze was blowing across the Kimber estate. My neighbor recognized his mistake at once. His face turned a ruddy color, he cleared his throat several times, and then, with visible effort, muttered an apology.

I suggested that he look in the bushes behind him, for the rank smell came from that direction. He picked up a stick and poked gingerly at the bushes, and presently there emerged a definitely deceased cat, his old pet Persian, which had been missing for days.

Mr. Kimber's complaint was the last gasp of opposition to my hospital that came from any of my neighbors.

CHAPTER TEN

"A HOSPITAL
BY ANY OTHER NAME ♦ ♦ ♦"

OPENING OUR ZULU HOSPITAL COULD VERY WELL HAVE involved us in fresh difficulties with our neighbors. But my wife and I hoped they were as weary of dissension as we were. Even the bitter-enders, we thought, might accept their legal defeat if we could avoid flaunting it in their faces.

Margaret saw a way this might be done. "All the opposition has been to a hospital. Why not call it the Mission Nursing Home—another name for the same thing?" And freely paraphrasing the aphorism on roses, she added, "A Zulu hospital by another name is just as sweet a victory."

And so under that name the hospital we'd dreamed of so many years opened its doors, on May 1, 1909, and not one of our neighbors took any hostile action.

We admitted twelve patients, transferred from the little cottage hospital, on the first day. Male patients were placed in a men's ward, forty feet long and half as wide, which had a dozen beds with excellent spring mattresses. Female patients were lodged in two upstairs women's

179

wards, each holding half a dozen beds. Our patients were at first apprehensive about such luxury, after sleeping all their lives on the ground, but in time they learned to relax in their elevated positions.

As soon as they were settled, Margaret and I walked along the corridors, once more inspecting the hospital. Its spaciousness in comparison with the cottage in Greyville still rather overawed us. The large and well-equipped kitchen, we viewed with particular enthusiasm. There food suitable for invalids could be prepared, something we could never be too sure of when it was cooked by a patient's relatives or friends. These relatives or friends would no longer be needed for that or any other duty. Margaret planned to train native girls as nurses, to dress wounds, give medicines and attend patients' needs.

We stopped to admire and talk about improvements we might later make in the operating room, the comfortable room for missionary patients, and the sizable matron's room. And then we passed on to look into the smaller rooms—a nurses' dormitory and their dining room, an office, and a drug room.

Afterward we went outside to walk over the verandas and balconies, which held a dozen beds and would be a fine place for recuperating patients to lie enjoying the fresh air and sunshine. Since we planned in the beginning to take but a dozen patients, we didn't dream that these outside accommodations would soon be regarded as a necessity rather than a luxury. Very shortly we would be obliged to raise our estimated maximum of a dozen patients to twenty, and even that latter figure was, much of the time, mere wishful planning.

To staff the Mission Nursing Home with meager funds was a problem to be treated lightly, or not at all. A sturdy Scandinavian woman, Miss Nilsen, was engaged to act as housekeeper and cook. I expected to do all medical and surgical work, with what assistance Dr. Bray and Dr. Pearson could give me. And Margaret, never one to shirk a superhuman load, planned to be head nurse, business manager of the institution, and Superintendent of Nurses in charge of training. She was also largely responsible for raising five children, including a son William who had arrived but a short time before (and later six), and for entertaining a flood of visitors.

Visitors were, in fact, the shoals on which her plans backed up. Some dropped in and others stayed for days or even months . . . fellow missionary workers, acquaintances met in back-country jaunts, friends from Durban, from America, or complete strangers with introductory letters from people we'd known. Over 900 visitors (not 900 individuals, of course, because many paid us repeat visits) came to our home every year. Since they were for the most part pleasant people who brought us glimpses of South Africa or of countries beyond, they added interest to our lives and were always welcome. But they were a responsibility that left Margaret too little time to train three native girls in their duties as nurses.

To find even three Zulu girls willing to study nursing had been difficult enough, for none in all South Africa had ever trained for that career before. They were as wary as their parents of any path not worn deeply by other native feet. Two of the girls chose the new path in a spirit of derring-do rather than from any strong urge to become nurses. The third, Elizabeth Njapa, a girl of nineteen, wished to become a nurse in order to support a half-caste daughter of five, born out of wedlock. Elizabeth had not gone beyond the sixth grade in a mission school, where she had been an intelligent and dependable student. Because of her affair my fellow missionaries were fiercely opposed to my taking her into the hospital. Since we could find no substitute, and Elizabeth herself was determined to become a nurse if given the chance, I ignored their objections.

She was plain looking, and matured as she'd been by her experience, she had an air both girlish and maternal. Fine eyes, a warm smile and innately gracious manners gave her at times, however, an appearance of serene comeliness. She was to become one of the most dependable nurses it was ever my experience to work with. But in the beginning, she was not much more than a helper, working under Margaret's guidance, for my wife had scant time to devote to her training.

Patients increased beyond our expectation shortly after the hospital opened, and a nurse was needed to train student nurses and to relieve Margaret of a portion of the ward work.

Before anything could be done to fill this need, word reached me in early October that my father, then nearly eighty, was critically ill and wished to see me before he died. Nothing less urgent could have persuaded me to leave the hospital started only months before, even though my furlough was then three years overdue. Hurriedly Margaret and I closed the hospital, packed, and sailed for America with our children. My father lingered on for several days after I reached his home in Iowa.

A short time later I recalled our need for a nurse, and sent an advertisement to a nurses' journal. The single reply I received was from a Miss Martha S. MacNeill of Florida, who enclosed a photograph of a young woman of almost spiritual beauty. That Miss MacNeill was a young nurse yearning for adventure, or that she had mischievously assumed an expression for the camera that she believed saintly enough to gain her a place on the staff of a mission hospital, did not occur to me. On the strength of her photograph and a letter describing her experience, I engaged Miss MacNeill and asked her to meet us in New York a few days before we sailed.

The Florida nurse appeared on the appointed day. And while the photograph had not exaggerated her beauty, it had given no idea of her pert and mischievous expression or of her small stature. She was but five feet tall and weighed only ninety-nine pounds. The feather-weight size suggested immaturity, and the nurse certainly looked no older than seventeen. I doubted if she were strong enough to move heavy patients in bed, or old enough to assume responsibility. But she assured me that she was extremely strong, and that she was really twenty-three.

Everything she told me was true. What Miss Mac-Neill—or "Mac," as she came to be known—failed to tell us until long afterward was that she'd exaggerated her age to the extent of several years in order to begin her nursing career while still in her mid-teens. Youthful pranks, including the placing of a roughly clothed, man-like dummy under the bed of a nervous new nurse, had nearly caused Mac's dismissal several times. Nevertheless, she'd graduated as a full-fledged nurse at only twenty.

The girl could never have been mistaken for a missionary. But her eagerness and enthusiasm so outweighed this shortcoming that I decided she would do. She returned to South Africa with Margaret and me. Despite Mac's cheerful personality, it was for us a sad passage. South African schools were then unsatisfactory, and we had left three of our children—Jessie, Mary and Robert —with their grandmother, to receive an American education. We had an uneasy feeling that our whole family might never again be together. And that proved true, except for a few brief weeks when I was on furlough in 1918.

Upon our arrival in Durban, we took rickshaws to our home, and we had scarcely stepped into the house before Elizabeth Njapa appeared. The other two girls who had worked in the hospital had found other work, she informed us, but her desire to become a nurse remained unchanged. We introduced her to Mac and the two young women looked at each other with the pleased expectancy of two boarding-school girls sure at first glance that they were going to like each other.

The white nurse was eager to recruit other trainees, so I sent her out to the girls' school at Inanda Mission. There she spoke enthusiastically to the girls about her career, which she regarded as most romantic. Hadn't it brought her to South Africa? Miss Phelps, the principal of the school, and a very practical soul, failed to share this romantic view. And so a clash of personalities developed between the hardheaded principal and the young nurse, taking concrete form in the desire of both to train one particularly promising girl.

The girl was Nomhlatuzi Bhengu, an attractive student with honey-colored skin, and dark-brown eyes that were large and vivacious. Perfect teeth gave her a dazzling smile, and when she sang, her voice had the deep, warm resonance of organ tones. She was in reality a Zulu princess, for her mother had been the "Great Wife" of a chief, the wife chosen to produce a male heir. When she gave birth instead to a girl, and the chief's favorite wife produced a son which died, the woman was charged with witchcraft and driven from the kraal. She came to Inanda Mission, working to pay for her board, and there her daughter Nomhlatuzi was raised. Nomhlatuzi always received from the other girls the deference due a chief's daughter. As a consequence, she had a haughty pride far from desirable in a nurse.

She was Miss Phelps's star pupil, better at her studies than any other girl, and more skillful as well at cooking, crocheting, embroidery work and anything else demanding mental and manual dexterity rather than physical effort. The girl was strongly drawn to Miss MacNeill and to the romance of a nursing career. Miss Phelps warned her that there was then no position open to African nurses, while she could easily find a teaching position because of her scholastic record if she completed her schooling. Nomhlatuzi refused to be guided by this well-intended advice. In the end the principal had to concede defeat.

Another student Miss Phelps was sorry to lose was Julia Magwaza. Her father had been an early convert to Christianity. Practicing its teachings, he had divided a grant of land he inherited in Zululand among the men of his tribe. It was one of the first efforts of a native to help his own people in any such practical and unselfish way.

Later he moved from Zululand to build a home near Inanda, and there his daughters were educated. Julia had the character that was to bring distinction to every one of her brothers and sisters. She was a good student, a girl of irreproachable integrity, yet so quiet and unassuming that it took time to discover her solid and trustworthy traits. She was graduating from the girls' school in a short while. Her father learned the purpose of the nurse's visit, and agreed to allow her to come to the hospital following graduation.

Edna Mzoneli was the only other girl Miss MacNeill could find who cared to study for a nursing career. She had been ill much of the time at Inanda, and not being able to keep pace with the other girls, she'd been sent home. Mac found Edna there—a tall, gaunt and awkward girl, with a cast in one eye. Unhappy at home, and seeing no prospect of either marriage or any other career than nursing, she felt that three years of training under Miss MacNeill could be no worse than other misfortunes which had plagued her. Her father, far from objecting, remarked grumpily that his daughter was too stupid for anything else.

Mac thus had her first class of four probationary nurses. She began with characteristic energy and enthusiasm to train them to take temperatures, to make beds, to bathe and handle patients. Likewise she taught by precept, and her strength being all that she had claimed, her example was strenuous. I had to protest when she came bearing patients half again as large as herself to the operating room. With twenty to as many as thirty patients, Miss MacNeill had little time for classes, but she did write a series of lectures. During off-periods, her green probationers could be found sitting in the halls memorizing these notes.

All the student nurses, except Elizabeth Njapa, were eighteen years old, but at times our little Superintendent of Nurses acted more youthful than her charges. She was more likely than the probationers to giggle at amusing mishaps; she relieved dicipline by mischievous pranks; and she was more effective than an older, more dignified superintendent would have been with young girls. To lighten routine, Mac staged plays that frequently satirized the more serious part of hospital life. And she planned and rehearsed plays and other entertainments with fully as much zest as the student nurses. Nomhlatuzi took the lead in all plays, for nothing Mac could say would persuade any other girl to take a part more important than the chief's daughter.

Under Mac's tutelage, the girls soon became able

nurses—in some respects even better than their instructor. For while Mac was tireless in her efforts when a patient was seriously ill, and never relaxed until the crisis was past, she had little sympathy to spare for those on the road to recovery. With recuperative cases, Julia Magwazi was the better nurse, having infinite patience, and a serene calm that soothed those in her care. They were devoted to her, and almost equally so to Elizabeth Njapa. Elizabeth was given less and less ward work, however, because she was so dependable in the surgery. I could tell her to prepare for an abdominal operation and then dismiss the matter. When I went to the operating room, every instrument, every dressing and suture would be in its place. Her standard of performance was rare enough even among white nurses.

Molding Nomhlatuzi Bhengu, most brilliant of the four, and the tall and awkward Edna Mzoneli to the pattern of a good nurse was more difficult.

Nomhlatuzi expected praise as her royal prerogative and was easily bruised by criticism. Naturally lazy, she performed her duties in the way that gave her the least trouble. Once she placed a hot-water bottle against an unconscious patient's leg without bothering to wrap it in a towel. The patient's leg was burned before the bag was discovered. As a disciplinary measure, Margaret removed Nomhlatuzi from the wards and assigned her for three weeks to kitchen duty. The girl brooded over this treatment, but she saw no way to avenge herself until one day when we were showing Lady Gladstone around the hospital. Nomhlatuzi decided to let the visitor see her wearing the beadwork and bead apron of a heathen maid over her kitchen dress. The plan of the inspection tour was changed at the last moment, and Lady Gladstone was first shown the kitchen, while Nomhlatuzi was in her room putting on her beadwork. The girl was hopefully waiting in the kitchen in her strange attire when she was discovered, long after our visitor had left the hospital. Her disappointment at having failed to give Lady Gladstone a false idea of the hospital was intense. And afterward, when her sister nurses learned of the incident, she found it hard to bear their teasing.

Another time, when we were leaving for church, Nomhlatuzi appeared in a white dress of her own design, cut revealingly low. Margaret sent her back to change into a more suitable dress. In her resentment, the girl reappeared with a high-necked dress of heavy black wool under her white one.

Margaret choked back her laughter. "Why, Nomhlatuzi," she said, trying to keep a straight face, "you must have been reading the fashion magazines. Black and white is the style this year."

It was a sweltering day, and the girl was miserable in the wool dress before the services ended. Style or not, she never repeated the experiment.

Edna Mzonelli was even more of a problem. At Inanda she'd been considered poorly balanced. Frequent spells of weeping or hysteria after she came to the hospital seemed to confirm her teachers' opinion. Her worst outbreak occurred after her sister's baby was born in the hospital. Edna began screaming and flailing her arms as if demented.

Margaret shook her to break the grip of hysteria. "Go to your room, Edna," she then said quietly. "And don't come back until you can behave as a nurse." Her shoulders shaking uncontrollably with sobs, she was led away by two other probationers. Half an hour later she was back, completely composed, to see her sister's child. Apparently the incident impressed on her the stern demands of her career; never again to our knowledge did she weep or give way to hysteria.

None of Miss MacNeill's student nurses was employed in the male ward. For this ward, I was training two orderlies, young men in their early twenties who acted both as helpers and as male nurses. One of these young men, Edward Ntuli, was slow, quiet spoken and in all ways efficient. The other complemented him perfectly by being his exact opposite. Johnathan Shabani, the second orderly, was the son of a preacher, but whereas his father had been known for his good works, Johnathan almost destroyed the Zulus' slowly developing confidence in hospitals.

Not long after I began training the orderlies, Miss MacNeill came running one night to our house. Breathing hard from excitement, she explained that someone had thrown stones through her window. The Zulus had such high regard for the hospital that I thought at first she was joking. Realizing in a few moments that this was not one of her pranks, I followed her back to her room.

Johnathan Shabani stood in the hall, the whites of his eyes showing vividly as he pointed a shaking finger at smoldering places on her floor. I stepped into her room and found in addition to the rocks of which Mac had spoken a number of cinders too hot to hold. Trying her window, I found it still locked. Obviously Mac was mistaken in thinking that the rocks had been thrown from the yard. But it seemed equally improbable that they'd been hurled over the transom, which was open hardly more than an inch.

In spite of his Christian upbringing, Johnathan was inclined to be superstitious, and he now suggested, "Maybe the devil throw them up from his furnace."

"Nonsense!" scoffed Mac, though neither she nor I could think of a more plausible explanation.

Taking a flashlight, I walked around the hospital grounds, but found neither footprints nor vandals.

The following night Johnathan came to my house sputtering with excitement. He claimed that someone had thrown stones into his room from a neighbor's yard. This time I called the police, and when two Zulu policemen arrived, I sent them with Johnathan to search the grounds. He led them to the darkest corner, presumably a good hiding place for hooligans. And while the policemen beat the bushes with their clubs, hot cinders began falling around them from a perfectly clear sky. Several coals burned the hands of the policemen, making them yell. The three men stopped searching and stared skyward, but no more cinders were falling.

Johnathan's teeth began chattering. "*Spirits!*" he whispered hoarsely, and started running.

The policemen easily outdistanced him and soon disappeared.

From then on I had to handle the nightly series of mysterious disturbances without police assistance, for they wanted nothing to do with spirits. Regardless of how often I searched, regardless of what traps I laid, however, I could uncover no clue to the mystery.

Meanwhile our patients were bordering on a state of panic because of the frequent manifestations of "spirits." Johnathan added to their uneasiness by suggesting they place a "tickey" (a thruppence piece) on their bedside tables to find out whether the spirits would accept the bribe to show they meant no harm. Even Mac grew jumpy from strain, and her patients recognized the reason. If a single native had decided to defy the staff and had bolted from the hospital, I imagine every Zulu able to stir would have followed. It would have been hard after that to convince the natives that the hospital wasn't bewitched.

One night of peace we did have, however, when Johnathan was sent on a medical errand. My hope that the hoodlums responsible for the disturbances had tired of their fun was dashed following his return. Stones and hot cinders were thrown through a ward window that night.

I calmed nervous patients as I went my rounds in the morning. Spirits would no longer trouble us, I assured them. Johnathan listened to these reassurances with astonishment.

"How do you know, Dr. McCord?" he finally asked.

"I know all about spirits."

During the remainder of the day, I caught him many times watching me, his wide mouth puckered with a half-suppressed grin.

As the sun began setting, I called him to my office. "I have work for you down town in the dispensary, Johnathan. You'll work there in the future. You'll have time to pack and leave before dark."

He tried to learn my reasons, but I would give none. A short while after he left the office, Mac appeared, disturbed at losing one of her two male helpers. But I would give her no reasons, either, merely saying that the change would work out for the best.

And it did. "Spirits" no longer bothered us.

Johnathan remained in the dispensary for several years, before leaving to find more exciting work. I could learn nothing of his whereabouts for months. Then one day when passing a Zulu theatre, I saw a concert advertised, and out of curiosity, I paid sixpence to go in. The curtain rolled back to reveal Johnathan, in a red cap, a red sash, and a uniform dazzling in its array of colors. He led a chorus of male singers, and their performance was decidedly worth the admission.

Johnathan was at last in his own element. Any man who could conceal hot embers in a hidden receptacle and by some sleight of hand make them appear to fall from the sky without being detected certainly belonged on the stage.

It was Johnathan and other young Zulus who caused trouble in less ingenious ways, however, that forced me to abandon the training of orderlies. If they had all been as trustworthy as Edward Ntuli, the experiment would have been successful. But they were not, and eventually nurses were placed in charge of all our wards.

Miss MacNeill's four probationers could soon carry out their duties without any large amount of supervision, and it was then possible to expand the hospital work providing a full-time doctor could be found. My own time was about equally divided between the hospital and the Beatrice Street dispensary, and I couldn't devote more time to the hospital without neglecting the dispensary.

But how was I to find a doctor at the modest salary we could pay? Margaret and I received only $1,000 a year, with an additional allowance of $250 for our five children. No other doctor would give his services for so little unless the work seemed of greater importance to him than his personal interests. In discussing this with our Mission, I learned that the son of a senior missionary, Mr. Goodenough, would within a few months graduate from an Irish medical school. Charles Goodenough as a boy had had unusual missionary zeal, and I thought he might be willing to make the necessary financial sacrifice.

When Dr. Goodenough reached Natal, to become my associate, I found him a personable young man, and

pleasant enough in manner, but his religious inclinations
had largely evaporated. His interest in the Mission Nursing Home, it was soon clear, was not impelled by any deep
concern for native welfare. He simply hoped to gain experience there that would later be useful in private practice. I couldn't blame him for this self-interest, but it was
nevertheless disappointing.

For a young doctor innocent of experience, he was
also remarkably opinionated, particularly if he could back
his views with the teachings of his Dublin professors. This
wasn't uncommon in young physicians, and I thought
sobering experience might develop a more flexible attitude.

One Sunday evening Margaret and I went to church,
leaving Dr. Goodenough in charge of the hospital. A
woman patient was then in the beginning stage of labor,
but as the case promised no complications, I felt it would
give my associate no difficulty.

I overlooked the difficulties inexperience can create.
Scarcely had we left when Dr. Goodenough ordered Miss
MacNeill to prepare instruments for a pubiotomy. The
nurse had justifiable doubts about the young doctor's ability to perform the operation. And she was sure I wouldn't
have left the hospital if surgery might be necessary. Never
backward where a patient's life was at stake, Mac told the
doctor that if an operation had to be performed it could
await my return.

Dr. Goodenough was incensed. "I believe I'm the
best judge of that, Miss MacNeill. Now go prepare the
instruments as I asked. And remember to include a Gigli
saw."

"But we have none," she said, suddenly hopeful.

"What! No Gigli saw? Very well, I'll make one."

While Dr. Goodenough made the saw by filing a

piece of wire, Mac asked Elizabeth Njapa to prepare instruments for the operation. Then the white nurse called
the police station nearest the church where Margaret and
I were attending services.

We were listening to the sermon when a note,
brought to the church by a native policeman, was handed
to me by an usher. It said that I was wanted at the hospital on a case involving the life of a patient.

Hastily we left the church. I mounted my motorcycle
and my wife climbed onto the pillion seat behind; we
sped toward the Berea. Mac was standing on the hospital
porch, wringing her hands, when I drew up in front. Her
relief at seeing me was so great that she leaned over the
porch rail and was suddenly violently ill. After she could
speak, she told me what was happening.

Without waiting for her to finish, I dashed upstairs.
Dr. Goodenough, with his new saw, was entering the operating room. I asked if anything was wrong.

"Luckily I took measurements of our confinement
patient," he said reprovingly. "The woman couldn't have
a normal delivery. I'm about to undertake a pubiotomy."

"I doubt if it will be necessary," I said.

"I know differently," my associate said stiffly. "Wait
a bit, Dr. McCord."

He strode down the hall, returning a minute later
with a textbook. Flipping through the pages, he found the
section on pubiotomies and sought to prove his point. Still
unconvinced, I argued against the operation. Our argument was interrupted by a wail from the surgery.

I opened the door and saw Elizabeth Njapa holding
a newborn babe. Dr. Goodenough had nothing further to
say.

Mac was not a girl to forgive a young doctor for giving her such a scare. But not until several weeks later,

when Miss Jones, a missionary, came to the hospital, did she find an opportunity to repay him in kind. Miss Jones was exhausted from overwork, and needing no medical attention, I merely placed her in the room reserved for missionary patients and gave orders that she wasn't to be disturbed.

Making his rounds with Miss MacNeill the next morning, Dr. Goodenough started to enter the missionary's room. Seeing her opportunity, Mac slipped between the doctor and the door.

"Miss Jones isn't to be disturbed yet, Dr. Goodenough."

"Oh! Wants to wash up and brush her hair before she's seen, eh? Very well. We'll drop by later."

As Dr. Goodenough entered another room, Margaret appeared with Miss Jones's tray. Mac had a chance to whisper her secret plan without being observed by the doctor.

Half an hour later, when he entered the missionary's room, he stopped and his jaw sagged. The missionary lay motionless, her face powdered a ghastly white, her hands crossed over her chest. She appeared dead. The doctor recovered and dashed across the room, intending to attempt a resuscitation. His alarm was too much for three feminine observers. Miss Jones could no longer restrain her laughter, nor could Mac and my wife, who stood in the doorway.

Dr. Goodenough never quite recovered from the blow to his dignity. Six months after he came to the hospital, I was recalled from a vacation because he had accepted a Government position and wished to leave at once. Government service gave him the necessary seasoning. Later, when he entered private practice, he did such good work that by the time of his death in the influenza epidemic of 1918, he was a well-established and popular physician.

The principal of the Inanda Mission School had been correct in saying that there was no provision for African girls to become registered nurses. When our native nurses completed their three-year courses and left the Mission Nursing Home, to give their places to a new class of probationers, few positions were open to them. They could work only in Government hospitals, in mission schools, or in their home districts. I had foreseen that some might marry and give up nursing, but that would not mean their training had been wasted. They could still serve their neighbors after marriage, earning money for medical assistance that would otherwise be expended on the hocus-pocus of witch doctors.

To discover the effect of our training, I watched the lives of our first nurses more closely than those of later years. When classes grew larger, it became impossible to know each girl as a personality, or to follow the myriad paths of a large group through the years. Our first class of nurses had less education than student nurses in later years, yet neither in loyalty to their calling nor in accomplishment did they suffer by comparison. They were pioneers, and their lives were marked by the courage, the discipline, and the self-sacrifice so often found in the breakers of fresh trails.

Perhaps our most successful nurse was Elizabeth Njapa. After passing our hospital examinations successfully, she married a libertine more interested in women than work. If she had hoped to make a home for her daughter Ivy, the marriage was no solution. It lasted but a short time.

Elizabeth then moved into her stepfather's kraal,

near Adams Mission, to nurse her mother through her final illness. When her mother died, she tried to continue nursing in the kraals near her home. We paid her daughter's expenses at Inanda to free her for this work. She and her stepfather were so uncongenial, however, that she left his kraal and an independent nursing career to work at Inanda Mission.

There she was a nurse and general helper for several years, until she had an opportunity to become the nursing superintendent at a small hospital in Zululand, run by a Government District-Surgeon. Her dependability made her a pillar in that hospital, and in off-duty hours she devoted herself to her daughter. The girl was a credit both to her mother and to the education she received in mission schools. Elizabeth herself served in the Zululand hospital for many years as matron, a position of remarkable trust for one of her race. . . .

Julia Magwaza, an equally steadfast character, found employment as a ward maid at the Government Addington Hospital in Durban.

This hospital did not welcome native patients, though they would be brought in from the lawn where rickshaw boys would sometimes dump them when sick. They would be placed in the Zulu ward, which, like the mulatto, Indian and white wards, was in charge of a ward superintendent known as a *sister*. She was a registered nurse, and serving under her were probationary white nurses who took the temperatures of patients, gave medicines, made beds and looked after the wards. Eventually the probationers rebelled against caring for native patients, and they were then allowed to limit their attention to nothing more than the taking of pulse and temperature. After a few syphilitic cases reached the Zulu ward, they refused even this meager service. Zulu ward attendants and ward maids were then employed to care for native patients. Thus Julia became a ward maid.

Better educated and trained than most of the white probationers, she was quite capable of handling any normal case and was experienced besides in midwifery. Yet the white student nurses, never bothering to discover this, looked upon her as little more than a native helper. Their attitude changed after she gave a startling demonstration of her qualifications.

Julia had had considerable experience in confinement cases in our hospital, and one evening she recognized signs that a patient would have her baby within a few hours. She called in the mulatto midwife. The midwife, who knew less than Julia about such cases, decided after a brief examination that the woman wouldn't have her baby until morning, and went off-duty.

Julia was certain the midwife was wrong. With growing apprehension, she watched her patient going through what she was sure were the final stages of labor. She couldn't find the ward superintendent, and no white probationer would listen to her. When the native ward maid who was to relieve her came on duty, Julia said quietly, "I must deliver a baby. You'll have to help me."

Two white probationers, who had never observed a delivery, noticed their preparations and asked if they could watch.

"Of course," Julia said, without turning.

And then to the astonishment of the white girls, Julia took the child, tied the cord, washed up, and made the mother comfortable.

Since there wasn't a white probationer in the hospital who could have delivered a baby, Julia was solidly established in their esteem. They often called her to help with their white patients or with confinement cases.

And so greatly did they respect her knowledge that they begged her to coach them when preparing for their Government examinations. Their faith was fully justified. One probationer she coached received the highest grade in the Addington Hospital in her examination, while another received second honors. Yet their instructor, because of her brown skin, wasn't even eligible to take the examinations for which she'd prepared others.

Julia enjoyed the respect of the probationers and her superiors during the several years she remained at the Addington Hospital. After falling in love with a handsome young native, she left the hospital to live at home while awaiting her wedding day. An epidemic of enteric fever broke out among the girls of the Inanda Mission School a few days after she reached home, and she abandoned wedding preparations to nurse the sick girls. When the epidemic subsided, she married. Her unstinting labor at Inanda had drained her strength, and when she contracted pneumonia, just a month after her marriage, she had so little resistance that she died.

Nomhlatuzi Bhengu, the prettiest, the most brilliant and in many ways the most trying of our nurses, completed her training and then married our orderly, Edward Ntuli. He was intelligent and with further training could undoubtedly have served his people ably in a medical way. There was, however, no medical training a male native could take at the time. In order to earn enough to marry our headstrong young nurse, he became a magistrate's interpreter and clerk.

Nomhlatuzi Ntuli continued nursing, although no less proud, no more inclined to exert herself physically after marriage than before. When on a case, she never allowed others to forget that she was the daughter of a chief. She kept every woman in a kraal scurrying to carry out her orders, thus relieving herself of the drudgery. Nevertheless she was a capable nurse and did a great amount of good, particularly in confinement cases.

Edna Mzoneli, whose father had consented to his daughter entering the hospital because he considered her stupid, appeared to have little to recommend her for nursing. She was frail, and the emotional, mental and physical demands of the work were severe on her. Frequently, from a sense of frustration, she would weep hysterically. These outbursts, as mentioned earlier, reached a climax when her sister's baby was born. Margaret's rebuke on that occasion brought about a remarkable change in the girl.

She sensed that hers was a dedicated calling, that as a nurse she was something more than the girl everyone believed weak and stupid. Thereafter she gave herself so completely to her studies and duties that my wife and I were sometimes concerned for her health.

Edna gave in to her former feeling of frustration only once. Because of overwork and lowered resistance, she developed a cold that lasted days. Discouraged, she wrote a brother she loved and respected to say that she had a fever of 101 degrees and wished to come home. It happened that her brother also had a cold. He wrote that he had a fever of 101½ and was still doing his work, and he expected her to do likewise until she finished her three-year course.

Nothing could prevent Edna from working beyond her strength. So I sent her home not long after that to rest and upholster her bones with more flesh. She was back in the morning, carrying her brother's baby on a pillow. She wanted me to examine the baby, which was suffering from the same disease as other children in her own and neighboring kraals. None of the other natives would allow her to bring one of their children to the hospital, for they were sure a white doctor knew nothing of "a black man's disease." The black man's disease was measles.

Having insufficient space for a contagious ward in those days, I tried to take only surgical and maternity cases. But I made an exception of Edna's nephew, placing him in an isolated bed.

"I tell them they must keep the children inside, in their blankets, and bathe them in warm water," Edna explained. "But they will not listen to me because I am only a girl. What shall I do?"

A run-down girl could not be expected to handle alone an epidemic that, if what she told me were true, extended over an area of many miles around her home. Yet there was no alternative. Many measles cases were appearing every day in the dispensary, to be treated and given instructions and sent home. I couldn't leave to help her.

Told what she must do, Edna left with new assurance. From many sources, I learned what happened next. She asked the pastor of the church near her home to call a meeting. When the church was filled, she walked up the aisle and stood in the pulpit, a gaunt young woman but no longer awkward or lacking confidence.

"This is not Edna speaking," she said firmly. "I am the voice of Dr. McCord." The strange announcement startled into silence the natives who had started murmuring when she stepped into the pulpit. Everyone in the crowded little church listened as the girl once despised, once the object of laughter, told those who had formerly ridiculed her how to save their children's lives.

Stranger still, they heeded her. Children with measles weren't allowed to spread the contagion playing with others. Little boys with blotched faces weren't sent out to tend cattle. Kept inside, between warm blankets, the children recovered where previously many had died. Much credit for this lay in Edna's unceasing efforts by day and often nights as well, for a period of six weeks. She nursed those suffering the most, visited kraal after kraal, and on some days traveled as much as ten miles afoot seeing patients.

She was little heavier when she returned to the hospital, but she looked stronger and more assured, perhaps because she had won the respect of her people for her untiring efforts during the epidemic.

Edna completed her training, and then was given the position of assistant matron in our hospital. She had received an allowance of ten to twenty shillings monthly as a probationer, and five pounds a month after becoming the assistant maton, but there was no evidence that she spent any of this on herself. Unlike the other nurses, who occasionally bought a dress or cheap jewelry to wear off-duty, she always dressed humbly. One day the girl brought to my wife's room a small sack of money, which she counted to show Margaret that she'd saved every penny she'd earned.

"I am a person," she said gravely.

Margaret smiled. "So am I, Edna."

Edna's face remained grave. "You have always been a person. I have been nobody. But now I am a person. Now I am a nurse."

Margaret was touched, for she sensed the years of frustration and the feeling of inadequacy that had beset the girl before two events changed her outlook. One was the discovery, at the time her sister's child was born, that a nurse must have more than normal self-possession. The other was the knowledge that as a nurse she alone of her people had been able to bring an epidemic to an end.

Edna showed Margaret a long, formally phrased letter in which she explained to her brother that she was sending him the money she'd earned because it was his insistence that she continue nursing which had made her a person.

Not long afterward she married, but she still felt consecrated to her career. Ceaselessly she traveled over the steep hillsides to assist in confinement cases or to nurse the sick, and not even advanced pregnancy could keep her at home. The drain on a constitution never too strong caused her to lose her first baby. When she again became pregnant, she sought my advice.

I warned her not to do any more nursing until her baby was born. In the meanwhile she needed more food and rest, and was to remain at home regardless of how much her services were needed. I would have liked to build her up physically before her confinement, but I was leaving in a short while to enlist in the Medical Corps of the United States Army.

During my absence, the influenza epidemic struck in South Africa. Death daily took a heavy toll in Durban. In the hinterland, kraals that had once been the homes of happy families became the last resting places of a vanished people. The epidemic struck indiscriminately, in some kraals taking the young and leaving only a wrinkled old man, an aged crone, or a woman without husband or children. Or in other cases the older members of the family died and there remained only a young child or orphaned brothers and sisters.

At Adams Mission the influenza was severe. A schoolroom was made into a hospital ward, and the missionaries tried to care for the boys until there were so many ill that the load became insupportable.

Mr. Leroy, principal of the boys' school, miraculously escaped influenza himself, but he was nearly exhausted from carrying the responsibility for so many patients. Durban doctors, already overworked, could not help. The missionaries could do no more than they were already doing, but as some were themselves sick, it was not enough. Not knowing where else to turn, Mr. Leroy sent an appeal to Edna, who was then nearing the end of her pregnancy. She answered that Dr. McCord had ordered her to remain at home until her baby was born. The principal struggled on, while more boys fell ill each day. Then, desperate for help, he sent another urgent message to Edna.

She responded to his second appeal. Heavy with child, she trod the miles-long trail to Adams to take charge of the ward of sick boys. She bathed their hot bodies, cleaned up the ward that Mr. Leroy and the other missionaries had been unable to clean properly, changed and washed sheets, and laid out those who succumbed to the disease. Day after day, night after night, the nurse worked to save her patients, allowing herself only snatches of sleep when she dropped off from complete exhaustion in the nearest chair.

When the epidemic subsided, and the last patient left the ward, Edna's strength was almost spent. More tired than ever before in her life, she wanted nothing but the luxury of a long sleep between warm blankets. Yet in a daze of fatigue she forced herself to clean and scrub the ward before leaving, so that it would be ready once more for classes.

The trail to her home seemed endless, and frequently she had to rest because of the heaviness of her body and her difficulty in breathing. Her hazy mental state, though she didn't suspect it, was the result of influenza as well as fatigue. She only knew that she must plod on. Her child stirred within her, and she must reach home before it was born.

There was no time after reaching home to take the rest her body craved. Labor pains had begun. After long hours, her first living baby was born. She was too weak to do anything for the child; her mind was already in a stupor. Breathing became more and more difficult because of the congestion of her lungs. She died two days later, without ever leaving her bed. Her baby, sick with influenza, lived only a few hours longer.

No doctor, dying in his fight to stop the ravages of an epidemic, no medical researcher, falling victim to the germs he studied, ever gave his life more truly to the cause of medicine than this native girl, Edna Mzoneli.

CHAPTER ELEVEN

ALL WORK
MAKES A DULL DOCTOR

DOCTORS PRACTICING IN DURBAN, A VAST DISTANCE from the great medical centers, were at a disadvantage in their efforts to keep pace with the march of medicine. Medical journals, it's true, informed us of the latest techniques and drugs. But we could not observe the innovations at important hospitals and the techniques of famed surgeons, hear visiting medical lecturers or attend meetings of large medical associations. To fill this need, the Durban doctors belonged to the British Medical Association, largely to exert pressure for better medical legislation, and formed a local group, known as the Durban Medical Society, which met monthly.

This society was an informal little club which met at members' homes, and at each meeting sandwiches and whiskey or coffee were served in midevening to prevent the sessions from becoming overly serious. Many of my most pleasant memories of South Africa concern our meetings. More important, they helped me as well as my colleagues to keep abreast of our profession at a remote part of the globe.

We exchanged experiences, wrote papers on techniques observed on our visits to Great Britain or (in my case) the United States, discussed problems of ethical procedure, and described our experiences with the latest drugs. At times we brought unusual cases to meetings, thus benefiting from many judgments before treatment or an operation was undertaken. The papers we prepared often obliged us to dig into matters we might never otherwise have delved into so thoroughly. My report on the drugs used by Zulu witch doctors and herbalists required just this sort of digging.

Whatever might be the personal differences of members on other matters, they were friendly colleagues when they met as the Durban Medical Society. At the time that Dr. Sam Campbell and Dr. Archie McKenzie opposed my Zulu hospital, for example, they remained cordial at our informal meetings. The one exception to our professional good feeling, the one discordant note in our society, was Dr. Winfield Wright.

Dr. Wright was of picturesque appearance, having the face of an angry lion, glowering eyes that peered from beneath cavernous brows, and hair as black as an Indian's that fell over his broad and swarthy forehead. Coming to South Africa long after I did, he soon proved himself an able physician, holding a staff position in the Addington Hospital for several years before taking up native practice. He seemed to feel that this made us rivals, a feeling I couldn't share because too few doctors were interested in giving the natives the medical care they needed. Dr. Wright was aggressive and fiery tempered, and these traits had irritated his colleagues to such a point that there was lively argument the evening we discussed whether to admit him to the Durban Medical Society. In the end he was admitted as a matter of professional courtesy. Those of us who had urged this course presently recognized our mistake. Dr. Wright took violent exception to many of the statements of other doctors, and often criticized severely the methods we advocated.

I earned his lasting enmity one night because of a comment on one of his criticisms.

That evening I'd brought a native patient to the meeting. The man had a large sarcoma of the left knee, a type of case rarely seen in Durban. After giving the pathologist's report, I was describing how I intended to amputate at the hip joint to save the man's life when Dr. Wright brusquely interrupted.

"Dr. McCord, if you amputate at the hip joint, how will you avoid shock?"

"By putting my patient under profound anesthesia, there will be no shock."

"Ah, but there will be!" Dr. Wright said dogmatically. And he launched into a dissertation on the alarming percentages of fatalities, due to shock, following hip-joint amputations. "Now to prevent death from shock," he went on, "the operation must be performed with spinal anesthesia."

As the other doctors had heard repeatedly Dr. Wright's discourses on his pet specialty, spinal anesthesia, they settled back resignedly when he began once more to relate in detail many operations where he had successfully used this technique. "Of the hundreds of cases I've operated on with spinals," he concluded, "only one death has followed the operation, and that was due to heart failure, twelve hours afterward."

I laughed. "If one of my patients died of heart failure twelve hours after an operation," I said, "I'd call it death from shock."

The roars of laughter from the other doctors irritated Dr. Wright. And it did not make him feel any more kindly toward me when I was able to report at our next meeting that after operating in my usual way, my patient had shown no trace of shock and had made a remarkably easy recovery.

The most unusual case I was able to bring before my fellow members was an extrauterine pregnancy. These cases, as mentioned earlier, are relatively more common among Zulus than whites. A native woman in this instance had appeared on diagnosis to have an ovarian cyst. To remove it, I had operated in the cottage hospital with the help of Dr. Pearson and Dr. Bray. We were all astonished when, instead of the cyst, I removed a perfectly formed baby, which had broken through the Fallopian tube, drawn sustenance from the umbilical cord and placenta, and after reaching full term outside the normal birth channel and dying, had by the action of calcium salts in the mother's blood turned as hard as stone. The mother made a quick recovery after the operation. And the "stone baby" was viewed and discussed with great interest by the members of the Durban Medical Society. Unquestionably, few doctors in America or Great Britain would encounter a stone baby in a lifetime of practice. For if a mother had an extrauterine pregnancy, it would be discovered at the end of the nine-month term if not before, and would be removed by surgery long before it could become calcified.

While visiting in America, at the time of my father's illness, I stayed at Rochester, Minnesota, for several weeks to observe the techniques at the famed Mayo Clinic. Upon my return to Durban in 1911, I described their methods to Dr. Bray, then president of the Durban Medical Society, and he insisted that I write a paper on the Mayo Clinic for our next meeting.

My fellow members listened to this paper with rapt attention and an incredulity at times verging on skepticism. Even by American standards, the methods of the Brothers Mayo were then novel and unconventional, and my British-trained colleagues imagined that I was gilding the truth.

They found it hard to believe what I told them about the extent to which the Mayos had systematized the payment of fees according to a patient's wealth. Within a few days, Mayo financial agents could discover a man's approximate financial status. He was then charged fees based more on his income than on the surgery or treatment required. A man earning $100,000 a year might pay $10,000 for a major operation, while a $100-a-month clerk would pay perhaps $100 for the same surgery. And even the $100 might not be charged patients in more straitened circumstances. A farmer who had an operation at Mayo's was discovered by their financial agents to have a mortgage on his farm. He had been a hard worker, but ill health and poor crop prices had made it impossible for him to pay off the mortgage. When the farmer left the hospital, he was not only charged nothing; with his receipted bill, he was given a check for $100 to employ a hired man until he was strong enough to take over the work without undoing the benefit of the operation.

No operations were undertaken at the Mayo Clinic. The Mayo brothers performed their brilliant surgery at near-by St. Mary's Hospital. As I described the operating theatre at St. Mary's, and how Dr. Charlie Mayo, with half a dozen pieces of cheesecloth tied over his face, kept up a rapid-fire discourse while he operated, I saw the doctors of the Durban Medical Society exchange knowing smiles. I told of one operation where "Dr. Charlie" caused a famed group of surgeons to grow more and more nervous as he searched for a lost kidney stone, a small one no larger than a grain of wheat. After many minutes, Dr. Charlie glanced up and said mildly, "Gentlemen, I lost that stone, and there's nothing to do but find it." The faces of the famed surgeons were gleaming with perspiration before Dr. Charlie, still quite unruffled, discovered the stone he'd dropped.

The moment I laid my paper aside, Dr. Milner-Smythe of the Addington Hospital pounced, with the air of a lawyer who has caught an opposing witness in a contradiction. "Dr. McCord, how could Dr. Mayo talk with all those layers of cheesecloth over his face?"

"It would take more than half a dozen layers of cheesecloth to keep Dr. Charlie from talking," I said, laughing. Even Dr. Milner-Smythe joined in the general laughter.

Not long after I read this paper, Dr. Bray's two-year term as president neared its end, and he drew me aside at a meeting to ask if I would succeed him. I told him that I didn't think it was appropriate for an American to head a society of British medical men. Besides, I wasn't a drinking man, and as a missionary, I didn't feel that I could serve drinks at my home. When Dr. Bray chose to overlook these objections, I proposed a compromise. If he'd act as secretary, providing the refreshments and arranging the programs, I would agree. And on this basis, I was elected president.

With such an able secretary, my presidency would have been a pleasant experience except for the increasingly antagonistic and critical attitude of Dr. Wright. And, shortly before the end of my term, he laid himself vulnerable to the enemies he'd been making.

He mailed a circular letter to his patients, describing types of medical treatment he was prepared to undertake.

These letters he sent out in such numbers that his loyal patients were able to pass along a great many to other doctors' patients. In effect this served as broad-scale advertising, to the British medical man the most unethical practice in which any doctor can indulge.

The doctors of the Durban Medical Society were especially incensed that one of our members should be guilty of such an offense, for it had been our desire to live up to a rather stiff code of ethics. Members immediately began laying plans for condemning and expelling Dr. Wright at the last meeting I was to conduct as president.

Learning of these plans, Dr. Wright came to see me. Making no effort to spare himself, he told me what he'd done, and then asked bluntly, "What are you fellows going to do to me?"

"Dr. Wright," I said, "you've made enemies, and now they have you where they want you. The real question is: What will you do?"

Looking more than ever like an angry lion, he thrust out his heavy jaw. "I'll fight to the last ditch."

"There will be no fight," I pointed out. "You haven't a leg to stand on. Your letter is all that will be needed to vote you out of our society. You'll be lucky if the Medical Association doesn't follow our example and revoke your license to practice."

His face had a grayish pallor. "I suppose you're right. What would you advise me to do?"

The position in which his question put me was a difficult one. His antagonistic attitude had disrupted many of our meetings. Yet the man was placing himself at my mercy. I could either give him no advice and allow him to ruin his career, or tell him how to save himself.

After a long pause, I said, "The only thing you can do is eat humble pie—take the attitude of, 'Yes; I see now that my letter might be construed as advertising, though I intended it only as a private letter to my patients. All I can do now is apologize and assure you gentlemen that I won't repeat the mistake.' "

"And what will be your attitude as president?" he asked.

"If you act as I suggest, I'll do what I can. But you'd better let me do the talking. If Dr. Campbell's barbs goad you into losing your temper, you'll swear at us all, and your position will then be hopeless."

Greatly cheered, Dr. Wright said, "I'll control my temper and do as you say."

The meeting was held at the Addington Hospital, because none of the members wished to have what promised to be a disagreeable affair in any home where Dr. Wright was a guest. A solemn group of doctors gathered in a room of the hospital, and after I took up briefly a few routine matters, I explained the purpose of the meeting and introduced Dr. Campbell, who was to read the indictment against our colleague.

Sam Campbell could when so inclined state matters in a way to make the blood of even a placid-natured man simmer. Dr. Wright, never of an equable temperament, squirmed in his chair as the long indictment was read, clause by clause. His face grew flushed, and several times he started to rise to protest. Each time I caught his eye and signaled him with a stern look to restrain his mounting wrath.

The moment Dr. Campbell finished, I rose before the accused man could reach his feet. "Dr. Wright," I said, "you admit the principal points in this charge, do you not? And you claim that you never intended your personal letters to patients to be made public, or intended to advertise in an unprofessional manner?"

In a voice hoarse with emotion, Dr. Wright muttered, "That is correct."

"Admitting your fault," I continued, before he could add anything, "do you wish to apologize to the Durban Medical Society for your error and promise that nothing of this sort will again happen?"

It was difficult for him to get the words out: "Yes; I apologize, and I so promise."

Then, before Dr. Campbell or any other member could think of a way to turn back the meeting to its original course, I said, "Can we ask any more of Dr. Wright?"

No one spoke, and so Dr. Wright remained a member.

His continued presence at meetings, however, made us all so uncomfortable that we eventually disbanded the Durban Medical Society.

A few years after that Dr. Wright lost his license after being tried and convicted of performing an illegal operation. He served a two-year sentence and then returned to Durban to become a "dietitian," under which designation he practiced for the remainder of his life. If he also illicitly practiced medicine on the side, no one succeeded in proving it.

Exchanging ideas with fellow members of the society had often acquainted me with new techniques or drugs useful in my practice among the Zulus. In later years this knowledge had to be picked up in less congenial ways. No permanent good came from my defense of the antagonistic Dr. Wright, and some loss may have resulted from it.

CHAPTER TWELVE

IMPACT OF WAR

THE LOSS OF OUR SUPERINTENDENT OF NURSES MARKED the beginning of four years of disruption and confusion in my Zulu medical work. Miss MacNeill had agreed to serve for three years, just long enough to train our first class of girls, and she had imbued the trainees with her own enthusiasm and energy. Yet we saw her depart with the mingled regret and relief you'd feel in separating from a beloved friend whose restless vitality had proved exhausting.

Miss Bates, the older nurse who replaced her, was unfortunately her opposite in too many ways. Only the plain and unflattering adjective *fat* could describe her physical appearance, and she had neither the energy nor the enthusiasm of the irrepressible Mac.

Despite certain misgivings about her, we felt optimistic. The universal Zulu prejudice against trying anything new had been broken down by our first class of nurses, and we had little difficulty enrolling seven girls in the second class. With but a single exception, all of these girls held out high promise. The exception was Sibyl Mini, whose father, Chief Stephen Mini, had led the mission natives of the Natal Native Horse at the time of Bambata's Rebellion. Nomhlatuzi Bhengu had left us with lingering doubts about training another Zulu princess, and only after I had made it clear to Chief Stephen Mini that his daughter must regard herself in our hospital as an ordinary mortal would we accept her. Our doubts, as it turned out, were more than justified.

The training of these girls had barely begun when both the Mission Nursing Home and the dispensary felt the impact of history in the making. It was 1914, and in August of that year the World War began.

Many Boers (or Afrikanders, as they then preferred to call themselves) were sympathetic to the German cause, either from British antipathy or because of German propaganda, and this segment of the population hoped to remain aloof from the war. Both Louis Botha, the Prime Minister of South Africa, and his able supporter General Jan Smuts were determined to support the Empire. Beyers, de Wet and other Afrikander leaders thereupon organized a force to oppose the Government. Botha and Smuts were faced with the difficult choice of either suppressing a rebellion of their own people or backing down on their promised support of Great Britain. They chose the former course. And to avoid the bitterness that would result from a racial war, they decided to suppress the rebellion entirely with Afrikander troops.

The Zulus, with no conception of the European struggle responsible for the Afrikander uprising, were unable to comprehend what lay behind the skirmishes between men of the same race. Prudence made them conclude that it was no time for any natives, even those needing medical attention, to travel the roads. So widespread became this feeling that but half as many patients came to the dispensary. The hospital never entirely paid its way, its deficits being met from dispensary income, and with a fifty per cent drop in that income both the hospital and the nurses' training program were threatened. Nor could overhead be reduced in any way, expenses having been hewn to the bone.

I had saved a few hundred dollars before the Afrikander rebellion began, however, so I decided to keep the hospital open and to continue training our nurses until that money was gone. It was a fortunate decision because the Afrikander rebels were defeated by November. Yet it was nearly six months from the beginning of the civil war before the dispensary work returned to normal.

Meanwhile warfare continued in South Africa, though against Germans rather than rebellious Afrikanders. Botha and Smuts were determined to eliminate the German influence partly responsible for the uprising by defeating the Germans in south-west Africa. This portion of Africa was exceedingly arid, and supplying water to the South African troops that reached the region by land and sea was a greater problem than the German force opposing them. Lack of water made a sustained battle difficult for either force. It was this condition which dictated military strategy in the campaign. Botha and Smuts harassed German troops whenever possible, but even more effectively they exhausted the Germans by threatening one objective after another, and then withdrawing. In this type of campaign there were few casualties. And the German troops, given no chance to rest, were soon in no condition to fight.

A German commander, who saw the effect of ceaseless marching on the morale and stamina of his men, is said to have exclaimed, "This is no war—it's a hippodrome!"

The "hippodrome strategy" nevertheless worked so

well that the Germans surrendered unconditionally to Botha in July of 1915.

Smuts was then given command of an army which invaded German East Africa. Here neither dryness nor the numerically inferior German forces were the real enemy. It was a pestilential country of bogs and vast swamplands, of tropical downpours and steaming jungles, and though Smuts defeated the Germans within six months, the casualties from disease filled the South African hospitals for months afterwards.

This campaign was the last military action against the Germans in Africa, but there was sporadic mob action against individual Germans throughout the war. South Africans are like Americans, and unlike the British, in their potential for violent action. The sinking of the *Lusitania*, for example, made even respectable business and professional men of Durban lose their perspective. Men I'd known for years, and had always thought of as quiet, courteous and socially polished gentlemen, were leaders in mobs that emptied the store and burned the goods of German-born Mr. Baumann, whose two sons were fighting in the British Army.

Another store in Durban, that of Karl Gundlefinger, who was strongly British in his sympathies, was burned because of the German name of the owner. Gundlefinger's British employees were deprived of jobs, and a British insurance company had to make good his loss, but as against these costs the mob had proved its loyalty. Abashed by their own actions, some of the solid citizens responsible for the violence had themselves sworn in as deputies the following morning to help prevent further rioting.

With the American declaration of war, I enlisted in the British Army and was commissioned a captain. To-

gether with Dr. Bray and other doctors, I was a member
of an examining board that decided whether returning
soldiers, either wounded or merely exhausted, were fit
for further service, should have additional hospital treatment, or should be honorably discharged, with a pension
if disabled. We doctors would slip into uniform and spend
our afternoons examining veterans. But Dr. Bray, always
the Irish rebel, though conscientious in reporting for
duty, stubbornly refused to wear his British uniform.

The time I spent with the examining board was time
lost to the hospital and dispensary during a period when
both creaked under the stress of an influx of patients and
an inadequate staff. And Miss Bates was making so little
progress in training her class of nurses that the new girls
were incapable of carrying the load, which then fell on
Margaret.

Providentially, the room kept in the hospital for missionary patients proved the means of seeing us temporarily through the crisis. Dr. Lawrence of the Mt. Silinda
Hospital in Rhodesia knew that the room could be had by
any missionary without charge either for the room or
treatment, though we did make a small $5 weekly charge
for board. So when one of his nurses, Miss Lundquist, developed a cancerous growth in her breast, and he lacked
the facilities to remove it in his hospital, he sent the nurse
to the Mission Nursing Home.

I removed the growth, but to discourage any recur-
rence, I felt that the operation should be followed by six
months of X-ray treatments. Miss Lundquist was reluctant to remain away from Mt. Silinda for so long, knowing that with the wartime shortage of nurses, it would be
hard to replace her. We could find no substitute to take
her place until it occurred to me that Miss Bates had
come from Rhodesia and was longing to return.

Miss Bates gladly replaced Miss Lundquist at Mt. Silinda Hospital. And Miss Lundquist, her conscience at peace, became our Superintendent of Nurses. She was an attractive young woman, with a strong sense of responsibility. Under her guidance, which was but for a short time, our student nurses made rapid progress. After Miss Lundquist's X-ray treatments ended, she returned home to marry a young missionary in Rhodesia.

The hospital and the nurses' training program limped along haphazardly until we were able to employ an equally capable Superintendent of Nurses, Miss Frances Horne. After staying with us a year, however, she responded to the call for army nurses. A Miss Jenkensen then served as a temporary substitute, but not having full qualifications herself, she couldn't give her student nurses adequate training. A short time later we engaged Miss Rice, an experienced nurse who had worked for the Free Methodist Mission. She trained that part of the class still with us until 1918. Edna Mzoneli of the previous class served for a while as assistant matron, assisting Miss Rice both in the hospital and with the training.

The multitude of cooks unfortunately spoiled a promising broth. The death of two of our student nurses from consumption could not be blamed on the succession of superintendents, but lack of supervision and the discouraging effects of trying to learn the methods of different white nurses might well be responsible for several failures.

Sibyl Mini, the Zulu princess, was lazy and untrustworthy, and had to be dismissed. When on night duty, she stole off to a place where she'd not be observed and slept through the night, leaving patients to shift for themselves. Another girl, who lacked the energy to do the work, also had to go. A third girl, perhaps as the result of insufficient supervision at the time, had to be discharged because of immoral conduct. Of the seven student nurses in the class only two, Rhoda Syvetye and Flora Cele, completed their training.

As the months passed, I felt more and more strongly that though Great Britain and my own country were allies, my place was in the American rather than the British Army. In May of 1918, I acted on this conviction by resigning my commission, and after doing this, I began at once to settle my affairs so that I could close the hospital and sail for America to enlist. My primary purpose in this was to serve in the American Army, but a secondary reason concerned the Zulus. I hoped while in the American Army to find a doctor to become my associate in establishing a native medical school.

The decision to take this step had evolved slowly, beginning with a series of events, the first of which was the calling of a meeting by some one-sided reformers shortly after I moved to Durban. The men who called the meeting invited a number of people to a hall for the purpose of organizing a Native Reform Association.

Many influential Durbanites felt as keenly as I did that laws affecting the natives were unjust and oppressive, and we attended the meeting hoping that the new organization would fight to change these laws. We were disillusioned quickly enough. The sponsors intended to effect reforms not in the inequitable laws, but in the natives themselves. In brief, they planned additional regulations to harass the already bedeviled Zulus! Those of us hoping for fair play promptly lost interest in the Native Reform Association, and after a second meeting, it died a natural death.

The short-lived organization had nevertheless served

a purpose. It brought together for the first time a number of people who felt that laws proving a constant irritant to the Zulus should be modified. We, the dissenters at the meeting of the first organization, formed a second that we named The Native Affairs Reform Association. Its purpose was to study the relation between the white and African races, and to bring pressure for the revision of inequitable laws affecting the natives.

Speakers familiar with native problems addressed us or read papers. At one meeting I was asked to prepare a report on the phase of African people's problems that to me seemed most important. I agreed to report on medical conditions among the Zulus.

To amplify my own observations, I wrote to scores of magistrates, missionaries and missionary doctors who might be in a position to know from personal experience the medical conditions in different parts of the colony. Their answers trickled in for weeks, building up an appalling picture. From sources I believed reliable came instances of poisonings by herbalists and witch doctors; instances of brutal killings, by beatings or other means, of men or women accused of practicing witchcraft by smellers-out.

One such instance, which still makes me cringe, was reported by Dr. Morledge, a District Surgeon of Zululand. A smeller-out accused a young man of practicing witchcraft on a young girl, and of causing her illness. Relatives and his former friends dragged the supposed practicer of witchcraft to a hut. There, while they held him down, they passed sharpened reeds through his rectum, abdomen, diaphragm and up into his lungs, until death ended the youth's torment.

In preparing my paper, I didn't confine myself to presenting native medical conditions as they existed. I went even further, recommending measures to overcome the superstitious treatment of disease by providing the Zulus with adequate service in country districts. This could be done, I believed, by giving the best-educated young Zulus five years of medical training to qualify them as medical aides. My report led to a spirited discussion, much of it centering around the controversial proposal for medical training. In the end, when The Native Affairs Reform Association passed a resolution condemning existing native medical conditions and recommending that something be done, I knew nothing would be. Experience had taught me that resolutions are easily passed, and as easily forgotten.

Twice before I'd seen that happen. At a General Missionary Conference in Durban I had talked on the influence of superstition on native health and had advocated a five-year medical course for a selected group of Zulus. The Conference believed that conditions such as I had described could not wait five years for correction, and had instead advocated a two-year medical-aide program to train natives in first aid, hygiene, nursing and simple medical treatment. Later the deplorable medical conditions among the Zulus were considered at a British Medical Association meeting and a resolution was passed that "Health conditions among the natives of Natal and the lack of provisions to remedy them are a disgrace to a civilized community." But the civilized community wore its disgrace lightly, nothing being done.

So now, with three resolutions passed and native health conditions being as bad as ever, I tried once more to present my case before leaving for America. I made a plea to the Durban Medical Society to exert its influence in having a Government commission appointed to investigate health conditions among the African peoples. Once more I pointed out that the cheapest and most effective way to improve conditions was to give educated Zulus five years of medical training and then send them into country districts as medical aides. Dr. Bray supported me in this proposal, perhaps more from friendship than conviction. Most of the other doctors, however, thought little of the idea and weren't reluctant to say so.

This was no surprise, for new medical ideas are accepted slowly. Even my nurses' training program, already proving its worth, was still controversial. To give my fellow doctors something concrete to dwell on, I sent my latest paper and recommendation to the *South African Medical Record*, where it was printed.

The chance that it would result in any positive action was so remote that I was determined to establish a native medical school myself, without other help. And I hoped while serving in the American Army to find a doctor to assist me in opening the school and in training young Zulus in medicine.

When we reached the Durban pier with our baggage, Dr. Bray was there to say good-bye, wearing the uniform he disdained to wear while on duty. We were touched, knowing that it was his way of paying his respect. When we said farewell, it was for the last time. Dr. Bray died before I returned to South Africa.

We sailed for the United States by way of Singapore, Hongkong, Shanghai, Tokyo, and the Hawaiian Islands, hoping by this devious route to escape the German submarines preying on Atlantic shipping. This precaution, we learned later, nearly proved a misfortune, our ship escaping by only a few hours an encounter with the German raider *Emden*.

I enlisted at Cleveland, Ohio, and was commissioned a captain in the American Army Medical Corps.

Ten days after receiving my commission, the Armistice was signed. Fighting ceased, and with an end to battle casualties, no more doctors were being sent overseas. But there was still much medical work to do in caring for the war wounded, in "delousing" servicemen to prevent the spread of epidemics, and in examining those ready for discharge.

When the men disembarked at East Coast ports, they were given antiseptic treatment, fresh clothing and medical examination, and those in good health were then transported to camps in various states, where they were to remain until discharged. It was my duty to accompany these trains; a medical officer was assigned to each coach. Generally we were given forms covering the men in our coach a minute or so before the train left the station. This left us neither time to examine our papers until under way, nor any chance to do anything if they weren't properly filled out. Sometimes we delivered a confused set of forms to a human sort of superior at our destination. Or, again, we might hand them to the type of officer who enjoyed throwing his weight around, in which case we'd have an uncomfortable time of it.

On inland trips, medical officers ate together in one coach. This gave me a chance to look over the doctors, always with the hope of finding one or two who might fit into my plan for a native medical school. My quest for the right men at first met with no success. Either my fellow medical officers were planning to return to successful practices and were too material in their outlook, or they were disinterested in foreign practice.

One day I was having luncheon with three other officers, while the train ran southward through West Virginia, and a religious discussion arose at my table. Two of the officers were giving me the worst of an argument when the fourth officer stepped in, both feet firmly planted in my defense. He was a young lieutenant, probably in his late twenties, with fair and prematurely receding hair; there was purpose both in his blue eyes and in his manner. Decisively he stated his arguments, citing instances from his own experience, and he carried the offensive so effectively to our opponents that I stopped talking to listen, with a certain amusement at his seriousness.

When the other two officers returned to their coaches, the young lieutenant and I remained for a while at the table, getting acquainted. I discovered that he was Dr. Alan B. Taylor, who had entered the Army directly from his hospital internship. I told him something of my own work in South Africa. Lieutenant Taylor's eyes lighted with interest, and after a time he admitted a secret yearning to try missionary work himself. The more I talked to him, the more convinced I grew that he was the man I wanted. So I began deliberately "selling" South Africa to him by pointing out every particularly picturesque hill or tumbling waterfall or mountain valley that recalled similar beauty spots in Natal. Taylor, who had the same mental picture of an equatorial Africa that I'd once had, was astonished to learn that Natal had beautiful rolling hills and swift waters rather than pest-ridden jungles.

By the time we reached Newport News, Dr. Taylor was half convinced that he'd like medical missionary work. He invited me to call and meet his wife, at the near-by camp where they were staying. I did so that evening, and met Mrs. Taylor, who had been a nurse at the Canadian hospital where Dr. Taylor had served his internship. She was a large woman, with strong and handsome features, and the reserve characteristic of her Canadian background. Although I didn't know it then, she was quick to sense the humorous aspects of a situation.

She withheld judgment when I described the beauty of Durban, and the fruit and flowers that could be had there for so little. But when, in my enthusiasm, I brought forth pictures of the natives, she made a convincing show of being horror stricken at the scanty attire of the women. Could a good woman live in a place where people dressed like that? I didn't suspect that she might be secretly amused at my embarrassed efforts to squirm out of the unfavorable impression I'd made. And I left that evening not at all sure I had succeeded. All I was certain of was that the Taylors were the right couple, if they'd come.

Yet, knowing they might remain in America, I continued my search for a doctor who might fit into my medical-school plans. In traveling through the West, I became acquainted with another able medical officer, Dr. J. W. Morledge of Cleveland. He agreed to come to South Africa if I succeeded in raising money for the medical school and his salary.

On one of my last trips as a medical officer, I was in charge of a coach taking men to Fort Sill in Oklahoma. An incomplete and incorrectly filled-in set of forms had been handed me before the train started, and when I reached my destination and delivered them to a major, he refused to listen to my explanation that they were exactly as they'd been handed to me. Roaring and fuming, he threatened to keep me virtual prisoner until the forms could be starightened out. The prospect of a week or longer at Fort Sill looked less gloomy when I learned that Mattie MacNeill was Superintendent of Nurses at the military hospital there. But I had time for only one visit with Mac, when I gave her news of her friends in Durban, before orders came that spared me whatever punishment the major was planning. I was ordered to Newport News to receive my discharge.

The discharge was not immediately forthcoming, so I had several months of additional duty there, and a number of visits with the Taylors, who had at last decided to go to Africa. And then, a civilian once more, I secured permission from the American Board to solicit contributions for a native medical school, and set out upon a fund-raising campaign. It was not easy to raise money for a project on the opposite side of the earth, even with photographs to give it a semblance of reality. But when I had exhausted every possibility, I had $30,000, partly in cash, partly in pledges. Later, during the depression years, I was to wish most heartily that the pledges had been paid in cash.

I met Dr. Taylor in Boston to tell him the results of the fund-raising. He was aghast at having pledged his future to what must have seemed to him an idealistic and impractical venture. He told me bluntly that he thought $30,000 far from sufficient for starting a medical school, a statement I could hardly deny. To limit his loss of time if the project proved as impractical as it appeared, he said he'd agree to remain in Africa for only seven years. If by then the medical school showed no signs of materializing, he would reserve the right to reconsider his position and withdraw.

Knowing the grip that Africa can take on anyone living there long enough to feel at home, I laughed. "Dr. Taylor, if you spend seven years in Zulu medical work, and then find that you could leave it, I wouldn't want you back."

I returned to Natal with my family in 1920 to reopen the hospital and dispensary, and to prepare for the opening of the first South African native medical school—a venture with enormous odds against it. Where the money to pay the expenses of the school was coming from, I did not know. And besides these expenses, I must find a means to pay the salary of Dr. Taylor, when he came to Africa the following year. And the year after that, when Dr. Morledge was to join us, I was committed to the payment of a second doctor's salary. Some might call my course blind faith, others sheer recklessness. Yet despite all these uncertainties, I left America with buoyant spirits.

CHAPTER THIRTEEN

MEDICAL SCHOOL
ON A SHOESTRING

THE NEWS SPREAD ABOUT DURBAN, SHORTLY AFTER MY return from America, that I planned to establish a native medical school. Both the public and the medical profession regarded the idea as mildly insane.

This reaction in Durban was less disappointing than the hostile attitude of Dr. Alexander Kerr, the Scotch principal of the South African Native College at Fort Hare. When I wrote him, outlining my plans, he answered brusquely that he had no patience with a medical school which would turn out half-baked doctors to practice on a long-suffering public. If anything could have dampened my enthusiasm, it was this letter from a man known to be sympathetic to the natives, and one on whose moral support I had counted.

However, I refused to be disheartened even by Dr. Kerr's chilling disapproval, nor did I feel it entirely unjustified. I was trying to start a native medical school—a venture certain to arouse strong prejudices—on a financial shoestring. I had no experience teaching medicine, very little equipment to devote to the school, and no one to assist me until Dr. Taylor reached South Africa. Still, I believed that I could teach young natives how to care for their people in remote districts in a far better way than they were being cared for by their present medical men, the witch doctors.

The first step was selecting a group of young Zulus intelligent enough to train. I found six bright-eyed, alert boys who spoke English fluently and were eager to study medicine, though none had more than two or three years of what we regard as a high-school education. I explained my plan. The boys would receive the best medical education I could give them, but when it was completed, they could not register as doctors, lacking as they would the necessary British medical degree. Nevertheless, they could use their training by practicing as native doctors without Government recognition. With the optimism of youth, the boys were content with this limitation, and wished to begin training at once.

Before that could be done, they needed scientific foundations. Adams Mission had made impressive advances since the beginning of the century, and now had an able science teacher. I sent the boys to study under him—in chemistry, biology, zoology and physics. And then, while they prepared for more specialized studies, I started work on the dormitory and classrooms they'd need two years later.

After this work had begun, I was able to devote myself to the hospital and dispensary, which were fast returning to normal. Little effort had been required to accomplish this, for the news of my return had been quickly noised about and when I went to open the dispensary, patients stood waiting at the door. Zulus who had postponed surgical treatment presently filled all the beds in the hospital as well, when it opened several weeks later. Miss

Rice returned to the hospital as head nurse and matron. Within a few days, she began training our third class of nurses—ten girls in all, winnowed from the applicants for their education, intelligence, character and seriousness of purpose. So many native girls were now eager to become nurses that we could select only the best, and, under competent supervision, they were within a short time taking care of patients like old hands.

Roads in Natal had improved, and I had brought back a Buick car to save time in making back-country calls. And when Dr. Taylor reached Durban in 1921, I bought a motorcycle, with a detachable sidecar, for his use. By exchanging these vehicles, depending on our needs, we reached patients requiring emergency treatment more quickly than in the past.

I'd always dreamed some day of having a younger doctor to relieve me of the drudgery, gradually unloading more and more of my responsibilities on his shoulders until I reached retirement age. But in bringing Dr. Taylor to South Africa, I had to abandon this dream. He was an ambitious man, with the ability to back up his ambition, and such a man couldn't be used as a medical errand boy. So from the time of his arrival, I had him assist me in operations. But I could not claim to have taught him surgery, for he was soon inviting in visiting surgeons, and learning techniques from us all. He had real aptitude as a surgeon and I was soon sure that he was the kind of a doctor I'd hoped to intrust my work to upon retiring.

The question was: *How could I keep him until my work was done?* Not by placing him in charge of the dispensary, certainly, since his principal interest lay in surgery. Only by immersing him in the routine of the hospital was he likely to find sufficient interest in the work to remain permanently. It would mean leaving more and more of the surgery to him as the years went by and as he acquired experience. But that was a small price to pay for a successor able to carry on my work. The truth was that at fifty-two, after twenty strenuous years of surgery, I was quite willing to leave that phase to a younger man. The human side of my work, and the portion I was most interested in, was in the dispensary, particularly in pediatric work and the maternity cases that started there and ended as delivery cases in the hospital.

After reaching this decision, I said one day to my associate, "Dr. Taylor, I'm going to place you in complete charge of the hospital."

He was delighted, and threw all his energy and enthusiasm into his phase of the work. And in doing so, he became so absorbed in it that I felt there was a good chance that he'd no longer think of his term of service in Africa as but seven years. His tenure was for life.

Every morning on my way to the dispensary, I dropped in at the hospital to discuss any problems that had arisen. And we still operated together, at first with him acting as assistant, later with Dr. Taylor operating while I assisted and administered the anesthetic with a special apparatus of my own devising. Responsibility for the hospital was Dr. Taylor's, however, and it was he the nurses called in night emergencies, while I could, for the first time in years, enjoy uninterrupted sleep. A tireless man, content only when his full energies were utilized in work, he went his rounds in the hospital swinging his stethoscope and whistling his favorite tune, "Till We Meet Again."

For my part, there were still back-country calls, although buses reached farther and farther into the hinterland every year. Sometimes I left a mired car, or pushed a motorcycle with a flat tire up muddy hills, waded swollen streams, slept on the dirt floors of native huts, or dropped asleep in sodden clothing after walking miles through driving rains. But with better bus service, patients could usually reach the dispensary, and I discouraged back-veld trips, which all too often were unnecessary.

Five of the students I'd sent to Adams Mission came to the hospital to begin their medical studies in 1923, one having been dropped because he was not to be trusted. Before I could do more than start the first medical classes, however, I was called to Capetown, the capital of the Union of South Africa, to testify before a Government commission inquiring into the use of native beer.

An old Durban friend, Dr. C. T. Loram, met me at the Capetown railroad station, and drove me to his home, where I was staying. He had been an inspector for the native schools when I first knew him, but he had worked up to the position of Minister of Education. At that time he enjoyed telling of a boyhood classmate who had been held up to him as an example. "Charles," his instructor had said sternly, "why don't you apply yourself as John Jones does? Twenty years from now, you'll be blacking his boots." And Dr. Loram would add with a chuckle, "Now I'm Minister of Education and Johnnie Jones is in jail!"

He was as large a man as I am, an inch over six feet in height and weighing 225 pounds, and as homely as Abraham Lincoln. Once during a sudden downpour, Dr. Loram had offered to escort a strange woman to a street car, but after a shocked glance at his face, the woman had gasped, "Go away, you naughty man!"

He had been born in Natal, and his strong sympathy for the natives had led him to study all phases of their lives, until he became an authority. The new Prime Minister, General Jan Smuts, had for this reason appointed

Dr. Loram to the Native High Commission to advise on native affairs.

After a good dinner, Dr. Loram and I discussed medical education for the natives, and he reminded me of my paper, *The Zulu Witch Doctor and Medicine Man*, which I'd read before the Native Affairs Reform Association six years previously.

I laughed, and said, "At that time, I suggested training the Zulus in medicine. Since then, however, my ideas have expanded. I'm planning to train all the native races of South Africa in my school."

"The South African Native College has a similar plan," Dr. Loram told me. Noticing my startled expression, he asked, "Haven't you heard of it?"

"Not a word," I admitted.

"Why not run down to Fort Hare and talk to Dr. Kerr before going any further with your own plans?"

When I spoke of Dr. Kerr's chilling letter, Dr. Loram smiled.

"He's a first-rate educator, and sympathetic to missionary work," he informed me. "And don't let his bark scare you away."

Heeding his advice, I stopped on my return trip at Fort Hare, on the outskirts of the small town of Alice, eighty miles inland from Port Elizabeth. The interdenominational South African Native College takes its popular name from the ruins of an old fort, which lie in the school grounds. The principal of the school gave me a momentary shock because of his remarkable facial resemblance to Dr. Loram, but his plumpness was more emphasized because he was considerably shorter. And instead of the stern and uncompromising man I expected to find, Principal Kerr greeted me with the warmth of an old friend, showing a generous desire to be helpful.

As I talked to him, I began to realize that his objections to my medical school had been directed not at my aims but at my means of accomplishing them. Where I planned in terms of tens and hundreds of pounds, he was able to speak in thousands and tens of thousands of pounds because of his Government backing. For every pound a student at Fort Hare paid in board and tuition toward his medical education, the Government contributed two pounds—up to a certain point. Thereafter, the Government matched the student pound for pound.

My little medical school shrank rapidly as he talked, but I was more delighted than otherwise that it was so. It wasn't the first time I'd promoted an idea, only to have others, with more means and better facilities, do the job better than I could.

"The more ambitious natives demand an education equal to that of white doctors, or none at all," Principal Kerr went on. "So, beginning with the matriculation requirement, we'll give the first year of the medical course, sending students to England for their last four years. Later on they'll spend two years here, and three in England. Eventually the whole medical course will be given at Fort Hare. Graduates, of course, will be able to register as fully qualified doctors."

"That all sounds fine," I said, "except for one thing. A foreign education often acts as a barrier between a native and his people. I'd rather see the whole course given in Africa from the first."

Kerr admitted that many missionaries and educators felt the same way, but Fort Hare College was not yet prepared to give a full medical education.

"Where would my boys fit into this program?" I

asked. "They haven't passed their matriculation examinations, and aren't eligible to enter Fort Hare."

"Why not send them down here to study for their matriculations?" Kerr suggested. "After they pass, they can start their medical course."

This could be done, he explained, if I'd pay $250 yearly for each student, far less than it would cost me to educate them. The Government would then be obliged to match this contribution with $500 grants, which would not be spent at Fort Hare, but would accumulate to help defray the student's expenses in England.

Rather than decide myself, I told the boys of this attractive proposal upon my return to Durban. I was still willing to give them their medical training, but they could not be registered doctors upon completing it. If they passed both their courses at Fort Hare and at a British medical college, they'd qualify for practice anywhere in the British Empire, but a high hurdle would be the matriculation examination.

The African natives are natural optimists, and my boys were no exceptions. They laughed when I suggested they might fail in their examinations. Of course they'd pass! I couldn't blame them for choosing the more glittering opportunity. But it was nevertheless with regret that I saw them leave. My medical school lay in ashes. My only consolation was that the Fort Hare medical school had risen, phoenixlike, from those ashes.

In 1924 an alliance between the labor forces and the Republican Afrikanders brought the downfall of Smuts's Government, and James Barry Munnik Hertzog became Prime Minister of the Union. Hertzog immediately toured the Dominion. When he visited Fort Hare, Dr.

Loram and Principal Kerr urged him to initiate a program to provide better native medical care. The new Prime Minister appointed the Loram Commission to study the problem and make recommendations.

The commission made an able investigation, taking testimony from doctors, missionaries and magistrates throughout the Dominion. It then recommended that the Government establish a medical school to give natives the same education offered white students in Great Britain. Graduates would be allowed the same qualifications and privileges as white doctors trained abroad, but they would not be obliged to receive their education in an alien environment.

Sir Edward Thornton, the Secretary of Health, foresaw the passing of many years before such a program would provide a sufficient number of native doctors. He therefore made an alternative proposal to give native medical aides a shorter period of training. This shorter training would not, of course, entitle medical aides to rank as doctors.

The natives, the missionaries and most magistrates approved of the Loram Commission's proposals, but a ground swell of opposition began sweeping in on the Government from the medical profession. When I had suggested the training of medical aides at a meeting of the Durban Medical Society in 1917, the members had objected on the grounds that such a program would lower medical standards and discredit the profession. Now that the Loram Commission was recommending equal medical qualifications for natives, many white doctors still apparently felt the program would discredit them. Probably what these doctors in reality objected to was any program making it easier for natives to practice medicine.

The Government awaited the medical profession's

opinion of the Loram Report before taking any action, and an important issue at the South African Medical Association meeting in 1930 was therefore the discussion of the report. In general city doctors approved of the report. Back-veld doctors, practicing in the remote districts, bitterly opposed it, largely for economic reasons. They would be competing against native physicians if the Loram proposals were followed.

After a long and rather warm discussion, with considerable farfetched eloquence, the matter was passed on to the Federal Council of the Medical Association, the governing body of the Association. Individually the members were mostly, I believe, in favor of the Loram Report, but the Council hesitated to cause a split in the Association by approving it. Their recommendation, as might be foreseen under the circumstances, could be condensed to a single sentence: "The time is not right for such a step."

The Loram Report was thereupon deposited in a governmental pigeonhole, where it has since remained.

Meanwhile, four of the boys I'd sent to Fort Hare had, as I had feared, failed in their matriculation examinations. And the fifth, who passed his examinations and returned the following year to begin his first year of medical training, was expelled for misconduct.

The Loram Report, with its practical proposal for training South African natives to meet the medical needs of their people, had been effectively waylaid. My medical students were scattered, with the exception of Edward Jali, who came to work for me in the dispensary. The funds with which I'd hoped to train them were gone, either in buildings or in paying their tuition and board at Fort Hare. With the coming of the depression to America, pledges of support for my school were no longer being paid, making it unlikely that I could revive my own plan.

The most discouraging aspect of all this was that the natives of a large portion of South Africa could look forward in illness and in childbirth to nothing better than the superstitious ritual, the ignorant "surgery," or often the poisonous concoctions of their witch doctors.

It was disheartening, but no more so than similar setbacks when I had been trying to establish a Zulu hospital. I was determined to keep working for some form of native medical training, and I could see that some progress toward such a program had been made. Now many city doctors recognized that natives in rural districts would never receive adequate medical care until other natives were given medical training to work in the field. Dr. Taylor and I started to make it our mission, whenever we were with other white doctors, to win additional converts to this idea.

CHAPTER FOURTEEN

DISEASE
ON GRAY WINGS

THERE WAS A CHRONIC NEED FOR MORE SPACE IN THE Mission Nursing Home, and the reason for this is easily explained. No beds whatsoever were provided for natives in the Government hospital when I first came to Africa, and when the Zulus were brought there, they were placed on the floors of closets and other out-of-the-way places. By 1920 there were only twenty-five beds for Zulus in the Addington Hospital. And they were the only beds provided for natives in the outlying districts, for 20,000 native industrial workers in Durban, and for thousands of household servants. In part the shortage of accommodations was met by our hospital, but it was so small that it sometimes held double the number of patients for which it was designed.

Since a man can spread his energies just so far, I couldn't maintain my dispensary practice and take more patients in the Mission Nursing Home, even if it had been larger. But with the coming of Dr. Taylor, the problem of providing for more patients could no longer be ignored.

And so, in the years following the first World War, we enlarged the hospital repeatedly, though never enough. Each time wards were added, more nurses were needed. Additional facilities in the way of bathrooms, rooms for storing equipment, drugs, linen and other supplies were also required. And after the nurses and new facilities were installed, the hospital was as crowded as before. Meeting one need always appeared to create new ones.

Enlarging our plant in the early days was invariably a knotty problem, since we had no endowments or wealthy backers. Expansion was sometimes paid for by small bequests or by borrowing. On one occasion it was financed by a singlehanded promotional campaign of Margaret's. On another, by Dr. Taylor's efforts in organizing a Hospital Board. And once, strangely enough, a plague of Anopheles mosquitoes was indirectly responsible.

The original Mission Nursing Home, built to accommodate fifteen to twenty patients, held on occasions as many as thirty or forty, and it took all the time I could spare from the dispensary. It was not large enough, however, to absorb the full energies of the young and ambitious doctor who took charge in 1921.

Enlargement in many ways was desirable, both to increase the number of patients we could take and to reduce the inefficiency that always results from overcrowding. An adequate operating theatre, for example, was needed. So were maternity and baby wards, to prevent the scattering of mothers and babies throughout the hospital. Government health officers conceded that most of the native tubercular patients entering the Government hospital died of the disease, while many of our T.B. patients returned home either cured or arrested cases. But the good we could do in treating such cases was severely limited by the smallness of our "outside ward," the veranda, which needed widening and additional supports. These additions, however, would cost between $7,000 and $8,000, while we had virtually nothing.

Margaret saw a glimmer of hope of raising part of this sum when she learned that money left to charity in the will of Mr. A. A. Smith, before his death a prosperous merchant, had not yet been disbursed by the son who was acting as trustee. Margaret invited the son and his wife to afternoon tea, and afterward conducted them over the hospital. She spoke of our need for an operating theatre to replace the relatively small room then serving as a surgery. Looking over the small surgery with a thoughtful eye, young Mr. Smith asked how much an operating theatre could cost. Margaret told him that the work could be done for $1,000. The young man mailed her a check for that amount a few weeks later.

Though the windfall was very welcome, it wasn't sufficient for the additions needed, and my wife turned her thoughts to ways of raising the remainder. The best possibility she could think of was to ask for contributions from employers whose servants or native employees we had cared for, at very low fees, in our hospital.

Typical of such cases was the treatment we gave a prominent lawyer's favorite servant, following a bicycle accident. The boy lost control of his bicycle on one of Durban's steep hills, and turned into the curb to stop his swift flight. His left knee joint was shattered when he was hurled against the curbing, and when I examined it later in the hospital, it resembled a sack of small, loose bones. Though there appeared little hope of saving the leg, I nevertheless tried to do so. And after repeated operations to remove small pieces of bone, the boy returned to work for the lawyer. While his leg was stiff, it's true, it was better than one carved of wood.

In the hospital I had cared for numerous servants or business employees hurt in some such way, and I had also delivered the babies of many female servants. If the babies were boys, they were often enough named McCord, adding to my hundreds of namesakes in Natal. The honor had begun to pall, but at least the numerous McCords kept our work fresh in the memories of Durbanites both at home and in their places of business.

Margaret felt that all this service deserved support, particularly from business firms. However, we bore the scars of our long battle to open the hospital, and we weren't very optimistic. Some influential people had opposed the hospital at the start, and was it likely they would now contribute to its enlargement?

Margaret intended to find out. She called on one of the leading businessmen to ask his advice. He listened sympathetically.

"I don't think you have a chance of raising the money you need while the Mission Nursing Home is a private hospital," he said. "But if it were a missionary hospital— that would be different."

"We intend to give it to the American Board when we retire," my wife explained.

"Well, why not do so now? Make things easier all around."

We talked it over and saw no reason why the transfer should not immediately be made, nor did our lawyer. In a few days, after the papers of transferral had been drawn and signed, Margaret returned to call on the businessman. Having already seen the notice of transferral in the paper, he hardly gave my wife a chance to ask for a contribution before he took the list she had prepared and signed his name, pledging a gift of twenty pounds. She left his office feeling slightly dazed.

Three other businessmen she called on each pledged twenty pounds with little urging on her part. And then a lawyer, who had apparently come from the office of one of these men, stopped her on the street.

"What's that list?" he asked.

Margaret explained that she was trying to raise money for an enlargement of the hospital.

"I see. And why haven't you called on me?"

"I'm only calling on businessmen whose servants or employees we've taken care of in the hospital."

"Let's see that list."

The lawyer glanced at the names and the amounts pledged. And then, to my wife's astonishment, he signed his name for a contribution of twenty pounds.

Something startling had happened since we'd fought for the right to build our Zulu hospital! The attitude of the whites toward the natives had undergone a distinct change. And the Mission Nursing Home, quite without our suspecting it, had built a reservoir of good will. Proof of this lay in the success of Margaret's campaign. Not a single business house refused to contribute!

The funds she raised built a large operating room, with a separate anesthetic room; a maternity ward large enough to accommodate a dozen confinement cases; and a baby ward. The porch was also widened by two feet, and the wooden posts supporting it were replaced by concrete pillars, so that it was strong enough and spacious enough to take twelve to fifteen patients—as many as we had expected to accommodate in the original hospital. These additions doubled the capacity of the hospital and appeared to answer our needs for years to come—an illusion we were quickly forced to banish.

Another effect of the improvements was to reinforce Dr. Taylor's contention that the Government should recognize the Mission Nursing Home as a hospital fully qualified for the training of nurses. From the time he had obtained subsidies for our training program, he had with amiable and tireless persistence sought this recognition. Government officials had put him off with excuses, but he had made friends even when failing to accomplish his purpose. Now, with the enlargement of the hospital, officials made an inspection, and our nurses' training program was approved. Our graduates could for the first time take the same examinations as white nurses and, if they passed, could become registered nurses. How our native nurses fared in these examinations will be spoken of in later pages.

It had proved a wise move to place Dr. Taylor in charge of the hospital, for he was a good executive and was fast becoming a skillful surgeon. Under his guidance the work would undoubtedly continue to expand. And it became even more important to keep him after Dr. Morledge of Cleveland came to South Africa, and then, because of strong family ties in America, left again.

Even though Dr. Taylor found the work absorbing, however, one point clearly troubled him. He had not received an appointment as a regular medical missionary, and the American Board was not responsible for his salary, traveling expenses, or pension upon retirement. It was I who had employed him and had guaranteed his salary, which came entirely from dispensary funds. His salary, but a fraction of what he could earn in private practice, was too small to allow him to lay aside anything toward retirement. Under such an arrangement, he might work until he was seventy, and then have neither a pension nor savings. I was afraid this drab prospect might make him decide to end his service in Africa at the time he returned to America on furlough in 1928.

My own furlough, fortunately, came a year earlier, and I left for America determined to have him appointed a medical missionary.

I went to the American Board offices in Boston soon after reaching the United States, and called on one secretary after another to urge the appointment. I pointed out that it was unfair that Dr. Taylor should remain in a position inferior to that of the other missionaries, and that if he were not given an appointment, we would very likely lose the man most essential to the continuation of the medical work in South Africa. Although all the secretaries were sympathetic, none would give me any positive assurance. Knowing that the American Board tries to reach a unanimous decision of its members, I felt that one secretary must be opposing the appointment.

I could not discover which one it was, however, until a friend advised me one day that it was Mr. Brewer Eddy, a determined man who usually swayed others to his viewpoint by a rock-firm stand.

Diplomacy was never my strong point, and it infuriated me that the results of all my years of work in South Africa might be lost through the stubbornness of one man. I charged into the office of Mr. Eddy, who was dictating to his stenographer, and looked plainly annoyed.

"Mr. Eddy," I said, with no effort at politeness, "I'll take but a minute of your time. And I'll make only one point, because if I made more than one, I might confuse you."

Pencil poised, the stenographer grinned encouragement. And Mr. Eddy, accustomed to speaking plainly himself, likewise grinned.

"That one point," I went on with heat, "is that our

mission hospital is a going concern that was built without any help from the American Board and has been carried on for twenty-five years without a cent of expense to the Board except for my salary. Those properties now exceed $40,000 in value. Half that value has accrued since Dr. Taylor joined us, a large part of it due to his work in building up the hospital. He's the man to carry on after I retire, but in refusing him missionary status, you'll lose not only his services but in all probability a $40,000 property as well. What are you going to do about it?"

Mr. Eddy smiled and said, "Sit down, Dr. McCord."

He began questioning me, showing by his questions that he'd never previously given the matter more than passing thought. But he was interested now; he saw that if a less able doctor succeeded Dr. Taylor, the South African properties might be frittered away. I explained that it would be better for the future sake of the work to let me be responsible for my own salary and have the Board pay Dr. Taylor's, if that was necessary to assure his appointment. In the end, Mr. Eddy appeared won over to my views, and we parted in good humor.

Before I returned to Natal, Dr. Taylor received his appointment. It was well he did, for not long after he returned from his furlough, in 1930, he was desperately needed. The worst malarial epidemic in Natal's history spread through the province, an epidemic that was, oddly enough, to play a part in the expansion of the Zulu hospital.

Natal had never had a malarial epidemic of any proportions prior to the twentieth century, so far as I could discover. This is somewhat astonishing in view of her subtropical climate and the heavy rainfall during the spring months of September, October and November. What had spared the province a malarial outbreak was her mountains, which rise to a height of 5,000 feet perhaps forty miles from the ocean, and diminish to 500 feet not far back from the coast. Swift torrents sweep every gorge and valley during the rainy season, flushing out all rivers and pools, and carrying mosquito larvae to the Indian Ocean.

The gray-winged Anopheles mosquitoes responsible for malaria have small chance to breed under such conditions. In the low, swampy territory of Zululand to the north, however, they find ideal conditions and there malaria is endemic. But traveling Zulus could not spread the disease to the south until natural conditions had changed.

The change came when an ambitious Government in 1904 extended the railroad from Stanger, fifty miles north of Durban, on northward into the heart of the Zululand malarial district. Anopheles mosquitoes locked into coaches in Zululand were brought back with every returning train. That winter, while starting work in the Durban dispensary, I had my first case of malaria. Fearing it might be plague, I took a specimen of the patient's blood, and sent it to the Government hospital. There the presence of malarial parasites was discovered.

The following summer, on New Year's Day, I took a hiking tour with my friend Reverend Johannes Astrup. On our tour, we learned of many deaths from malaria the previous summer. The weather after our return continued warm, with only light rains. The ground remained damp, absorbing the gentle rainfall, leaving little overflow to scour out the sluggish streams and rivers. Pools appeared in every hollow, even on the flats between Berea Hill and the Indian Ocean. And in the still waterways and stagnant pools of the river valleys to the north of Durban, Anopheles mosquitoes imported by train from Zululand bred, and billions of wriggling larvae swarmed.

Clouds of mosquitoes were soon attacking natives, including malaria-carriers from Zululand, and a sufficient number thus carried the parasites to spread the disease among a people having no acquired immunity. By late January and for weeks afterward patients suffering from malaria streamed through my dispensary.

Now, the first cases posed a problem in treatment. I was afraid the Zulus would throw away quinine pills. They were accustomed to *drinking* medicine, their witch doctors always preparing it in liquid form. So, to be sure my patients would take their treatment, I dissolved quinine in strong hydrochloric acid, added pepsin for easier digestion, and colored the mixture with methyline blue analine dye for visual effect. The appalling taste convinced the Zulus that it was strong medicine, and they drank it down. That achieved the desired end. There were no fatalities if they took quinine before the disease was too far advanced. But in a few cases, I had to administer the drug hypodermically.

Malaria took a heavy toll that year in the river valleys between Durban and Zululand, a toll that could have been reduced if there had been any native medical aides or enough nurses to visit those too sick to come for treatment.

I laid in a large stock of quinine, expecting a repetition of the epidemic in 1906. Torrential rains the following spring washed clean the pools, rivers and streams, and malaria did not reappear. So for years I was reminded of my unfortunate foresight whenever I went to the drug room. I had little use for quinine, nor did anyone else. Demand for the drug in the first World War inflated its price, and I sold out the entire stock at a handsome profit. The windfall came during the Afrikander rebellion, when the flow of patients had slackened because natives were afraid to travel on the roads, and it helped keep the hospital open.

Anopheles mosquitoes continued to breed in small numbers in Natal, but without causing another malarial outbreak until 1930. The weather that summer was mild and there were frequent light rains. Under these conditions, mosquitoes bred in enormous numbers. A malarial epidemic, far more terrible than that of 1904, swept over the country. Not confined to river valleys to the north of Durban this time, it struck, often in malignant form, among the hill kraals and to the south of Durban as well. A person bitten by mosquitoes carrying malarial parasites might fall ill within two or three days, and die within a week.

Sick Zulus trudged into the city, and the Assistant Officer of Health of the Union had quinine tablets distributed to them without charge. The reaction of the natives was just what I had imagined during the earlier epidemic that it might be. They threw away the free tablets and came to the dispensary to buy my "blue medicine" at twenty-five cents an ounce. The Government health officer was annoyed when he learned of this, and asked me to come to his office. I explained my reasons for coloring the medicine and for giving it in liquid form. The health officer still considered my method unfair.

I smiled at him. "I prefer to give medicine in the only way I can be sure the natives will take it. However, there's nothing to prevent you from using methylene blue and giving quinine in liquid form."

The health officer, an able but a stubborn man, refused to bow to native prejudice in this way. And so the Zulus courteously accepted all the pills he distributed and, when out of sight, tossed them away. They had no faith in either pills or free treatment, and quinine pills looked to them like a feeble remedy for a powerful sickness.

All day long I treated ambulatory malarial cases in the dispensary, and at night I helped Dr. Taylor in the hospital with the more serious cases. Most patients were relieved by quinine administered orally or hypodermically, but a few, reacting badly to quinine, had to be given atabrine. And there were malignant cases that reached the hospital too late to respond either to drugs or other treatment. The dead were removed to make room for new arrivals, and before long patients lay in the aisles, under beds and even in the halls.

One night, when the hospital designed for forty patients held exactly twice that number, Dr. Taylor felt that overcrowding had gone far enough. He gave orders that no more patients were to be admitted. And then, exhausted from days of overwork, he turned in for a few hours of sleep.

At two o'clock in the morning, a bus reached the hospital with nearly thirty sick natives. They had chartered the bus at Greytown, a hundred miles away, and now having reached their destination, they refused to leave. Those who were well enough loudly clamored for admission, and nothing the matron could say would quiet them. Dr. Taylor was awakened, but he was no more successful in persuading the busload of sick natives to leave. At last, growing resigned, he asked nurses to make room for them by crowding patients more closely together on the floor, in hallways, on the dining room tables and floor, and anywhere else that space could be found.

The hospital was never again packed so tightly, although the epidemic lasted for several months, finally being brought to an end by cold weather. At that time a large number of former malarial patients had unsettled accounts and no means to pay. Ordinarily this was no problem; we allowed patients without money to work out their bills by doing odd jobs in the dispensary or hospital, or by garden chores. Patients who had recovered from malaria were willing to discharge their debts in this way, but so many workers would have created chaos. Some other means of payment had to be devised.

The epidemic had demonstrated that the hospital was still too small, so Dr. Taylor suggested that the unpaid accounts be settled by the making of cement blocks, to be used in future expansion. He had wooden forms made, and the blocks were shaped by filling the forms with a mixture of cement and sand, the sand being dug up from the hospital grounds. Only men worked at this; the fees of women and children were discharged by the labor of male relatives. For months the manufacturing of blocks went on around the hospital, until there were unsightly piles everywhere. Neither Dr. Taylor nor I had estimated in advance the vast number of blocks that would result from the work. We had a fresh problem to solve—and promptly, too, if we were to avoid the complaints of neighbors.

Dr. Taylor talked to a Norwegian builder, known to be a good construction man. Making a rough count of the blocks, the Norwegian thought there were enough to add a four-story wing to the hospital, and his bid was quite reasonable. Dr. Taylor was eager to order the work started at once, because of a recent increase in the number of nursing trainees. I was equally eager, but more cautious. I reminded him that however much we needed the addition, he must first find a way to meet the construction costs.

Dr. Taylor gave that some thought. It occurred to him that we'd borne the brunt of caring for natives during an epidemic, and part of our proposed addition was to house native student nurses. This was certainly public work, and, as he saw it, public work deserved public support. So he haunted Government offices to voice his theory and request a subsidy of $5,000 to build the new wing. Repeated refusals failed to discourage him because he had half expected that. But to the delight of us both, he eventually made his point and was granted the subsidy.

The hard cement blocks were excellent building material, and when the last one had been used, we had a new wing with a basement, three floors and an attic. The basement gave us workrooms and a sitting room for the non-technical staff; the first floor, a new men's ward; the second floor, a dormitory for the two-score nurses now in training; and the third floor, their commons. The epidemic had the unlooked for result of adding half again as much space to the hospital, making it possible to accommodate forty to forty-five additional patients. It again appeared—though mistakenly—to be quite large enough for years to come.

It was not long, though, before the increasing number of patients and student nurses made it necessary for Miss Cooper to have the assistance of two white "sisters" —the British term for ward supervisors. Sharing the student nurses' quarters, these sisters found the constant laughter and gay chatter of the native girls wearing after a hard day of work. They asked for separate quarters so that they could rest when off-duty. There was no space in the hospital to provide such privacy.

As it happened, we had purchased an acre across Mc-Cord Road from the hospital years before, in time building a laundry at the back of the property and adding tennis courts for the staff and nurses. There was ample space left for a white sisters' bungalow. Construction would cost a good deal, however, and the only money we had for the purpose was $1,000 that Steven Rich of Verona, New Jersey, had sent us from his uncle's estate. The money was to be used for some useful work dedicated to his uncle's memory, but it wasn't sufficient to build the bungalow.

When the white nurses were approaching the end of their endurance, an old friend, Emory D. Alvord, came to Durban for a vacation. Alvord was a former agricultural missionary who had become a Government inspector of native schools in Rhodesia, and in one way or another he had acquired an amazing array of skills. He was a large man, with boyish enthusiasm and boundless energy, and as restless as a weather vane. He had intended to stay at the beach, only to find within a few weeks that he'd seen enough of salt water. Dismayed at the prospect of remaining idle during the balance of his holiday, he begged me to find some work he could do. That left me wide latitude, and so I mentioned our need for a sisters' bungalow. But I added that he was supposed to be having a vacation.

"That's right—and I intend to enjoy it!" he cried eagerly. "Now, what about this bungalow?"

I hunted up the architect's sketch. He looked at it carefully.

"We'll borrow iron frames from a builder," he said briskly, a minute later. "I'll see about sand and cement and bricks. Can you find me some native workmen?"

"You're going too fast," I said. "I have only a thousand dollars—"

"That will be plenty," Alvord interrupted, "if I do the work."

And do the work he did! He kept twelve native workmen scampering to supply him with materials as they were needed, but all the construction was of his own hands. The workmen were almost too exhausted to drag themselves home at the end of a day's work. Yet Alvord, doing the greater share, appeared as fresh at the end of a day as when it began. He enjoyed himself hugely, and within but a single week, by laying 500 bricks a day, he completed a five-room bungalow. The white sisters promptly established themselves in it.

It was our last construction before depression days.

Now the depression was eventually to have a beneficial effect on the hospital, but its immediate effect on all missionary work in South Africa was severe. As the American economy contracted, contributions to missionary work decreased. One missionary after another was recalled by the American Board because there was no longer money to pay their salaries.

The Board remembered my offer to take my own salary from dispensary funds if Dr. Taylor received a missionary appointment, and asked me to transfer the burden of my support to the Medical Department of our Mission. Dr. Taylor's salary, as luck would have it, was still continued.

In 1931 the Board wrote the Secretary of our Mission that still further retrenchment was necessary. To reduce the number of missionaries, a portion of the work had to be eliminated. The Board suggested that this could perhaps best be done by closing the girls' school at Inanda.

I called a meeting of the Natal Mission to consider the proposal. It had a chilling effect on the missionaries. They recalled that when the girls' school at Adams had closed at the time of Mrs. Ireland's death, it had never re-opened. Might not the same thing happen to Inanda? Closing the school would at the very least deprive 200 girls each year of their high-school educations and domestic training. That would be a loss both to the girls and to the hospital, which selected many of its nursing trainees from

the most promising Inanda graduates. Yet none of us saw
any way to raise $3,000 a year to keep the school running.

It was my place as Chairman to suggest a way to do
this, if it could be done. So I turned to Dr. Taylor, who
sat beside me, and whispered, "Would you care to risk the
payment of your salary from hospital funds to save Inanda?" He hesitated momentarily, realizing that his salary
was insufficient to meet the deficit, and then nodded.

After announcing his decision, I added, "Of course
that won't meet the entire $3,000. We'll have to cut cor-
ners in other ways, perhaps by taking fewer girls, but at
least the school will remain open."

It looked like a hazardous step because our hospital,
like most others, was not quite self-supporting.

Yet forcing ourselves to assume the added burden
had a fortunate result. We had to face the fact that the
hospital had been built up by bequests, by money borrowed on my personal responsibility, by an occasional
Government subsidy, and through the generosity of
friends. It had no regular backing except the small subsidy
granted by the Government for the training of nurses.
And now, having grown too large to depend upon such
haphazard financing, it needed more stable foundations.

Dr. Taylor circulated among business and professional men to learn how this could be achieved. These
men felt that the hospital should have a board to advise
and assist on financial matters. Obviously this was sound
advice. Dr. Taylor immediately organized a Hospital Advisory Board of twenty members. I was made an honorary
life member, Dr. Taylor as Superintendent of the Hospital was a member, and other members were chosen from
the Natal Provincial Council, the Durban Town Council,
the Union of South Africa Parliament, and from among

the lawyers, businessmen, medical men and missionaries of the province.

The Advisory Board took an intense interest in the hospital and everything connected with it, including Dr. Taylor's salary. When the members learned, at one of the early meetings, what he was paid, there were indignant murmurs of protest.

"The Superintendent of our hospital is not going to be paid such a niggardly salary!" a member cried. "We'll double it."

Dr. Taylor smiled and shook his head. "Thank you. But I don't feel that it would be fair to accept more than our other missionaries."

The board members had an approximate idea of what Dr. Taylor could earn in private practice, and his willingness to work for so much less left them temporarily speechless.

After a pause, another member said, "Well, tell us what you want, Dr. Taylor. What can we do for you?"

"We're handicapped in every way by cramped quarters," my associate answered promptly. And he explained why more space was needed for patients, nurses and facilities. "We need an entire new wing," he concluded.

"How much will it cost?"

"About $100,000," Dr. Taylor said.

I thought he'd asked for too much, too soon. None of the other board members appeared to feel that way, though they were thoughtful.

"I doubt if we could raise that much while the hospital is owned and controlled by a foreign missionary society," a man said, after a few moments. "Financial control would have to remain here in Durban, in a local Board of Management."

After a discussion, the Advisory Board decided to

convert itself into a Board of Management. But would the American Board sign over ownership of its valuable hospital plant to this new board? Lengthy correspondence settled all points touching on the question. The American Board, up to its chin in financial problems, was actually relieved to relinquish its property rights in return for financial support of the hospital.

A constitution agreeable to all concerned was drawn. Under its conditions the hospital—to be known henceforth as the McCord Zulu Hospital—would remain for all time a missionary institution run for the Zulus. Practical control remained as before with the American Board, but responsibility for the hospital's finances and management would rest with the Board of Management.

When the constitution was signed, the hospital board launched a drive to raise $100,000. Contributions from two businessmen gave us a quarter of that sum the day the drive began. Numerous smaller donations soon brought the total raised to $75,000. The success of the drive seemed so certain by then that negotiations were started to purchase land on which the new wing of the hospital was to stand.

Three acres adjoining the hospital—once the estate of its determined opponent, Mr. Kimber—were ideal for the purpose, but the owner asked $37,500, half again what the property was worth. The member of the Board of Management handling negotiations offered $25,000 as the most we could pay. Disgruntled at his failure to sell at an exorbitant price, the owner offered the three acres to the Berea Nursing Home. The doctors in charge of the home had no immediate use for the property, but rather than allow their institution to become known as the nursing home behind the native hospital, they offered $25,500, an offer the owner promptly accepted.

We felt that we'd suffered a crushing defeat. There was no other land for sale near the hospital suitable for the addition. So it was necessary to revise our thinking. And in doing this we saw the possibilities in the unused land adjacent to the hospital and behind my home. Since we couldn't expand sidewise, the only alternative was to erect a higher building than we had originally planned on the remainder of the property. No time could be wasted if this was to be done, for a regulation limiting the height of buildings in the district to three or possibly four stories was even then being drawn up by the Town Council.

The Board of Management asked a firm of architects to start at once on the designing of a six-story hospital, 104 feet in height. The architects rushed these plans through and they were approved before the Town Council could pass limiting restrictions.

The new wing, though it was to be connected to the older hospital by bridges at the first, second and third floors, would in reality be a separate building, ninety feet long and forty wide, with an identity of its own. For this reason, and because my associate's efforts were largely responsible for the addition, the Board of Management proposed that it be named the Alan Taylor Wing. The proposal pleased Dr. Taylor.

Excavation for the wing started while I was on furlough in 1937, and the cornerstone was laid before my return. In British territories, this demands an impressive ceremony and an important dignitary to lay the corner block. It was laid for the Alan Taylor Wing by the Administrator of Natal.

Except for the cornerstone, the building had not progressed much beyond the basement walls when I returned to Durban. But it rose rapidly from then on. Each morning when I climbed the scaffolding to see how much work had been done in the previous twenty-four hours, I could observe distinct progress.

Dr. Taylor had planned to take his furlough following my return, but he could not bear to miss any part of the construction work. Month after month he postponed his departure. Then, when he had delayed his furlough long enough to see the building completed in November, he decided to remain for the opening ceremony.

We planned an elaborate ceremony, for the opening of this large, modern hospital wing was an important landmark in the medical progress of the Zulu race. Invitations were sent to men of prominence throughout South Africa, but not only to such men. Anyone who had attempted to improve the lot of the natives or had shown an interest in their affairs was remembered. And no one who wished to attend, regardless of race, whether wealthy or humble, was refused an invitation.

A crowd of approximately a thousand assembled before the speaker's stand on the veranda of the old hospital the day of the opening. Two men who had championed native medical education, and had worked for the welfare of the natives in many other ways as well, were on the stand. They were Jan H. Hofmeyer, the Minister of Mines, Labor and Social Welfare, who was to announce the official opening, and Sir Edward Thornton, who was the principal speaker. After they had addressed us, Dr. Taylor and I also spoke. Last of all, in what was perhaps the most moving part of the ceremony, the native nurses took their places on the veranda, and sang in chorus, their voices carrying in the open air with a deep and beautiful resonance as they rendered the "Zulu National Anthem" and "God Save the King."

During the ceremony, I could not keep my thoughts from straying. My mind flitted back to incidents half-forgotten, incidents that had played their part in the erection of this hospital for the Zulus. It was the work of many hands, over many years.

The McCord Zulu Hospital with its new wing might be said to have begun with the pioneer medical work of Dr. Newton Adams in Natal, a century before the ceremony we were holding. His work among the Zulus had been followed by Dr. Bridgeman's and mine, and now there was Dr. Taylor to carry it on. The Board of Management had helped in the work, and so had many others. . . . There was Margaret, who had encouraged my hardest ventures, who had administered anesthetics and had assisted at countless operations, and had communicated her own patience and integrity to our first nurses. . . . There were Katie and Uqibelo in the dispensary . . . Miss MacNeill and Miss Rice and Miss Cooper in the hospital . . . the native nurses, with their loyalty and sense of service. . . . And there were our Zulu patients, who had also helped by their willingness to pay for their medical treatment. . . . All had had a hand in building the hospital. But the greatest change the years had wrought, the thing which had made the hospital in its present size possible, was the different attitude of the whites toward their primitive brothers. Without that change, there could have been no Alan Taylor Wing. . . .

When the last notes of "God Save the King" had died away, Mr. Wallis Dyer, Chairman of the Board of Management, handed the key of the new wing to Mr. Hofmeyer, and he unlocked the front door. Spectators, white, black and Indian, were then free to inspect the building.

Margaret and I escorted a group of friends through the northwest door to look first of all at the large new kitchen, which would prepare food for the entire hospital. A service elevator in one corner would take trays on wheeled wagons to all floors. Leaving the kitchen, with its shining equipment, we passed through pantries, storerooms, the workroom, the garage and the furnace room, with its enormous tanks for the storage of hot water.

We entered the passenger elevator, explaining to our visitors that it had cost half as much as the original unit of the hospital, and rode up to the first floor. There we stepped out into an eight-foot corridor running the length of the building. On one side was a men's ward, large enough for thirty patients, or more with a little crowding. And opposite it were semiprivate wards and rooms for food and medicines. Bulging into the ward was a glassed-in cubicle, where the floor nurse had her office and could watch both the patients in the men's ward and those in the semiprivate wards as well. Bathrooms, lavatories and sluice rooms stood at the end of the passage, and near them were chutes to carry soiled linen to the basement and refuse to the furnace room.

All floors except one were identical to the first, though some of course were for maternity or women's wards rather than male patients. The exception was the fifth floor, and we now took our visitors there to show them the nurses' dormitory, which had fifty beds, and a large dining room with enough tables to accommodate nurses in both the old and new units of the hospital.

Afterward Margaret and I took our guests up to the sun deck, stepping out into the brilliant sunlight. There recuperating patients could sit or lie. Resting our elbows on the parapet, we looked down upon the city of Durban, at the white sails of yachts scudding across the bay, at a south-bound steamship, its wake milky white against the glistening blue of the ocean. And then, turning our backs to the parapet, we pointed out the hills of Inanda, where the girls' school still instructed Zulu girls; Margaret's birthplace of Umsunduzi, and the northeastern hills of Mapumulo, beyond Esidumbini where we had stayed with Laura Mellen and where I had first studied the Zulu language. From the sun deck, we could likewise make out the curving line of the Maritzburg railroad line, and the many roads winding through the rolling green wilderness of hills.

Dr. Taylor stepped from the elevator, coming to join us. His face glowed with almost boyish delight, and it was plain to read there his feeling of pleasure. He was a man whose heart was easily moved, and even a less warmhearted man than he might have felt his emotions stirred by the ceremony we had just witnessed.

A few days later, with quite evident regret, he flew to England to catch a ship for America, leaving me in charge of the hospital that had become the largest interest in his life.

CHAPTER FIFTEEN

WHO SERVES
HIS PEOPLE BEST

FREQUENTLY ENOUGH THE DEFEAT OF A CONSTRUCTIVE program by a small and self-interested minority is just what is needed to insure its eventual success. The defeat of the Loram Commission's native medical training program worked out in precisely this way.

City doctors throughout South Africa felt the sting of their rout at the hands of back-veld physicians, and many formerly only lukewarm toward medical training for natives now became determined partisans of such a program. In the Government, too, were men unwilling to concede defeat. Among Government officials who saw the quashing of the Loram program as nothing but a setback were Sir Edward Thornton, the Secretary of Health of the Union, and Mr. Jan Hofmeyer, the Minister of Mines, Labor and Social Welfare. Sir Edward Thornton was a large and robust man whose air of reserve did much to conceal a compassionate nature; he could work most effectively by convincing individuals or small groups of the rightness of his cause rather than by dramatizing his efforts. Mr. Hofmeyer was a more affable but a no less determined man, and he had strong support from the Afrikanders in all branches of the Government. These two officials worked quietly but tellingly, winning converts to their view that medical neglect of the natives must not remain a permanent condition in South Africa.

Their unobtrusive campaign led the Government to inquire as to what was being done to meet the health needs of the native races. Sir Edward and other officials testified that nothing whatsoever was being done. So a commission was appointed to find a workable plan for meeting these needs. To avoid controversy, the commission shrank from publicity, and was scarcely heard from again until it presented its report. The report was almost identical to the medical-aide program I had presented to the Durban Medical Society, and had later published in the *South African Medical Record* in 1918.

Principal Kerr's testimony before the commission on the cost of such a program, however, was something of a shock, for he said that it could not be carried out for less than $300,000. The burden to taxpayers would in all probability insure the defeat of the program. Government officials then thought of the immensely wealthy mine operators who owned the rich gold and diamond mines of South Africa and benefited more than any other group from native labor. Why shouldn't they return a fraction of their profits to the people from whom their earnings derived?

The Government made a proposal to the Chamber of Mines at Johannesburg, the organization representing the mine operators, that it pay the entire cost of the medical-aide program. The Chamber of Mines, figuratively speaking, gulped at the suggestion, but thereafter its reaction was not one of blind opposition to the program but of cautious inquiry into its soundness. Numerous conferences with Government officials followed before the mine owners were satisfied that their money would be wisely spent. Then it was handed over to the Government, and by the Government to Principal Kerr. True to his conservative Scotch instincts, he invested the entire amount in time-tested securities which would provide sufficient income to support the medical-aide program.

To decide what training should be given young native medical aides, a committee was appointed to determine the eligibility requirements and to chart the course. It included Principal Kerr; several faculty members of the Lovedale Native College; Dr. Neil MacVicar, of the Victoria Hospital at Lovedale, who had devoted his life to medical work among the natives; Dr. Cluver, who was later to become Secretary of Health for the Union; myself and several others.

We decided, to begin with, that medical aides should at least have a Junior Certificate (equivalent to the second year in an American high school) to qualify. Except for this basic requirement, we placed no rigid obstacles before students wishing to take the training, but we recommended that preference be given in most cases to those who had passed their matriculation examinations. Nor was any student to be barred because of insufficient means to pay entrance fees, tuition and board. In cases where applicants lacked means, but were of good character and proven ability, scholarships would be granted.

We also decided that students should be given a five-year course. Three years would be spent at the South African Native College at Fort Hare, where they would study botany, zoology, chemistry and physics their first year; anatomy and physiology their second; and pathology, bacteriology, public health work, and laboratory procedure their third. Students would then have a year's study of medicine, minor surgery, and midwifery at Victoria Hospital. And in their fifth and final year, at McCord's, they would study clinical medicine—similar to the work of an intern at an American hospital.

The training, in short, was very nearly what a white medical student would receive. But the native or non-European (the course was open to Indians and half-castes) who satisfactorily completed the course could practice only as a medical aide under the supervision of a white Government doctor. His salary would start at $900 a year, a large salary for a native or non-European in South Africa, and increase $50 a year while in service, eventually reaching a maximum of $1,500 annually. He could not augment his income by private practice, and if he left Government Service, he disqualified himself for further practice.

Manifestly it was unfair to require practically a white doctor's training, and then hedge medical aides with such restrictions, and I'm sure that every one on the committee felt this strongly. Chastening experience, however, had taught us that it was wiser to move slowly than to arouse the antagonism of the back-veld doctors and make no progress at all. The best we could hope for was that the medical aides might soon win a firm place for themselves. Then it would be possible to take the final step toward a full medical course and medical recognition for non-Europeans.

The training course would break virgin soil, so it seemed advisable to limit the first class to ten students, selected from among the many we imagined would wish to enroll. We anticipated dissatisfaction from those denied admission, and dissatisfaction there was, but for quite a different reason.

Advanced students at Fort Hare raised a clamor of

Concluding in my own language, let me say,
"*Nyi ya bonga Baba. Unga dinwa nango muso.*"
                                    Imina otobekileyo,
                                        Edward Jali.

A second letter, to Margaret, was written by Edward
after he commenced to work as a medical aide, under the
supervision of a Government health officer, Dr. Maclay.

Church of Scotland Mission Hospital,
P. O. Tugela Ferry,
April 9, 1940.

Dear Mrs. McCord:

I am sure that you would like to hear from me
more regularly than once a year, to know what I am
doing and how I am doing it. I am writing today from
a place called Mhlangana. It is one of Dr. Maclay's
clinics and is about twenty miles from the hospital.
I have already been at Collessie, fifteen miles from
here; at Keat's Drift, about twenty miles away; and
at Pomeroy, more than forty miles distant. From here
I will visit Mhlumayo and one other place.

Dr. Maclay takes me by car to each of these
places during the clinic days and leaves me there until
the next clinic day is due. In some districts I stay a
fortnight, in others a week. My duty is not to examine
the patients and prescribe some wonderful drug but
to teach the people better ways to live. It is the kind
of work a Christian should do, the work Christ did
while here on earth. He wandered from place to place
teaching the people. Now and again He healed the
sick and raised the dead.

Every day I visit the people in their kraals. I find
out about their health. As a rule there is almost always someone sick in each kraal but still trying to
work. Then my lessons commence. I may speak to a

mother, or to a hutful of men and women gathered around a dying friend, or to people I catch drinking beer. I tell them about the spread of disease. My best example is how T.B. is spread.

In explaining about this disease, I tell them there is no *Mtakati* [wizard]. In T.B. the *Mtakati* is the sputum. The *Zifenes* [baboons] he employs are the flies which, after feeding on the spit, carry germs on their hairy feet and in their stomachs. As they feed in other places, they brush off the bacilli from their feet in the same way as the *umtakati* [wizard] is said to carry medicine under his long finger nail and drop it in the road or in beer unnoticed. The flies also regurgitate as they eat. In this way they deposit or spit out the bacilli as an *umtakati* is said to spit out the medicine concealed under its tongue.

As I give such illustrations, my audience seems to believe. I tell them that a fly is the *umtakati*, not their neighbors. I give similar illustrations with almost all other diseases. Yet it is not always possible to teach in this way and we have much to contend with. In one place I was told that the district was swarming with *inyangas* [witch doctors]. Actually I was refused permission while there to see a patient I had come ten miles to advise. I do not know whether I was suspected of being a Government spy, or what, but I was told that only the *inyanga* could cure the woman's sickness.

In one of these districts where there are many *inyangas* I had to visit several chiefs and headmen. My experience with them makes me realize that if I were doing this for myself, without love for my work, I would never again visit a chief.

I arrived at one chief's kraal at 4 P.M. and was told I could not see him until the following day. I was shown to a kraal a mile away, where I spent the night in a hut that was filthy and swarming with cock-

they began to work in remote districts, has won strong support for the cause of native medical education. Durban doctors are today, I am informed, almost wholly in favor of full medical education for natives, to be given in South Africa. The Medical Association at a meeting at Durban before the war passed a strongly worded resolution favoring the establishment of a medical school at Durban, to be open to all non-Europeans, though primarily to give natives a medical education comparable to that given whites and with equal status afterward. Plans for the establishment of such a school were in fact in progress, but had to be postponed at the outbreak of World War II.

The plan may have setbacks, but I have no slightest doubt that it will eventually be realized. And I hold this view because of the proven success of the native medical aides.

Many men had a share in the development of the Medical-Aide Training Course. The part I had in originating and developing it was, in my opinion, more important than building the McCord Zulu Hospital or establishing the dispensary where I worked so many years. I feel that it was the most valuable work I was able to do for the Zulu people.

CHAPTER SIXTEEN

ONE FAMILY
WITH MANY NAMES

A ROMAN CATHOLIC PRIEST WHO CAME OFTEN TO VISIT the McCord Zulu Hospital once commented on the loyalty and trustworthiness of our nurses. Speaking of another hospital which had begun the training of native nurses, he said, "The staff there find their nurses won't accept responsibility. And they can't build the walls high enough or the bars strong enough to keep the girls in and the boys out. Here at McCord's," he added, "you have no walls or bars, nor are any needed."

What the priest said was true. Yet our girls were of the same blood as those who failed in other institutions, particularly in the Government hospitals. Why did they make such excellent nurses, whereas Zulu girls proved undependable in other hospitals? I believe the difference at McCord's came from balancing discipline with play, from treating the girls as responsible individuals deserving of trust, and from impressing upon them the ideals of their calling.

Undoubtedly we enjoyed an advantage in being able to choose our trainees. Girls with a strong urge to follow nursing preferred to enroll at McCord's, where they felt they'd become better nurses and would find a more congenial atmosphere. Thus we could select from an increasing number of applicants each year the girls of exceptional character and the highest scholarship. With this and the quality of their training in common, our nurses, whatever their names or individual differences, had characteristics as distinct as the members of a single family.

A composite picture of a McCord nurse would show a well-balanced girl, conscious both of her duty to her patients and of her own personal dignity. Religious principles guided her in her work and in her relation with others. Off-duty she studied hard, but she also welcomed play. She had a happy disposition, and got along well with her sister nurses. On Sundays, when having tea with the doctors and supervisory sisters, she was neither self-conscious nor servile. She considered, and quite rightly so, that her work was as important in its way as Dr. Taylor's or the matron's. She was part of the McCord family, a vital part. And the only walls or bars to restrain her were her own dignity and self-respect, her knowledge that as a trusted member of the hospital family, she must be worthy of trust.

Some other hospitals treated probationers as inferiors or incompetents who must constantly be watched, and who would even then prove unreliable. If they sensed from their superiors' attitude that only the worst was expected of them, what incentive was there to give their best?

The distinctive character of our nurses could be explained in many ways. One reason was that Dr. Taylor, who was more of a missionary than I, brought religion into the hospital in a way that made the trainees look upon nursing as a humanitarian calling, not as a job. Another reason was the influence and the long years of service of Miss Cooper, who mixed discipline with inexhaustible patience. Games, social evenings once a month, and teas following the Sunday service helped take the edge from the strict routine of practical training and studies. The social life of the hospital also allowed the staff and probationers to become better acquainted. Government recognition of our nurses' training program, giving our probationers an incentive to be more conscientious, also helped mold their character.

From the time the Mission Nursing Home started to train native nurses, we gave them training equal to that received by white probationers. But because the Government had not recognized our hospital as one qualified to train nurses, we could give our first two classes of girls only hospital certificates. This placed them at a disadvantage both in the wages they received and in the positions open to them.

Shortly after Dr. Taylor became superintendent of the hospital, he tried to obtain the Government recognition that the quality of our training deserved. This recognition might quickly have been granted had we been training white nurses, but because we were training natives, the Government delayed. Our third class of nurses was graduating in 1924, and these girls, like their predecessors, could be given nothing better than hospital certificates unless the Government acted.

Dr. Taylor began making frequent calls on any Government officials who might wield influence. As a result of his persistence, the Mission Nursing Home was investigated and approved as a training hospital. Little time remained, however, to prepare the ten girls of the third class for their examinations. Miss Cooper spared no effort. She drilled the girls in every subject on which they might conceivably be questioned.

In a sense our whole training program was on trial when the ten girls went to the Durban Technical Institute to take their examinations, and a very unequal trial it was. Our girls, but a generation removed from kraal life, were not only competing against white nurses; they were also forced to compete in English, to them a foreign tongue. Because of this language obstacle, it wouldn't have surprised me if all had failed. I felt very uneasy lest this might happen. When the results were posted, and all of our girls passed, my wife and I were overjoyed.

To train probationers for hospital duties and to pass Government examinations are quite different things. And so, from the time our hospital won Government recognition, the fact that the girls would eventually have to pass examinations in English was always kept in mind in the training. Year after year Zulu nurses proved the mental equal of the white nurses against whom they competed. One year, for example, thirty of the thirty-one girls we sent up for the Government examinations passed. In another year, when eight nurses from the whole Union of South Africa passed with honors, four were white and four black—two of the native nurses from our hospital, two from another mission hospital.

In the same year that the Mission Nursing Home became a recognized training hospital for nurses, Beatrice Msismanga enrolled in the nurses' course, at the age of eighteen. She completed her course three years later, passed her Government examination, and then, breaking with precedent, enrolled in our midwifery course. She was the first girl to take training in both nursing and midwifery. Her example was frequently followed afterward, our graduating nurses taking an additional year of work in midwifery to qualify in both fields.

The midwifery course, which could be completed in a year and a half if it did not include nursing, was started in 1925 with a class of two probationers. Midwifery students wore uniforms pale pink in color, to distinguish them from the nursing trainees, in their dark blue, or the graduate sisters in striped, lighter blue uniforms. They alternated clinical work on the labor and baby wards with academic work. Their instructors were graduate midwives; often, in later years, graduates of our hospital. The instructors were allowed two hours of free time every day, but they rarely took it. They could usually be found when off-duty on the lawn, instructing one or more backward pupils on clinical or academic points the students didn't understand. Because of the instructors' devotion to the girls under them, our midwifery graduates seldom failed to pass their Government examinations.

Zulu mothers, true to their conservative instincts, failed to rejoice at having properly trained midwives of their own race. Our graduate midwives had no call for their services for many weeks, and they began to feel their training was wasted. Then one night, when all we doctors were occupied at the hospital, an urgent call came from a Zulu woman living in a slum district of Durban. The woman was beginning labor, but as none of us could leave to deliver her child, Dr. Taylor sent Lydia Kambule, a graduate of our first class in midwifery. A boy accompanied her, so that she could send for one of us doctors if she experienced any difficulty. Several hours passed before the boy reappeared, still with Lydia. Her pose of composure poorly concealed her pleasure at having assisted at the delivery of a child, the first she had delivered without supervision.

Lydia had overcome the Zulus' prejudice against trying anything new, and thereafter she was in great demand. She delivered about thirty babies in an average month, which was all that time would allow. Her success also helped other midwifery graduates to become established.

Much of their work was in slum districts, less than a mile from the hospital, and after several of the girls had been annoyed by strangers, they were sent out in pairs, both for protection and to assist one another in confinement cases. These attractive young midwives, always traveling in twos, in freshly starched uniforms and with bags in hands, became a common sight as they strode briskly from case to case, in the poorer as well as in the outlying districts of Durban. Among the Indians, they were particularly in demand. An Indian woman attended by a male doctor loses caste, and she will call one only in extremity. A mother was charged ten shillings for prenatal care and the same amount for a delivery, making it possible for a "team" of midwives to earn as much as $150 a month, extremely high wages for natives. The midwifery course as a consequence became nearly as popular as that in nursing.

Each enlargement of the hospital made it necessary to increase the number of nurses and midwives in training to care adequately for the increase in patients. More probationers in turn required a larger staff. In 1933, Miss Cooper had two white sisters and two qualified native midwives to assist her in training the fourteen nurses in general training and the ten midwifery trainees. Six years later, she needed seven white sisters and three native nurses to train the forty-three student nurses and the fourteen student midwives.

The following year, in 1940, we instituted a plan that had never before been tried in South Africa, a preliminary training class for nurses. We hoped through a three months course to select the students best qualified. Sixteen girls, carefully chosen from among the graduates of Inanda Mission, were enrolled. Half of these girls were to be eliminated, leaving only the eight best to enter the regular nursing course.

The girls understood the conditions perfectly. And each girl was determined that she would not be among the rejected eight. Their instructors seemed equally determined to defeat the plan. The girls worked as if their futures depended on it, and their instructors spent all their spare time helping any girls who showed the least tendency to fall behind. When the three-month course ended, every girl had done so well in both clinical and academic work that there was but a trifling difference between the best girl and the worst. Only one fair decision was possible. The whole class was enrolled in either nursing or midwifery. Even though the preliminary nursing course failed as a means of selection on its first trial, it was potentially a useful means of choosing the girls best suited to nursing and was continued.

The method of selection and the character of the training gave McCord nurses a family resemblance, but there were of course the individual differences you'd find even in a family with much in common. This is well illustrated by Nurse Ellis Mangele, who was almost as broad shouldered and tall as a six-foot man, and Nurse Linda Langeni, a wisp of a girl, yellow-brown in color, who was such an excellent surgical nurse that she was given a staff position, then becoming known as Sister Linda.

Nurse Ellis, with a strength to match her great height, was a natural athlete. She had never played tennis before entering the hospital, but her powerful forehand drives and humming serves were before long too much for the other nurses to handle. She turned to male competition, and was soon beating all but the best men tennis players. Even George, our laundry foreman, the champion of the hospital, had a tussle to win from her. And when yo-yo became popular, several series of matches, with prizes for the winner, were held. Nurse Ellis took the prize so consistently that the others presently lost all interest in the game.

She was also a natural mimic, and her caricatures were a feature of the monthly social evenings. Motion pictures were sometimes shown at these social evenings, particularly travelogues which gave the nurses an idea of how other peoples lived. More often, however, the nurses provided their own entertainment with singing, skits and plays. It was in skits caricaturing the weird practices of witch doctors that Nurse Ellis excelled. Playing the part of either the witch doctor or his mistreated and long-suffering patient, she sent the other nurses into gales of laughter. Because of her reputation for comedy and her great stature, however, she was never given a part in the Nativity plays held on the last social evening before Christmas.

One night there were a series of skits caricaturing various members of the staff. One nurse appeared, smiling broadly, and in an imitation of my voice that might almost have deceived Margaret, said, "Good morning, ladies. I hope I find you all well this morning." I had to laugh with the rest, for that was my usual greeting for the nurses on my morning visits to the hospital. Another nurse bustled in as the laughter subsided, saying in an exaggeration of Miss Cooper's quick, nervous manner, "Here, here, girls —what are you doing? You mustn't do it that way, you must do it this way, you must do it this way." Last of all,

Nurse Ellis strode into view, swinging a stethoscope and whistling, "Till We Meet Again." Dr. Taylor's hearty laugh rose above the peals of merriment, for the big nurse imitated perfectly his gait, the manner in which he always swung his stethoscope, even the inflection of his whistling.

As she disappeared, other nurses brought out a portable bathtub. It was only a short time after the malarial epidemic, when the Mission Nursing Home was enlarged and the girls were provided with bathtubs in addition to showers. I assumed that the skit dealt humorously with the new tubs. To my astonishment, the nurse playing the part of the patient began disrobing. Feeling that realism was going too far, I sprang up, intending to escape. And so did Dr. Taylor and the other male staff members. Nurses posted near us laughingly shoved us back into our seats. We were relieved a moment later to see that the disrobing girl wore under her uniform a heavy black bathing suit. Before the other nurses had finished scrubbing her with the heaviest brushes in the hospital, she must have been grateful for it.

Nurse Ellis was more than mimic and athlete. Because of her size and forceful personality, she usually overawed even the most troublesome male patients. For that reason she was placed in charge of a men's ward. Her ward customarily quieted down the moment she came on duty.

There were, however, exceptional occasions. One night a former patient of hers left the hospital and then imbibed too freely in celebrating his recovery. He slipped back to visit friends in Nurse Ellis's ward. When she asked him to leave, the drunken man threatened her. He was too large a man for even Nurse Ellis to eject by physical force. Rather than attempt it, she crossed the road to ask some street workers to help her. Welcoming the diversion, they followed her willingly enough. And with little difficulty, they dragged the troublemaker from the ward.

Hardly had he been released, to go staggering along the hall, than his friends began bitterly accusing the workmen of unnecessary roughness. Their language was harsh and profane, and when they added to this abuse an invitation to fight, the sorely tried workmen said they could think of nothing they would enjoy more.

The drunken man's friends were nearly well and jumped from their beds as the street laborers started toward them. Feeling greater concern by now for her ward than for herself, Nurse Ellis seized the nearest workman, spun him around, and gave him a push that sent him reeling into the hall. She hustled one after another of the laborers from the ward in the same way. And then, having restored order, she pointed a shaking finger at patients responsible for the trouble and gasped:

"You . . . and you . . . and you . . . were going to fight. I shall report you to Dr. Taylor in the morning, and ask him to send you home. If you can fight, you are well enough to leave."

Amused by her vigorous stand, Dr. Taylor backed up her authority in the morning, and discharged all of the troublemakers. . . .

Sister Linda, the little nurse who was no larger than a Hottentot, would never have handled a similar disturbance in exactly that way, but in her quiet and efficient manner, she was equally competent in meeting any situation. She completed both our general nursing and midwifery courses, being so outstanding in both that she was invited to join the staff. By 1937 she had become the night sister, in complete charge of the hospital at night, except when she required Dr. Taylor's assistance.

During my last years in South Africa, white medical students were sent to our hospital by the Medical School of Witwatersrand University at Johannesburg to gain experience in obstetrics. They would observe the delivery of ten babies, and would then take sole responsibility for ten additional deliveries, with only a graduate midwife to assist them. For the sake of the patients as well as that of the young medical students, who were nervous when facing their first deliveries, Sister Linda was usually assigned to help them.

Her low, composed voice had a steadying effect as she asked, "Now, Doctor, do you want this knife?" A little later, she'd inquire, "Do you want these scissors, Doctor?" And, still later, "Do you want to tie here, Doctor?" If the medical students answered, "Yes," to each of Sister Linda's questions, they had a remarkably easy time of it. And few seemed to suspect afterward that they'd actually received their instructions from the little nurse.

When on my 1928 furlough, I visited Dr. Taylor's father in the upstate New York village of Mooers. The elder Taylor asked me to attend services with him, and I found that the meeting, held in a small hall, had the flavor of the Methodist camp gatherings of long ago. Plain farmer folk made up the congregation, their faces glowing with an unmistakable warmth and friendliness. Their religion, you could see, wasn't something they accepted on Sunday and shed on Monday. It was part of their way of life.

I was asked to tell Dr. Taylor's former neighbors about his work in South Africa. During my talk, a spry little man with a graying beard sprang up from a seat behind me, pranced across the stage, and startled me with a hearty thump on the back. "God bless you, Brother," he said, and bounded back to his chair. No one appeared to think that anything unusual had happened, so I continued

had remained with us, made a motor trip into the interior. We saw Victoria Falls, camped in stockaded areas of Kruger National Park—where lions, giraffes, hippopotamuses and other wild animals roam unmolested—and visited missionary friends in Rhodesia. We returned to Durban on July twenty-eighth, with but ten days remaining until sailing time. During those ten days, we were given a series of farewell parties, each of which was a gentle severance of certain of our old and warm ties with Africa.

The first of these was a farewell reception arranged by the Hospital Board and the hospital staff, and it had an odd note of coincidence. Years before the most vigorous opponent of my Zulu hospital had been the coffee merchant and mayor of Durban, J. Ellis-Brown. The principal speaker at the reception was his son, Rupert Ellis-Brown, also a coffee merchant and the Mayor of Durban! With wit and eloquence, the son, now a man in his middle years, praised me for overcoming the opposition of his father and others who had fought to prevent the building of the hospital. Nothing could more clearly demonstrate the changed attitude of the whites toward the Zulus within the space of a single generation than the difference in outlook of the elder Brown and his equally influential son.

Mr. Lugg, whom I'd first met when he was in intelligence service during Bambata's Rebellion, and who probably knew more about the Zulus than any living man, spoke from their viewpoint on what the McCord Zulu Hospital meant to the natives. Dr. Taylor then gave a speech of appreciation, and presented me with a handsome chair, hand-carved of African hardwood and of proportions ample for a man of my size.

In the morning paper there was an account of the reception titled, *Gratitude of the Natives,* and an editorial tribute to my work by a Mr. Curry, who had been a magistrate in the native court when I first came to Natal. I wouldn't have been normal if I hadn't felt a warming glow at the praise, but I also recognized its ephemeral nature. Newsprint is relatively cheap, and the newspaper praise of today is gone with the next roll of the presses. So what impressed me most was that these pieces were carried by the same paper that had once lampooned me with cartoon and limerick at the time it was thought that J. Ellis-Brown had blocked my plans to build a Zulu hospital.

In those days comparatively few Zulus reached the fourth standard in school, not many of our Zulu pastors could speak English and many found it difficult even to read the Zulu Bible. Well-nigh universal then was the feeling among whites that the Zulu should be kept in his place, "a hewer of wood and a drawer of water." In those days, too, I performed operations in the cottage hospital, and sometimes, against my desires, in a native hut or behind a bush. The majority of the public of that day had felt that such primitive surgical conditions were good enough for Zulus. Yet public opinion had so reversed itself over the years that the paper which had once lampooned me now wrote eulogies about my efforts to give the natives a little more medical equality. A newspaper seldom steps far ahead of public opinion; in this case, it reflected the view of the majority of whites of today that the natives should be given a helping hand. . . .

Three nights after the first reception, a second was held in the hospital. It was typical of our monthly social evenings, with only the "McCord family"—the staff, black and white, the nurses and medical aides—and a few friends present. On this, my last social evening at the hospital, the singing of such songs as "Deep River," "Swing Low, Sweet Chariot," and "Amagora e Mendi" seemed particularly moving; and the skits, more amusing than usual. Memorable in this way was a skit in which a student nurse played a Zulu Juliet. Though her acting was achieved only by a demure countenance and the expressive use of her eyes as she was wooed by three medical aides in the rôles of Romeos, she was such an able comedienne that she kept the room roaring with waves of laughter. After the skit ended, but before the laughter subsided, a young white doctor led an older white sister out before the gathering and in an impromptu sketch even funnier than the original, they parodied the romantic scene that had gone before.

At the conclusion of the party, Margaret and I were touched when the nurses presented us with a hearth seat, carved of the same mahogany-colored hardwood as the chair we had received earlier. Some kindhearted conspirators must have been at work, for on Sunday evening, at a farewell reception at the Congregational Church, we were given a tea table to match the chair and the hearth seat.

On Monday the Zulus of Durban and surrounding districts gave us another reception, where there were more speeches and other gifts—though we needed no remembrances to recall our years of work among them. After the last speech, I noticed Katie Makanya in the crowd. She had been my interpreter and assistant in the dispensary for forty years, and she had retired when I had, with a pension for her years of faithful service. Now I asked her to rise. Katie had grown plump with the years, and her broad face lighted with pleasure at being recognized. Her friends cheered when she stood up. I thanked her for her loyalty and her years of devoted service. I hope that I left no doubt in my listeners' minds that I could never have done so much for the Zulus without Katie's help.

The chess club I'd belonged to for many years gave

another farewell party, and presented me with a gigantic rook. It proved to be a tobacco jar, wrought by the skilled hand of an expert carver. For a nonsmoker like myself, it would serve equally well to hold candy.

Those last days in Durban were busy ones, for when we weren't saying good-bye to friends, black and white, we were packing or selling possessions we couldn't take with us. We stayed during our last week with Tom and Hilda Harle. Hilda and her brother and sister had lost their father in childhood, and after leaving their stepfather and mother while still quite young, they had made their own way until all married. They had been frequent visitors at our home, and we looked upon them practically as members of our family.

It had been my hope to leave Africa for the last time with a crowd of friends on the dock to call hearty farewells as our ship left the shores of the continent we'd come to love. But that was not possible at the time of our departure on August the eighth of 1940, in the second year of a second World War. Wartime precautions barred visitors from the docks. Not even Hilda Harle and her husband Tom could accompany us there; we had to say good-bye at their door.

Then our car sped toward the McCord Zulu Hospital, to give me one last look at the institution which was, in a sense, the result of my life work in South Africa, the best monument I could leave behind.

All of the doctors and nurses of the staff, all of the medical aides, all of the student nurses in their pink or dark-blue uniforms were there. Again we said good-bye to old friends. And then, as our car started to leave, the sixty nurses tried to sing a farewell song. They began bravely enough, but as the car gained momentum, the song gave 'way to shouts of, "Good-bye . . . good-bye . . . good-

condition, however, remains unchanged. You'll recall
that our African patients called you *Nkosi* or "Chief"
while I was always *Nkosana*, "Son of the Chief." I
thought that when the mantle of responsibility fell
on my shoulders that I might become *Nkosi*. But apparently the head of a chief must have gray hair, and
my head, with scarcely any hair, doesn't seem to
qualify, for I'm still known to the Zulus as the chief's
son.

It has been said that one measure of a man's
success is the extent to which the ideals and institutions he has built carry on. In that respect the hospital
you founded on the spirit of good will appears also
to be built upon rock. McCord's strength increases
with the years.

I can remember my misgivings, twenty-seven
years ago, when I started the 10,000-mile journey to
South Africa to join McCord's staff. You scarcely
gave me time to get settled in Durban before turning
over the hospital and the surgical work to me. However, you were good enough not to leave me to face
those new responsibilities entirely alone. I can recall
your cheery, "Hello," each morning when you
dropped in at the hospital, to give me a chance to discuss any troublesome problems that may have arisen,
before you went on to the dispensary. And it was also
reassuring when I was operating to have your substantial form at the anesthetic end of the table, and to
know that I would have the benefit of your twenty
years of surgical experience should I run into any difficulties.

Your reasons for turning over so much responsibility to a young doctor were not entirely clear until
I returned home on furlough, seven years later. My
father had just died, and friends urged me to take over
his large practice. By then, however, I was so deeply
immersed in my South African work, and finding it so

absorbing, that there wasn't the slightest temptation
to abandon it. That was, I suspect, exactly as you'd
planned it.

It seems remarkable, looking back on it, that
during the nineteen years we were so closely associated that there was never a single misunderstanding
or any sharp difference of opinion. Probably the
reason for that harmony was that we had the same
end in view.

In retrospect, it seems to me that the medical
work in Natal, which has meant so much to us both,
went through two distinct phases. Your work, in the
first phase, overlapped my own in the second.

In that first period, when the Zulus believed that
disease was the result of witchcraft and they had no
slightest conception of scientific medicine, you pio-
neered the work of winning them to hospital treatment, particularly surgery. Yours was also the pioneer effort in training native girls in nursing, and
young men in medicine. Against severe opposition,
you gradually won over South African whites to the
realization that sickness among native workers or
servants was likewise a threat to the health of the
white community since disease knows no color lines.
All this work was accomplished by charging fees
which, while small enough not to prove burdensome,
still allowed Africans to keep their self-respect in a
way which would not have been possible if they had
felt themselves objects of charity.

On these solid foundations I was able, in the
second period, to make what I like to think of as my
special contribution to the work. By the time I joined
the staff the white residents of Natal were won over
to McCord's, the native nurses had proved their
worth, and the hospital itself was modestly self-supporting. That made it possible for me to go with confidence to the South African Government to ask for

multiplied as the wounded flowed southward from North Africa. Yet somehow the work of the hospital was carried on.

A large share of credit for the functioning of the hospital during and after the critical war years should go to our native nurses, who were loyal, hard working, and willing to assume responsibility. One indication of their success is the fact that three native staff nurses are now responsible for major wards, and their work in every respect has been most satisfactory. One has carried on as Night Supervisor for over four years.

Not long ago, I was showing several doctors around our hospital. One was the staff doctor of a large Provincial hospital, and the other was Dr. Walker May, whom you'll remember as the Honorary Consultant of the Government hospitals. I commented on the work being done by our African nurses, and when I finished the tour, the visiting doctor turned to Dr. May.

"Is Taylor telling the truth? Are these native girls really running wards and accepting responsibility as he says? The native nurses at my hospital certainly won't. They just work to earn the money to have a good time. Have to watch them every minute. How do you account for the difference?"

Dr. May laughed. "Taylor's telling the truth, all right." Then, sobering, he paused for several moments. "It must be the religion taught here that makes the difference. The native is still in an evolutionary period where the teaching of religion is still a necessity."

Dr. May might be right, except for the suggestion that it will not always be necessary.

Another doctor from a Provincial hospital made very much the same comment after a tour of our hospital. "Dr. Taylor," he said, "it will be interesting to see how nurses trained in Government hospitals compare with those trained at McCord's in ten years time."

Thinking he was joking, I laughed.

"No; I'm serious," he insisted. "Your graduates are far ahead of ours in their treatment of patients and in their acceptance of responsibility. Perhaps it's because you're able to get a teaching and supervisory staff that feels a call to native work."

A doctor responsible for employing large numbers of African nurses in a Government nursing program admitted that he gave first preference to nurses trained at McCord's, Lovedale, Holy Cross and other recognized mission hospitals. And one of the highest ranking nurses in the Nursing Council has spoken strongly in favor of the continuance of nursing training in mission hospitals.

Probably there's no great difference between the girls who enroll for nurses' training at mission and Government hospitals. My guess is that when Government-trained native nurses fail it's because their superiors expected that they would. At McCord's and other mission hospitals, we instil the idea of service and expect our girls to live up to their responsibilities. Rarely do they fail us.

When you introduced the first Elementary training school for nursing trainees in South Africa in 1909, with a class of three student nurses, you started something that has long since proved its worth. Today we are training 150 girls at a time for nursing and midwifery. This has made it necessary to enlarge our staff of white sisters to superintend the training; in fact two white nurses, tutor-sisters, devote their entire time to classroom work.

A training innovation proposed by Tutor-Sister Emily Poole, and instituted in 1944, was the teaching of advanced nurses in "study blocks," which completely divorced their classroom and wardroom work. The ward sisters at first bitterly opposed this change, and it was difficult, because one-fifth more nurses were needed to staff the hospital and maintenance costs were correspondingly increased. At McCord's, where the training of nurses is regarded as of equal importance with the treatment of patients, the slightly greater expense has justified itself by the improved quality of the training. It is interesting to observe that this innovation, as well as every other essential step we take in training our student nurses, is prescribed in an outline recently issued by the Nursing Council as the goal South African hospitals should eventually strive to reach in their nurses' training program.

The Administrator of Natal in 1945 predicted that unless the trend of young white women away from nursing and toward business careers was not checked that the nursing profession in South Africa would pass entirely into the hands of African women. If you ponder on that statement, you'll understand why we attach such importance to training native nurses. The trend the Administrator spoke of still continues, and as a consequence we must prepare our girls for heavier duties it seems likely they must some day assume.

I regret that your long-cherished dream of training young African men for medical service has not met with the success of the nurses' training program. Well over a quarter century ago I came to South Africa to help in that phase of the work, and the training of African doctors on any substantial scale is still short of accomplishment.

Your plan to train young men in scientific medicine was regarded as a wild and ridiculous scheme, I understand, when you first proposed it in 1917. McCord's nevertheless did give young Africans some medical training at different times, only to have each program blocked for one reason or another.

It appeared certain when you left Durban that the native medical school was at last to become a reality. The half million dollars offered by the Chamber of Mines for this purpose had been accepted by the Department of Public Health, and a committee appointed to select hospitals for such training had recommended that it be given at the South African Native College, Fort Hare and McCord's. These plans came to naught because the training given did not prepare students for registration as doctors.

Now, with the war ended, and the Medical Association strongly supporting the establishment of a native school of medicine, the chances look brighter. The United Party Government accepted the principal of such a school and agreed to provide for it in the 1947 budget. That government has now fallen, but the new one seems equally willing to carry out the plan and has promised its support. So if you should decide to fly out to Africa not so long from now, you may find your dream taking solid form with bricks and mortar.

Incidentally, the University of the Witwatersrand at Johannesburg began in 1940 to train ten specially selected young Africans in medicine, and we are now getting two or three of their graduates every year. These native doctors, as well as our two Indian doctors, have earned the respect of our patients and of the staff, both brown and white. Their good work is a promise for the future, when more young Africans will be able to receive medical training.

Don't wait too long before you pay South Africa another visit because your friends may not all be here if you do.

Cordially yours,
Alan B. Taylor.